How to Light a Water Heater and Other War Stories

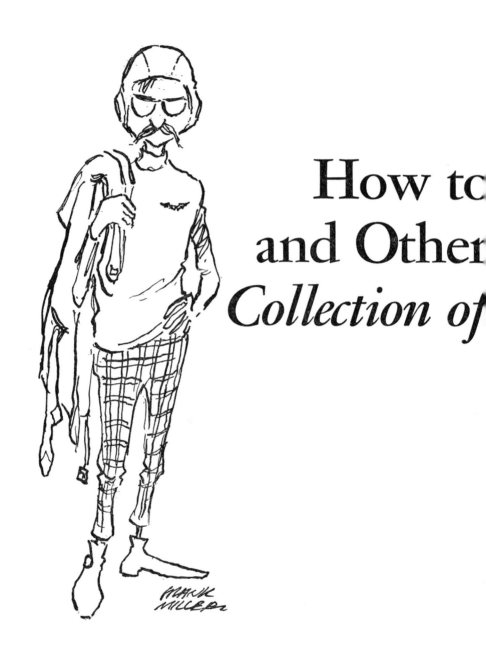

How to
and Other
Collection of

Light a Water Heater War Stories *a Random* *Random Essays by*

DONALD KAUL

Illustration by FRANK MILLER

The Iowa State University Press, Ames, Iowa, U.S.A.

Donald Kaul regularly writes the column "Over the Coffee"
for the Des Moines *Register*.

Frank Miller is cartoonist, *Des Moines Register and Tribune*.

© 1970 The Iowa State University Press
Ames, Iowa 50010. All rights reserved

Composed and printed by
The Iowa State University Press

First edition, 1970
Second printing, 1970

International Standard Book Number: 0-8138-0895-2
Library of Congress Catalog Card Number: 75-106602

Contents

Foreword

Donald Kaul is at least five different columnists, which is a pretty spectacular bargain for his readers. Fortunately for our sense of human limitation, he is rarely all five at once. And there are several kinds he can't seem to manage to become at all—a gossip columnist, for example, or the kind who trades newspaper space to press agents in return for Christmas presents.

It is one of the pleasures of following Kaul's column in the *Register* most days, as most of Iowa does, that one can never be sure which of the five columnists the paper-boy will bring this morning.

One day it will be the work of a grumpy, slightly eccentric State Conscience—necessarily self-appointed since Iowa hadn't thought it needed one. Thus his frequent, funny, indignation with the State Legislature (which represents us, doesn't it?) for dullness and childishness in a time of genuine crisis. This writing is more like moralizing than it is like joking.

A second voice of Kaul's is that of the domestic comedian, as indicated in the title of this collection. At its best, as in columns like "The Roots Take Hold," "Ain't Love? . . . Yeah, Ain't it?" and "TV Dinner a la Box," there is the underlying and even savage sadness for the basic haplessness of our circumscribed lives which has always distinguished good domestic comedy from the kind on exhibition in a television family series.

Fitfully, but always conveying a sense of pent-up energy released, Kaul tries to direct our attention to aesthetic matters. Since motion pictures are a favorite medium for this—see the columns on *The Sound of Music* and on *High School*—it is less quixotic than it might seem. Sometimes he even gets us to think about books, or architecture.

But Kaul is probably more often than anything else a social and political commentator of a particular kind: a cartoonist in words. Whether the cartoon invokes a scene, for he is fond of contriving scenes with several characters in speaking roles, or simply an image, he often extends an invitation to visualize which gives the piece extra dimension. There is "the man in the plaid cap with ear flaps and the galoshes with the buckles unbuckled" and "the girl with last year's face," and even O. T. Coffee himself, always the same physical specimen in spite of his transparent alias "a Des Moines man"— thin, defiant, and not quite coordinated. Yet if he suggests images frequently, he is also a writer, and can do it all with words when that is the only way to do it—as in his notions, two of my favorites, that President Nixon is to politics what Muzak is to music; and that Dean Rusk believes in the Tooth Fairy.

In his fifth, quite different kind of column, and the hardest to name, Kaul writes straight. In "A Plea for Rationality," in his memorable interview with T. J., in his reporting of the Chicago convention and reflections on the Detroit riot, he is a sensitive and straightforward reporter and commentator, proud of his craft and good at it, but not at all objective.

He is, perhaps, and it seems likely he will continue to develop with it, our first Iowa representative in the emerging field which has been called "the new journalism."

This is the journalism of men like Pete Hamill, Jack Newfield, Jimmy Breslin, Tom Wolfe, and others, in which the writer's personal involvement is part of the story.

Seymour Krim, a critic and new journalist, wrote: "I believe the new communicator . . . should speak intimately to his readers about these fantastic days we are living through but declare his credentials through revealing the concrete details and particular sweat of his own inner life . . ."

In his own way, and far from New York, Donald Kaul does this sometimes, too.

VANCE BOURJAILY

Preface

A S an art form, a daily newspaper column
is closely related to butter sculpture and sand
castle architecture. There is an intrinsic im-
permanence about it. The average column has
the half-life of a fried egg, which probably explains why so many persons, upon learning that
you write a column for a living, say "And what
else do you do at the paper?" It's no good explaining that it's a full-time job, they won't
believe you. Lately I've taken to responding
to questions of this sort by saying that I draw
cartoons under the pseudonym of Frank Miller
in my spare time. That generally seems to sat-
isfy *them,* if not Frank Miller.

But there's another class of person—intelligent, articulate, highly educated—who, upon
meeting a columnist, asks: "However do you
manage to come up with a fresh idea every
day?" That demands a more elaborate explanation.

There are two schools of column-writing, the toothbrush school and the nymphomaniac school. The first owes its existence to an anecdote told by Sydney Harris, the syndicated daily columnist for the *Chicago Daily News*. Harris recalls having lunch with Ilka Chase, yet another columnist, who said:

"Sydney, I don't know how you manage to write five columns a week. I have all I can do to turn out three."

Harris remembers replying:

"I should think that writing five would be easier than writing three. There's no logical rhythm to writing three columns a week. I've made turning out a column part of my daily routine. It's just something I do each day, like brushing my teeth."

Harris obviously has an easier time writing a column than most of us do, or he has a harder time brushing his teeth.

The other school of column-writing was given its name by another *Daily News* writer, Edwin Lahey. Lahey, for years a crusty, hard-hitting Washington reporter, is perhaps best remembered for the opening line he once gave an eyewitness account of one of the early atomic tests: "Megaton, Schmegaton. It was a hell of a blast."

Asked what it was like to write five columns a week, he replied, "It's like being married to a nymphomaniac." I'll accept that—on faith.

So, to get back to the original question, "How do you come up with a fresh idea every day?" You don't. But, if you work very hard at it, you can make it look as though you do, more or less.

In reading the pieces collected here, it is well to remember that they were written out of sheer panic, as an alternative to looking at a blank sheet of paper for eight hours. It is only fair to judge them on that basis. If you find them more interesting than most blank sheets of paper you've seen, my work has not been in vain.

These essays are loosely organized into five sections, with the accent on loosely. The first group tends to deal with national affairs, the second with Iowa and Iowans, the third with matters cultural, the fourth with domesticity in all its forms and the fifth with folk and their ways. You might argue with some of the categorization, but it won't do you any good. Where background material was thought necessary to an understanding of the column in question, it has been supplied by a marginal note.

DONALD KAUL

Prologue

IT'S BEEN more than ten years since I pulled my wagon over to the side of the road at the confluence of the Des Moines and Raccoon rivers, put my arm around my wife, and said:

"Bathsheba, here we will make our home."

And she replied: "You must be out of your gourd." But that's another story.

Up to that time I had never been west of Hamtramck, Mich., but I was attracted to Iowa by the opportunities it held out to a social satirist.

"Nothing much ever happens in Iowa," a colleague in Michigan told me, "but almost all of it is funny."

YET SUCCESS was not instantaneous. I had to work for my big break. I'll never forget how it happened.

I was down at the pool hall, shooting a friendly game of eight-ball, when a nattily-dressed stranger came up and challenged me to a game.

I accepted. We flipped a coin to decide who shot first, and I won.

"Age before beauty," my opponent said with a sneer.

"And pearls before swine," I replied quick as a flash, lining up my shot.

"Oh, you want to engage in a battle of wits, do you?"

"Yes. Too bad you didn't bring yours with you."

"Sir," said the stranger, "you shall either die on the gallows or of some dread disease."

"That," I responded, "depends on whether I embrace your principles or your mistress."

"Dolt! Bumpkin! Fool!" he sputtered.

"How do you do?" I said. "And I am Samson. Would you kindly lend me your jawbone?"

"Baw!" he cried and fled the pool hall in tears.

AT THAT MOMENT a man in a snap-brim hat and monogrammed suspenders walked up and said:

"Say, kid. I saw what you did to that guy and I like the way you handle yourself. Did you ever think of turning pro?"

"You mean, insult people for a living?"

"Yeah."

"It's what I've always dreamed of."

"Well, you need polish but I think you've got what it takes. I think we can make a columnist of you."

"You mean you'll let me write political satire like Art Buchwald and Clark Mollenhoff?"

"It's not going to be easy, you know. You have to be willing to pay the price."

"Anything, anything."

"No booze, no broads, no . . ."

"Forget it."

He proceeded to pull a huge roll of bills from his pocket. It must have been more than $50.

"See that?" he said. "Columnists make that much every week."

"Okay, I'll do it," I said. That was five years ago, almost to the day, and I've been writing this column ever since.

I've never regretted the decision. It has permitted me to be offensive to people in large groups, rather than one at a time. I have attacked more sacred cows during these five years than a devout bull could manage in a lifetime. It has been fun.

And the $50-a-week comes in handy too.

'Sire, ... the peasants are rioting'

Life Among
The Savages

WORD HAS it that the United States is going to get some "Reverse Peace Corps" workers.

It seems that President Johnson felt that the Peace Corps has been so beneficial to the Americans who have served in it, that he invited foreign countries to join in the fun and send us some young helpers.

So Argentina and maybe some other countries are lending us a few young people to help out in our poverty program.

It would be interesting to know what a Reverse Peace Corps worker from an underdeveloped country would say to his friends back home after a two-year tour of duty in the States.

HIS countrymen would probably say, "Tell us, Tom Tom, what are the natives of the United States really like?"

And he would reply, "Unbelievably ignorant but very friendly and grateful for anything you teach them."

"Like what?"

"Like making grass mats."

"They don't know how to make grass mats?"

"They don't know how to make anything. Your average American can't make a grass mat, throw a spear, build a fire or string a bead necklace."

"Incredible."

"Yes, the shortage of skilled labor in the country has reached the critical stage. And that's not the worst problem facing them, either. They also suffer from a shortage of certain natural resources."

"Which ones?"

"Air and water, principally."

"WOW! How'd they get in such bad shape?"

"I wasn't able to understand it entirely, but as best as I could get it, it had something to do with a mystical rite they call pollution."

"Pollution?"

"Yes. Americans seem to believe that if they fail to dump noxious substances into their air and water, their economy will fail."

"Boy, how silly can you get? I suppose you have to boil the water before you drink it."

"No. Nothing can live in the water Americans drink, not even germs. Fresh water fish, upon finding themselves in an American stream, have been known to commit suicide."

"How?"

"By jumping out of the water onto a bank and just lying there in the sun, waiting for merciful death."

"Poor devils. I suppose that Americans pretty much try and stay away from this filthy water of theirs."

"On the contrary. Most of them spend their weekends boating on it, swimming in it, plunging their children into it and positively wallowing in it."

"Disgusting savages."

"DON'T be too harsh on them. They have made contributions to world culture."

"Like what?"

"The telephone, the electric light, mass production."

"Those, oh sure. But you certainly can't compare those things with our contributions to world culture."

"You mean the wheel, fire, pointed sticks, that sort of thing?"

"Right."

"I suppose not, but in trying to understand the Americans you must remember that most of them think history started in 1776."

2

"That's as far back as their tribal legends take them, eh?"

"I'm afraid so."

"Boy, it sure makes you realize how lucky we are not to be one of the overdeveloped nations."

"I know it, but we shouldn't be too smug about it. But for an accident of geography, it could have happened to us."

The Uglier America

SAM CURRIER was standing in front of the Ingersoll Theater last week, wondering who Virginia Woolf was, when he nearly was knocked to the sidewalk by a man hurrying down the street. It was his friend, Albatross Ives.

"I'm sorry, Sam. I didn't see you standing there. My mind's on other things. I'm on my way to the monthly meeting of the Des Moines chapter of the League for an Ugly America."

"The League for an Ugly America? What is that, some sort of lunatic fringe organization?"

"I should say not. It's one of the most respected organizations in the country. As a matter of fact, we are considered the most powerful lobby in Washington."

"PRETTY effective, huh?"

"Effective? Next to us, Texas millionaires are a disenfranchised minority."

"What is it exactly that you do?"

"We have two major aims: To create ugliness where we can and to destroy beauty where we find it."

"That's a pretty big job."

"Yes, but we're equipped for it.

We maintain a special 10-man section that does nothing but encourage the establishment of junkyards in scenic areas. Another section is concerned exclusively with the erection of ugly public buildings."

"I'll bet that's a busy group."

"It certainly is. For example it took six of our best men, working night and day for two years, to get the new House office building built in Washington. Many have called it our masterpiece. It stands as proof of what Man is able to do in the way of repulsive building, given imagination, dedication and unlimited resources."

"Is that the building that cost $130 million?"

"RIGHT. What most people don't realize is that ugliness doesn't come cheap. You only get what you pay for."

"That's well put. Does the League have any other special divisions?"

"Several. The prestige section, of course, is the one devoted to the desecration of national monuments and historic buildings. We like to think of that as sort of an elite corps. It was through its efforts that the Truman balcony was built onto the back of the White House and the east front of the nation's Capitol was renovated beyond repair."

"Does most of the League's work have to do with buildings?"

"It used to but right now our most important work is being done by our natural resources division. At the moment we're promoting the damming up of Grand Canyon. It's one of the biggest projects we've ever attempted."

"I heard about that. Won't Grand Canyon make a pretty good-looking lake, though?"

"Yes, we've thought of that. That's why the damming up of the Canyon is merely the first stage of our plan. Once we get it

3

filled with water we're going to pollute it. With any luck at all, in 10 or 15 years you'll be able to visit the Canyon and see nothing but scummy water."

"I can hardly wait. Is the League's Des Moines chapter very active?"

"IT CERTAINLY IS. Buildings like Veterans Auditorium don't just happen, you know. What other city of our size has a civic auditorium that looks like the world's biggest two-car garage?"

"Say, wait a minute. Doesn't the whole basis of your society go against Mrs. Johnson's campaign to beautify America?"

"That's a perceptive question. Yes, it does and, to tell you the truth we were pretty worried about her at first. I mean, you start planting trees where the junkyards ought to be and you're well on your way to socialism. But we finally figured out a way to combat the campaign."

"How?"

"**Every time Mrs. Johnson plants a tree, we're going to erect a billboard in its shade.**"

"But will they let you do that?"

"They will when they see the slogan we're putting on the billboards."

"What slogan?"

"*Don't Be a Litterbug.*"

Commitment To Honor

THE UNITED States has assured the Cambodian government that it "will do everything possible to avoid acts of aggression against Cambodia."

I'll bet that clears up a lot Cambodia has been worrying about.

It would be interesting to learn exactly how Prince Norodom Sihanouk, Cambodia's chief of state, managed to extract such a reckless promise from our envoy, Chester Bowles.

An instant replay of the meeting would probably go something like this:

"Prince," says Ambassador Bowles, "your country is in dire danger of being overrun by card-carrying Communists."

"*Yes,*" *replies the prince. "It's one of my two great worries.*"

"But I'm authorized to tell you that the United States stands ready to come to your defense."

"**That's my other great worry.**"

"As you probably have heard, my nation is committed to keeping Southeast Asia free from the threat of the world-Communist conspiracy and we are prepared to fight to the last Southeast Asian, if necessary, to honor that commitment."

"I was afraid of that. Tell me, what specifically did you have in mind?"

"WE INTEND to fight fire with fire; an eye for an eye, a tooth for a tooth. If the Communists burn down one of your villages, *we'll* burn down one of your villages. If *they* blow up a bridge, *we'll* blow up a bridge. And if they persist in acts of terrorism, we'll bomb them back into the Stone Age.

We're going to teach them that the cost of aggression is high."

"I believe it. I don't mean to seem ungrateful, but isn't it a little unfair for you to concentrate all of your energies in Southeast Asia? Surely there are other parts of the world that need saving f r o m Communism—South America perhaps?"

"Sure there are, but none of those South Americans will sign a mutual defense treaty with us."

"How unneighborly."

"We think so. We keep scanning the Monroe Doctrine for loopholes, but so far we haven't been able to come up with anything."

"That's a shame. I don't suppose there's any chance that your government would consider not saving us from Communism, just this once?"

"*And break o u r solemn pledge to you? I should say not. Do you want us to get a reputation as a nation that doesn't keep its word?*"

"I can appreciate your problem. Would you at least consider agreeing not to save us without a formal declaration of war?"

"SORRY, THAT would be unconstitutional; a clear violation of the President's power to conduct foreign relations."

"Forget it then. I wouldn't want you to do anything illegal."

"The best we can do for you is to promise that we'll do everything possible to avoid acts of aggression against your country."

"Well, that's more than Mrs. Kennedy offered us. I'll take it."

"Prince, you drive a hard bargain but it's a pleasure to do business with a peace-loving monarchy."

"There's an old Southeast Asian saying: 'If friends can't agree to negotiate, who can?'"

The Perils Of Polls

A CURIOUS news item appeared in the paper the other day. Former Republican Gov. William Scranton of Pennsylvania told a college audience he believes the American people trust the honesty of the Johnson administration.

President Johnson has been called a great many things by Republicans and others in recent months, but that's the first time anyone's publicly accused him of trustworthiness.

It set me to thinking that perhaps this Credibility Gap business one is always reading about is no more than a myth, a fiction dreamed up by political analysts.

I decided I would do some original research on the subject by conducting a one-man opinion poll on the streets of Des Moines.

The first potential respondent I spotted was a thin, rather haggard-looking woman standing on a corner.

I approached her with my warmest smile and said: "Excuse me, madam. Do you trust the honesty of . . . "

"RAPE!" she cried and, pausing only to kick me in the groin, ran down the street.

IT TOOK me a few moments to pull myself together, a task made no easier by the disapproving glances of passersby. I finally got to my feet and went up to my second subject, a short, fat man walking a chihuahua.

"Pardon me sir," I began, "do you . . ."

"Don't bother me, buddy."

"You don't understand sir. I'm . . ."

5

"I understand, I understand. You want to sell me something. A magazine subscription or maybe some French postcards, right?"

"No, as a matter of fact . . ."

"You mean you don't want to sell me something? You want a handout? Get out of here."

"I'm afraid we're not communicating."

"Sic him, Fang."

The dog attacked me just as the lady whom I had interviewed earlier returned—with a policeman.

"That's him officer," I heard her say, "the one with the crazy look in his eyes and the dog on his leg."

The policeman began his investigation by saying, "Okay creep, reach for the sky. I'm going to put you where you won't bother no ladies for a long time."

"Officer," I said, "there's been a terrible misunderstanding."

"Yeah, that's what they all say. The last creep like you I arrested said he was conducting a poll."

"He tried to drag me into the alley, officer," the woman said.

"And the no-good bum tried to hit me for the price of a drink," the man with the dog said.

I summoned up a little carefree chuckle. "Under the circumstances I can understand your suspicion. However, in point of fact, I *was* conducting a kind of poll."

"A pervert like you ain't fit to live," the woman said.

"If you were conducting a poll, wise guy, what was your question?" the police officer inquired.

"I was attempting to find out whether the American public trusts the honesty of the Johnson administration."

THE THREE of them looked at each other for a moment, then simultaneously burst into laughter. It went on for several minutes. Each time it threatened to subside, one of them would say "Johnson" or "honesty" or "trust" and renew the hilarity.

"I'll say one thing for you, mister," the policeman said, wiping his eyes. "You've got a sense of humor."

"Yeah," said the woman. "He ain't even bad-looking—for a creep. I mean, if you like the Boston Strangler type."

"Why don't you give the guy a break, officer?" the man said. "A guy with an imagination like that shouldn't be in jail."

"All right," said the policeman, "I'll let you off with a warning this time but if I catch you bothering anyone again, you'll think you're the fall guy in a Lee Marvin movie."

"I get off work at 11 o'clock," the woman shouted after me.

Advertising, Soviet Style

ORTHODOX Communistic ideology is based on a number of highly questionable theories; one of them being that the state can anticipate the needs of the nation's economy and can arrange to provide for them.

This is utter nonsense. If a single family is unable to predict accurately what it is going to need on a two-week vacation, how can an army of bureaucrats perform a similar task for the whole country?

The Russians have long since recognized the impossibility of a totally planned economy.

In recent years they've been relying more heavily on supply and demand, letting the consumer tell the government what's

6

wanted in the way of goods.

Now they've discovered that even that isn't enough. There have been embarrassing instances of supply outracing demand. So . . . to increase demand, the U.S.S.R. has begun to ADVERTISE.

Nothing much at first, of course; just a few minutes of television time explaining the best features of an electrical appliance, a billboard announcing the virtue of a certain suit, a poster advising that you'll like a particular department store.

But this is only the beginning. Wait until the Russians really get the hang of the ad game. It'll probably go something like this:

A GROUP OF Soviet ad men, dressed in their paisley commissar uniforms, are seated around a long, oval table. One man, obviously the head commissar of advertising, stands and begins to twirl his horn-rimmed glasses as he addresses his colleagues.

"Well, comrades, I trust you all have been wearing your thinking helmets over the weekend, working on the problem of what to do about the lagging sales of our glorious auto, the PIG. Let's kick a few ideas onto the table to see which way the mine shaft crumbles."

A young man seated at the far end of the table leaps to his feet. "Comrade Ivan Ivanovich, I think I may have something. It's just off the top of my head but I thought I might push it into the mine field to see what explodes."

"Go ahead, Vassily, chicky baby, purge yourself."

"It is my suspicion that the glorious Soviet public is not understanding the significance of the auto's name. Comrades, you and I know that, in Russian, the initials P-I-G stand for 'Lenin's Greatest Achievement' but does

the public know it? We have to remember we are dealing with a public that has a glorious 12-year-old mentality. What the PIG needs is a new image, in short, a new name."

THE HEAD commissar stands musing for a moment, then turns to the man on his right.

"What do you think of Comrade Vassily's idea, Nikita?"

"There's an old Ukrainian saying, 'A paper tiger in the tank is worth two in the bush.'"

"Hmmm, good point. And you Boris, how do you feel about it?"

"There is much to be said for it, both for and against. The great danger, of course, is that its positive aspects might turn to negative ones."

"I think it's a brilliant idea," the head commissar says.

"So do I," says Boris.

"Me too," Nikita adds.

"Then all that's left to be done is to choose a name."

"I HAVE THAT, too, shouts Vassily, springing to his feet again. "It has a great deal of sincerity, yet is as uncomplicated as a Soviet election. We can call it the FORD which, in Russian, stands for 'The Last Time I Saw Siberia.'"

"I don't think you kicked a soccer goal with that one, Comrade. It's a fine name but the imperialistic American s w i n e have already used it."

"Comrades," s a i d Nikita, "bounce this idea around in your handball courts for a moment. Next week the glorious Soviet Union is sending a man to the moon. Why not name the car after him? He'll be a big hero on his return and we'll be able to tie in a promotional campaign that will boost sales."

"Great idea, Nikita Nikitavich. What is this cosmonaut's name?"

"Edsel."

This Was a Man

TO AN ENTIRE generation of American liberals, Adlai Stevenson was much more than a politician; he was their first cause, very nearly their patron saint.

Those of us who reached adulthood during the late 40s and early 50s were able to admire John F. Kennedy for his intelligence and style, and respect Lyndon Johnson for his energy and ability, but our deep affection was reserved for Adlai Stevenson.

Merely by being called an egghead, he transformed the derisive term into a badge of honor, something to be worn proudly among the philistines.

The basis for his enormous appeal to us, of course, was his wit and charm. He was a politician who wrote his own speeches and, moreover, wrote them with elegance and humor; a politician who dared to discuss issues on an abstract, as well as concrete, level.

To understand the full force of his appeal, however, one must understand the times that produced him.

IT WAS A VERY black era for the young American liberal. The most destructive war in history had ended only a few years before and already we were engaged in another.

The sickness that was Mc-Carthyism lay heavy on the land, spawning fear and suspicion.

And, worst of all, there was apathy. Nobody seemed to give a damn about anything. To many young persons searching for values, we were a truly dispirited nation.

Into this bleak environment Adlai Stevenson reluctantly stepped. He conducted a remarkable campaign, everything that civics textbooks say campaigns should be.

He didn't win, of course. I doubt that many of us had expected him to, really. Dwight Eisenhower was far too great a popular hero to be beaten.

Yet, in losing, he accomplished something.

HE DEMONSTRATED that even in a world gone insane, it was possible to remain a rational, civilized man; to react to age-old aspirations and to

Adlai Stevenson

8

treat ideas as if they really mattered. And that it was not only possible to do these things, but important. Many of us needed that assurance.

His second campaign, in 1956, was less satisfactory than the first. It was far more orthodox politically than that of 1952, but no more successful.

[*Stevensonians have long speculated on the outcome of those elections had the two candidates debated each other in the manner of the 1960 television debates. Stevenson most assuredly would have won the debates but it's probable that the people still would have chosen the inarticulate general over the eloquent humanist.*]

His tenure as United Nations ambassador, the post he held until the time of his death last week, was a disappointment to his followers.

I**T WAS EMBARRASSING** to see our champion forced into defending positions he could not have agreed with and into telling outright lies. Other politicians might lie but we expected more of Adlai. He was our pride.

It is even possible at this point to entertain the suspicion that Governor Stevenson would not have made a great president. Perhaps he was TOO rational, TOO objective, TOO patient. Perhaps his ability to see both sides of a question would have blunted his ability to act.

Perhaps. But his loss is felt like the loss of a personal friend. A fitting epitaph comes to mind from Shakespeare's Julius Caesar:

"*His life was gentle, and the elements*
So mixed in him that Nature might stand up
And say to all the world, 'This was a man.'"

Spy Goes Out
In the Cold

A WASHINGTON reporter has related an amusing experience he had with the CIA—and there aren't many of those around.

It seems that Ernest A. Ostro now of the Washington Star, answered a help-wanted ad in a magazine a few months ago to find that his prospective employer was the Central Intelligence Agency.

The agency was interested in him, he says, until it found out that he was happily married. His interviewer told him that the job for which they were considering him would keep him away from his family for at least two years; that what they really were looking for was a man with an unhappy h o m e life, preferably someone who was getting a divorce.

W**HILE OSTRO** didn't get the job, his experience throws some light on the hiring practices of the super-secret government agency. It leads one to imagine what a typical CIA job interview must be like:

Joe Loser, a cheerful, middle-aged man who has managed to evade steady employment for the whole of his adult life, knocks at the basement door of a boarded-up house.

The door opens immediately and a man in an olive drab suit says: "Who sent you?"

"The State Employment Service," Loser answers. "I went down to pick up my unemployment check and they said the CIA might have a job for me at this address. I told them I wasn't qualified but they . . . "

9

"You weren't followed here, were you?"

"No. And I didn't accept any candy from strangers, I'm proud to say. Look, I'm obviously not the man for the . . ."

"Follow me."

Loser is led into a small room at the rear of the basement where another man, wearing a drab, olive suit, is seated behind an oak desk.

"I SUPPOSE you're Mr. Loser," he says. "We've been expecting you. Come in and sit down. I imagine you're anxious to know a little more about the job."

"Not really."

"Oh a bit of a gambler, eh? We like that in our men. However, I must warn you that whatever you hear today must never go beyond the walls of this room. A slip of the lip may sink a ship."

"That let's me out" says Loser. "I'm a compulsive talker. As a matter of fact, I was kicked out of my fraternity in college for revealing our secret handshake to a sorority girl."

"Good. Then you know the terrible price that can be exacted for loose talk. Turn on that water faucet over there, will you, Clyde? I have a hunch this room may be bugged. One develops a sixth sense about these things after a time."

"I wouldn't," says Loser. "I barely use the five I've got."

"Now, let me ask you a few questions. Are you happily married?"

"Heavens no. My wife and I can't stand the sight of each other. We fight like cats and dogs."

"FINE. We find our agents in the field do better if they have no firm family ties. Do you drink?"

"Like a fish. One, sometimes two fifths a day."

"Excellent. An agent should be able to handle his liquor. You never know what you're going to be called upon to do in this business. You don't happen to have any subversive connections, do you?"

"Not unless you count my late mother, who was a Russian spy. I myself haven't belonged to the Communist Party since 1964, when I was thrown out for my support of Red China."

"Couldn't be better. We've been looking for a man with double-agent potential for some time. Clyde, I think we've got ourselves a boy."

"WAIT a minute gentlemen," says Loser. "This thing is getting out of hand. I don't want to work for the CIA—or anyone else, for that matter. All I want to do is collect my unemployment insurance."

"Sensational. That will make a great cover story in case you're captured behind enemy lines."

"What enemy lines?"

"Next week we're parachuting you into Washington, D.C., under cover of darkness. Your job: Find out whether J. Edgar Hoover is still alive."

• • •

I'M NOT SAYING that Lyndon Johnson is worried, but last week he sent Hubert Humphrey on a secret tour of the Middle East, trading new lamps for old.

• • •

10

The Dirty Dozen

OF ALL THE disquieting news that has found its way onto the front pages of newspapers recently, perhaps the most unsettling domestic story was that of the garbage collectors strike in New York City.

The collectors went on strike and New York's mayor asked the governor to call out the National Guard to make the garbage go away, but the governor said the Guard wasn't trained for that kind of work.

The governor then suggested giving in to the collectors' demands, but the mayor said no and the city shortly became the nation's first live-in garbage dump.

The incident does not bode well for the rest of the nation. Surely garbage collectors throughout the country—smelling victory in the wind, as it were—will begin making exorbitant salary demands, then striking until they're met. Unless . . .

UNLESS WE start giving our National Guardsmen antigarbage training. Garbage collectors wouldn't dare go out on strike if they knew a fully-trained, well-equipped National Guard stood by to take over for them.

And, of course, it would have some effect on the Guard. Should the retraining take place, can you imagine a conversation between a veteran Guardsman and a raw recruit?

"What's the matter, kid?" says the veteran. "You look down in the dumps."

"I am, Sarge. We had bayonet practice today."

"And you didn't do too well, eh?"

"No. I grabbed my rifle and yelled 'Kill!' Like I was supposed to, but just as I was about to stab an empty egg carton the wind picked it up and I wound up getting Corporal Schroeder in the foot."

"Cheer up. It was just tough luck. It could have happened to anyone."

"Yeah, but that's not all. I can't seem to get the hang of keeping the garbage and trash separate."

"It'll come, it'll come."

"But Sarge, we're going out on field maneuvers next week. I haven't got much time to get ready."

"There's only so much they can teach you in basic, kid. A Guardsman isn't a Guardsman until he gets his feet wet."

"SARGE, I'm scared."

"Sure you are. You wouldn't be any good if you weren't. Everybody is."

"Even you?"

"That's right. Every time I go out on a big garbage strike I get butterflies in my stomach. And anybody who says he doesn't is a liar."

"But, Sarge, you're a hero. You've got the Distinguished Service Medal with four lettuce leaf clusters."

"I know, but the first time I saw action I was so scared I couldn't remember which lever to pull on the Dempster Dumpster."

"No kidding?"

"If it hadn't been for a sergeant who slapped my face and brought me back to my senses, I might not be here today."

"Gee, maybe I'll do okay then."

"Sure you will. Just remember you've got a proud heritage to live up to. And don't forget our company motto."

"What is it?"

"Every litter bit hurts."

11

The Killers In Suits

THINK ILL of me if you will, but I am hopelessly prejudiced against war criminals.

I've been that way, I suppose, ever since the invention of war crimes—at the Nuremburg trials. I gloried in the treatment the mad-dog Nazis received there and, years later, I cheered when they brought Adolf Eichmann to the bar of justice.

Perhaps that makes me a bigot, I don't know.

The plain fact is, I just don't like war criminals. I don't want one to move next door to me. I don't want my sister to marry one.

However . . . I feel I must say a word in defense of Pvt. Michael A. Schwarz, a war criminal of sorts.

Schwarz is a 21-year-old Marine who has been sentenced to life imprisonment for his part in the murder of a dozen Vietnamese civilians—three women and nine children—at the village of Son Thang on Feb. 19.

PRIVATE SCHWARZ, a member of a five-man "killer team," admitted shooting the women and children. He was only following orders, he said.

Murder, the court-martial said.

So Private Schwarz, a ninth-grade high school dropout, is a convicted war criminal. That's ludicrous.

You take a young, dumb kid and you send him to boot camp.

"Follow orders, kid," you tell him. "We don't want you to think, we want you to follow orders. The penalty for disobedience of a command in a war zone is death."

And you train him. "Kill! kill! kill!" you yell at him. You even make him yell it back at you—"Kill! Kill! Kill!"—just to get him in the spirit of things.

Then you send him out into the field against an army that includes women and children. He does what he's told: kill-kill-kill. Maybe he becomes a trifle over-enthusiastic about his job.

"Wait a minute!" you say. "The third fellow you killed . . . the one just before the old lady . . . he was an unarmed, innocent civilian. You've just committed murder, son, and we're going to try you as a war criminal. That's because we're such a moral country."

"BUT WHAT about all that kill-kill-kill stuff you gave me in basic?" the young man asks.

"That was just a figure of speech."

"How about the following orders routine?"

"Naturally, we expected you to use your judgment about that."

And that's how Michael A. Schwarz gets to be a war criminal.

The ironic part is that had he been a bombardier and killed those same three women and nine children by burning them alive with napalm, he wouldn't have been a war criminal. He would have been a hero. He might have even gotten a medal.

Killing women and children somehow doesn't matter so much when it's done from the air. Who ever heard of a pilot committing an atrocity? Mistakes, yes; but an atrocity, never.

IF YOU'RE going to get serious about trying people for war crimes—any war, any crimes—you're going to have to begin with fellows in business suits.

12

The people who make the decisions which ultimately find their expression in war crimes wear business suits.

After them, you want to get after the people in uniform who wear a lot of gold braid—generals, admirals, people like that. They have some influence over the manner in which things are conducted.

After them you get the junior officers and after them the non-commissioned officers and after them—and not until then — you get the Private Schwarzes. That's where they belong in the chain of responsibility.

If you do otherwise, you're not looking for war criminals. You're looking for scapegoats.

• • •

RUMOR OF THE WEEK — When they get the heart transplant operation perfected, they're going to try it on animals.

• • •

The Symbol Of Dow

IF YOU'RE GOING to demonstrate against the war in Vietnam, you might as well demonstrate against Dow Chemical.

For Dow, maker of napalm, as much as any single organization, has come to symbolize what modern warfare has become: Utterly ruthless, totally dehumanized and highly profitable.

One might argue that war has always been thus, an unpleasant business altogether. Perhaps, but with a difference.

IN 1937 THE incendiary bombing of the Basque city of Guernica by fascist forces during the Spanish Civil War brought a cry of moral outrage from what we used to think of as the civilized world.

A few days after the attack The Des Moines Register carried an eyewitness account by a Spanish priest which began:

"I saw the bombing and burning of Guernica—one of the terrible crimes of this age."

And yet, by the rather elevated standards set later in the bombing of Coventry and Dresden and Tokyo and Hiroshima and Nagasaki, the bombing of Guernica was nothing, a trivial thing. *Our sensibilities have become so brutalized by 30 years of virtually unremitting horror that now, when one objects to the bombing of Vietnam on the ground that civilians— women and children—are being destroyed, the accepted answer is that war is war—civilians are bound to suffer. Yes, but by napalm?*

Napalm, by its very nature, is a monstrous weapon. It's not a new one. It was developed in

13

1942, used extensively in World War II and very extensively in the Korean War. Vietnam marks the first time civilians in great numbers have been subjected to it.

HERE ARE some excerpts from a scholarly monograph on napalm (reprints of which were handed out at the Iowa City demonstration Tuesday) written by two doctors for the July 13, 1967, issue of "The New England Journal of Medicine," hardly a radical publication:

"Children will suffer a disproportionately high mortality and morbidity because of the special problems, acute and chronic, presented by the burned child . . .

"Panic is more likely to be observed among napalm victims than those wounded by other agents. Seasoned troops, accustomed to bombardments with conventional agents, have been known to break from cover during a napalm attack. . . .

"Incendiary bombing is potentially as destructive as atomic warfare. Fire storms can be created by planned bombing patterns.

"The effects of a fire storm, with high-velocity winds, smoke, toxic gases and extreme heat, create the conditions for a medical disaster. Loss of life under such circumstances overshadows all other considerations.

"The saturation bombing of Japanese cities with napalm during the last months of World War II caused many more deaths than the atomic attacks on Hiroshima and Nagasaki."

THIS THEN is what the nationwide demonstrations against Dow Chemical are all about. The demonstrators are saying that Dow cannot escape responsibility for the uses to which its product is put. In fair-

ness, however, it must be pointed out that Dow is hardly unique among American corporations in this regard. Virtually all major firms supply war materiel.

There is, however, some concern on the part of like-minded people over the form the demonstrations are taking.

It is absurd to label a demonstration, the purpose of which is to get demonstrators arrested, "non-violent." Such action is provocative. It invites violence.

It is common knowledge that there are certain kinds of policemen who enjoy hitting people over the heads with sticks. It is wrong to encourage them in this proclivity and, having encouraged them, it is ludicrous to scream "police brutality."

But basically, the demonstrations of the type we've seen in Iowa City recently are wrong because they're ineffective.

The demonstrator who has just acquired a concussion and a police record may feel that he has made a sacrifice for his beliefs, but the sacrifice is a meaningless one.

He has convinced no one of the rightness of his beliefs and that, it seems to me, should be the direction in which his efforts are bent.

We live in a society that seems to be coming apart at the seams. It is, to put the best possible face on it, an imperfect society but it seems unlikely that if we allow its destruction a better one will rise from the rubble.

●   ●   ●

SOME DAY BIRDS will fly the ocean like men, in huge silver planes.

●   ●   ●

Poor, Poor Prexy

THE TWO great disadvantaged groups in the world today are the South Vietnamese peasant and the United States college president. Whatever else happens, in any given situation involving either of these groups, they're sure to get it in the neck.

Interestingly enough, the job of college president was considered a relatively good one—something on the order of a Latvian bank president—until a few years ago. That's when the Revolting Generation came of age and things have been sheer hell for campus administrators ever since.

Here is a typical day in the life of a typical contemporary college president.

He goes to his office in the morning and says to his secretary, "Well, what's the situation today?"

"It hasn't changed much. They still have the dean of men barricaded in the west wing of the girls' dormitory."

"Because he won't allow women students to stay out all night?"

"Because he won't make it mandatory."

"I see. By the way, I thought we'd made all of our dormitories co-educational."

"YES, WE DID that last fall when that group of boys hung you out of a third-story window by your heels."

"Young rascals. How can the dean of men be in the girls' dormitory then?"

"**Don't you remember? We changed it back this winter when that delegation of coeds threatened to fire bomb your home.**"

"It all comes back to me now. They said they didn't want to live with the boys because the boys only had one thing on their minds—student power."

"That reminds me . . . your wife called. She said that group staging a sit-in in your living room has threatened to go on a hunger strike if the food doesn't improve."

"What are they protesting, anyway?"

"*Permissiveness on campus.*"

"Oh, yes. Well, we'll see what we can do. How is the Board of Regents doing?"

"THE REGENTS are still cut off without supplies in Old Main, but we've got a contingent of classics scholars working to lift the siege."

"Those classics boys can do it if anyone can. What's their department motto again?"

"Alexander the Great is alive in Argentina."

"**Marvelous spirit. Why are the Regents under siege?**"

"The students are protesting the Coke machine in the union; it keeps running out of change."

"I told the board that issue was potential dynamite. Say, what about the rumor that the football coach was hanged in effigy?"

"There no truth in it."

"That's a relief."

"He was hanged for real."

"I WARNED him against being stubborn, I told him he should have given in."

"What did they want?"

"The students wanted the coaching staff to carry the players off of the field after a victory, instead of the other way around. Answer the phone, will you?"

"**It's not ringing.**"

"I've been hearing bells ever since that student protest committee gave me that savage beating in my office last week."

"What were they protesting?"

"Police brutality."

Hizzoner

Speaks

IT HAS BECOME something of a matter of prestige for a world leader to have his pithy remarks collected in a book. In the world leader racket, if you don't have a "Quotations From . . ." book to your name, you don't have a name.

The trend was started, of course, by "Quotations from Chairman Mao Tse-tung," the little red book that has become a bible for the Red Chinese and for young radicals throughout the world.

It was followed by "Quotations from Chairman L.B.J.," a tongue-in-cheek compilation of the thoughts of Mr. Johnson.

And now—at last—we have the wit and wisdom of perhaps the most quotable of all world leaders collected between hard covers. The book is "Quotations From Mayor Daley" and the subject, of course, is the Hon. Richard J. Daley of Chicago, Ill.

It is by far the best of the three books. Mao doesn't really get much better than "Political power grows out of the barrel of a gun," while Johnson's "We don't want our American boys to do the fighting for Asian boys" is even less prepossessing.

COMPARE THEM, for style, with Daley's ". . . The policeman isn't there to create disorder, the policeman is there to preserve disorder."

Or his classic:

"Together we must rise to ever higher and higher platitudes."

While one must comb the books of Mao and L.B.J. to root out an occasional gem, great quotes come spilling out of the Daley book in dizzying splendor:

"It is amazing what they will be able to do once they get the atom harassed," he said. Also:

"They have vilified me, they have crucified me, yes, they have even criticized me."

Yet there are parallels in the thoughts expressed in the three books and it may be of some value to explore them.

HERE, for example, are a few remarks that reflect the contrasting styles of leadership of the great men:

Mao—"Thousands upon thousands of martyrs have heroically laid down their lives for the people; let us hold their banner high and march ahead along the path crimson with their blood!"

L.B.J.—"Wouldn't it really be better for us, wouldn't it be better for the Soviet Union, wouldn't it be better for Great Britain, wouldn't it be better for Germany, wouldn't it be better for all the people of the world who are looking to us for leadership if we carried Ohio by 400,000 instead of 300,000?"

Daley—"When you get 500,000 people to the polls without a contest, it surely is an expression of confidence."

Here are thoughts on their native grounds:

Mao—"We, the Chinese nation, have the spirit to fight the enemy to the last drop of our blood, the determination to recover our lost territory by our own efforts, and the ability to stand on our own feet in the family of nations."

L.B.J.—". . . The true image of Washington is not that of power or pomp or plenty. It is, rather, that of a prayerful capital of good and God-fearing people."

Daley—"Chicago has been acclaimed as the nation's most exciting city, and we intend to keep it that way!"

On culture:

Mao—"An army without culture is a dull-witted army, and a dull-witted army cannot defeat the enemy."

L.B.J.—"There is, I think, a growing appreciation in America for the arts and a growing understanding and I think there is a growing demand among our people."

Daley—"We've demolished more buildings than any administration in the history of Chicago."

On a philosophy of life:

Mao—"In times of difficulty we must not lose sight of our achievements, must see the bright future and must pluck up our courage."

L.B.J.—*"Don't spit in the soup, we've all got to eat."*

Daley—"Looking back, you never forget the person who helped you get your first job."

Daley, by a mile.

On Banning the Bans

THE 17-NATION disarmament conference — s o m e t i m e s called the oldest established permanent diplomatic crap game in the world—reconvened in Geneva, Switzerland, a week or so ago.

They've been doing that for years; sitting around and talking, thinking the unthinkable. drinking the undrinkable, trying to save the world from its basest instincts.

Some of the older delegates must be well nigh worn out by this time. They need to be pulled out of the front line of disarmament for rest and recreation.

It would be interesting to hear the conversation between one of the old disarmament conference hands and his young replacement.

"Well," the old-timer says, "I suppose a young chap like yourself has some fresh and new approaches to the disarmament game."

"Oh, yes," says the replacement. "I think it's time to bring space-age technology to the problem of disarmament. Before I came over here, I fed all available data on disarmament into a computer and the machine came up with a revolutionary new proposal."

"What is it?"

"The computer suggested that all the nations of the world take their swords and beat them into plowshares. The idea needs a little work, but I feel it's basically sound."

"Yes, so did I when I proposed it 12 years ago. It was defeated unanimously. Even our own country voted against it. It was claimed it would bring about a worldwide economic depression."

"Oh. The powerful international sword lobby opposed it then?"

"Yes, and the plowshare manufacturers weren't too crazy about it either."

"WHAT SORTS of disarmament proposals have been successful over the years?"

"Ones with limited objectives. For example, Monte Carlo made a big hit at the conference a few years ago by promising not to

17

stage a nuclear attack against any of its immediate neighbors."

"**But Monte Carlo doesn't have any nuclear weapons, does it?**"

"No, but you have to start somewhere. The only other resolution to get unanimous support during my time here was the one requiring conference delegates to keep the safety catch on their revolvers during formal sessions."

"You mean the delegates come to the meetings armed?"

"Just the ones who don't have personal bodyguards. We passed the safety catch resolution right after an Arab delegate shot himself in the foot during a roll call. Many consider it the highlight of the disarmament talks thus far."

"Getting the r e s o l u t i o n passed?"

"*No, seeing the Arab delegate shoot himself in the foot.*"

"Don't you ever deal with the more significant aspects of disarmament?"

"Like what?"

"Like a missile ban, for example."

"We talked about it once, but the countries with an offensive defense posture wouldn't hear of it."

"**H**OW ABOUT an anti-missile ban then?"

"The nations with a defensive defense posture were against it. At this session, however, we shall consider a ban on anti-missile missile-antis."

"Never heard of them."

"**Neither had anyone else. That's why we think we've got a good chance of banning them.**"

"Do you think that there's any hope of someday outlawing nuclear weapons altogether?"

"*Yes, I do, but we'll have to go at it one step at a time. We have to learn to crawl before we can walk, walk before we can run.*"

"What do you think the first step will be?"

"The banning of the peaceful uses of atomic energy."

Stamp Out Extremists

I AM INDEBTED to the National School Boards Association for sending me their "information service bulletin" on the recent attempts of extremist groups to take over school boards and P.T.A. organizations around the country.

The bulletin states that "much of the turmoil currently disrupting many of America's school boards is traceable to irresponsible critics—extremist critics—who produce a death sentence on honest communication by destroying democratic

methods of argument and persuasion and by stifling responsible diversity and dissent."

It goes on to list "some signs which may indicate that your schools could soon become a target for extremist criticism." And the first sign it lists is:

"A sharp rise in attendance at school board or P.T.A. meetings."

Well, there you have it. Now we know what to watch for. Forewarned is forearmed. One can imagine a man trying to join a local P.T.A. that has been alerted by the bulletin.

He finds out the date of the meeting and after searching the school, he finds it, attended by four women, in a windowless, smoke-filled room.

"HELLO," he says. The women, startled, turn in their chairs to face him.

"What are you doing here?" one of them asks. "How did you find us?"

"It wasn't easy," he answers. "I didn't even know this school had a sub-basement."

"What do you want?"

"I'd like to join the P.T.A."

"What are you, some kind of lunatic fringe?"

"He looks like a right-wing nut to me, Ethel."

"No, I . . ."

"We don't need your kind around here."

"Scat."

"Ladies, please. Control yourselves. I come in peace. I'm no extremist. Look, here's my Diner's card."

"That doesn't mean anything. They can be forged. If you're not a neo-Fascist screwball, then why do you want to join the P.T.A.?"

"*I wish to take an active role in my child's education, to contribute my share to his intellectual development.*"

"Then why do you want to join the P.T.A.?"

"Shut up, Irma. I have an idea, girls. Let's give him a test to find out whether he's a radical right-winger."

"OKAY. Bernice, you're the chairman of Committee to end Parochialism, Provincialism and Uninformed Anti-Communism in Our Schools—as a matter of fact you're the whole committee. You administer the test."

"All right, but I still think we're wasting our time. We don't need his kind."

"Ask the questions."

"*Young man, do you favor arming the safety patrol?*"

"Only as a last resort."

"*Do you think godless atheists should be allowed to teach in our schools?*"

"Yes, but I think we should be sure that our children should be exposed to godFEARing atheists, too."

"*Have you or any of your close friends or relatives ever stifled responsible diversity and dissent?*"

"Never."

"*Is this country a democracy or a republic?*"

"Which is better?"

"*Are you in favor of fluoridation of drinking water?*"

"Only for young children."

"I THINK that's enough, girls. If he were a right wing extremist he couldn't have answered all of those questions correctly. I say take a chance on him, what do you say, Martha?"

"Scat."

"Fine, it's unanimous then. Welcome to the P.T.A., young man."

"*I'm sorry, ladies, but after mature consideration I find that I will be unable to join your organization.*"

"Why?"

"I promised my mother never to join a secret society."

• • •

RUMOR OF THE WEEK—Dick Nixon takes Sen-Sen trips.

• • •

19

Klan Talk

FOR ALL of its bad points, you have to give the Ku Klux Klan this much credit; it is much funnier than the average minstrel show.

A copy of the Constitution and Laws of the Women of the Ku Klux Klan (adopted in 1927) has fallen into my hands and much of it is too good to keep to myself.

For example, the constitution sets forth the names to be given Klan officers. The president is called "Excellent Commander," which is reasonable enough, but the rest are lulus.

Here they are, the positions followed by the proper Klan titles:

Vice-president—**Klaliff**
Lecturer—**Klokard**
Chaplain—**Kludd**
Secretary—**Kligrapp**
Treasurer—**Klabee**
Conductor—**Kladd**
Inner Guard—**Klarogo**
Outer Guard—**Klexter**
Investigator—**Klokan**
Board of Investigators—**Klokann (plural of Klokan)**

YOU MAY very well wonder what some of these people do; the Klokard for instance.

I'm glad you asked. The Klokard shall be responsible for the proper performance of all ritualistic work within the Klan and s h a l l disseminate Klankraft throughout the Klanton." Of course, what else would a Klokard do?

A Kligrapp "keeps an accurate and complete record of all the proceedings of the Klonklaves" and a Kladd collects "the countersign and password at the openings of a Klonklave."

To which one can only say, "For Krying Out Loud."

The year of the Klan (an Anno Klan) begins with the month of June but a Cycle is a 12-month period beginning with the month of December. Sounds Krazy, doesn't it?

But wait until you hear about the names they give the days, weeks and months. For use in official Klan documents the days of the week, presumably starting with the first day of the month (pristine clarity is one of the virtues the Klan Constitution lacks), are named "Dark, Deadly, Dismal, Doleful, Desolate, Dreadful, and Desperate," in that order.

The weeks of the month are designated as "Woeful, Weeping, Wailing, Wonderful and Weird."

The months of the year are: "Bloody, Gloomy, Hideous, Fearful, Furious, Alarming, Terrible, Horrible, Mournful, Sorrowful, Frightful and Appalling."

[There are those who might think that I'm making all of this up, but I ask you, how do you make up stuff like this?]

CAN'T YOU just hear a Klarogo talking things over with a Klexter?

"It's been a perfectly beautiful Appalling this Anno, hasn't it?"

"Yes, and it's about time. Last month was awful."

"No, it wasn't. It was Frightful."

And can you imagine the trouble the Klan poets have with the system?

"Fearful is the cruelest month," the poet says and someone replies: "If you think Fearful is bad, wait until you get a load of Hideous."

Have you ever tried rhyming Moon with Bloody?

Compared to those Klan girls, Edgar Allan Poe was a wide-eyed optimist.

To some, the Klan's nomenclature might seem a trivial matter, but in truth it has far-reaching significance.

It proves one thing beyond any reasonable doubt. It proves that it is not merely for show that the bed sheets that the Klan members wear come to a point above the eyeholes.

Lakeside Madhouse

I had complained to my editors that I never got a chance to cover any national disasters, so they sent me to the Democratic National Convention in 1968. It was a memorable experience, something on the order of being in the front rank of Pickett's charge or taking a guided tour of San Francisco during the earthquake.

CHICAGO, ILL.—This isn't a town, it's a nervous breakdown. I've seen a few things in my time—Detroit on V-J Day, New York when the Beatles were in town—but I've never seen anything like this.

The New Left is fighting with the Old Left, the Hippies are at odds with the Yippies, the A.D.A. is mad at the CIA and all of them are being picketed by the American Nazi Party.

Of all the things Chicago doesn't have in its hour of crisis, however, the thing it doesn't have the most of is communications.

When someone in Chicago says, "Keep in touch," he means, "Don't let go of my hand."

The Titanic had better communications than Chicago. About half of the cab drivers here are on strike as are many of the bus drivers.

If someone happens to have a phone you can't reach him on it and the air pollution obliterates smoke signals.

The nerve center of this madhouse is the Conrad Hilton Hotel, convention headquarters.

The Hilton has about six workable elevators or about one per 6,000 who want to use them at any given moment.

People gather in front of the elevator doors in great mobs and fight for places on board. They look like Europeans fleeing the Nazi invasion.

The Iowa delegation is somewhat isolated from all this hurly-burly. It's housed way across town in the Drake, an elderly, elegant hotel across the street from the Playboy Club.

The service is adequate, the elevators run on time and you can even get into the restaurants. It's a lot like Iowa, a little out of the way, maybe, but altogether sensible.

★ ★ ★

ABOUT TWO BLOCKS from the Drake, in the heart of a nightclub district, is a saloon called "My Place." Its sign says:
Topless
Bottomless
No Cover
—Naturally. There's nothing left to cover.

★ ★ ★

I WAS STANDING in front of the Merchandise Mart Sunday, waiting for Gov. Harold Hughes [of Iowa] to show up for his appearance on "Meet the Press."

I was out there alone when a dog of undetermined origins romped up. I tried to make friends with him, without success. It wasn't that he was hostile, merely suspicious.

At that point the governor drove up with his aides and got out of his car. I immediately aimed a searching political question at him.

"Governor," I said, *"how come McCarthy has thousands of screaming fans to greet him wherever he goes and all you get is a columnist and a mongrel pup."*

The governor looked down at the dog, then kneeled. The dog came right up to him and in a moment allowed itself to be chucked under the chin.

The governor, very quietly, said "Sit." The dog sat. He said, "Give me your paw." The dog gave.

The governor got up. "That's no mongrel," he said, "that's somebody's pet." Then he went inside and appeared on nationwide TV.

Which is the difference, I suppose, between important politicians and columnists. Not even dogs obey columnists.

Blame It on TV

CHICAGO, ILL.—Cab drivers, once one of the major sources of political wisdom in this country, are being ruined by television.

There was a time when you could jump into a cab at Chicago's O'Hare International Airport, ask a cabbie: "How does this political race shape up to you?" and he'd give you an answer you could put in the bank.

"The way it looks to me," he'd say, *"this guy Stevenson ain't got a chance. He seems like a nice fella but he ain't got Ike's moxie. People, they remember Ike from World War II, with the jacket and all, you know what I mean?"*

Sure, you knew what he meant and you went out and wrote it. And it was right.

YOU ASK A CAB driver in Chicago a question like that today and you get an answer like this:

"I see the convention as the manifestation of a frustrated party laboring in a frustrated city. Vice-President Humphrey certainly must be regarded as the front-runner in the contest for the nomination but whether his success will prove to be a hollow one will depend on his ability to heal the wounds of this bitter internecine rivalry."

Good night, Chet. Good night, David.

I SPENT $10 in cab fares yesterday trying to get cab drivers to tell me what grass roots America is thinking and all I found out was the results of the latest Gallup Poll.

It's television, strictly television. The drivers watch it, the people they drive around watch it, and they just pass the word back and forth.

Cut off from my primary source, however, I did not give up. I improvised. I sought out the opinions of others who make frequent contact with the public.

First I went to a policeman and said, "Excuse me, officer, but do you feel that the primary issue of the coming presidential campaign will be law and order and, if so, how do you feel this will translate into delegate votes at the convention?"

And the cop said:

"One more smart crack out of you, creep, and you've bought yourself a concussion. Get behind the barricade."

So I thanked him and went off to find a canny politician I know.

"SAY SPIRO," I said, "Do you believe that this is going to be an open convention and if so, will it be open from nine to five or 24 hours a day?"

And Spiro replied:

"Convention? What convention? I can only speak for myself but on the one hand there may be a convention and, on the other, you never know. But don't quote me."

Thus informed, I found a Yippie friend from Ottumwa who was sleeping in a cave during the convention.

"Pardon me, Zoltan," I said, "but do you believe the politics of the New Left have a chance of winning overwhelming grass roots support before next Tuesday?"

And Zoltan, telling it like it is, said:

"Grass roots? They're groovy man. Smoke 'em all the time. But I don't understand the question, baby. Yesterday was next Tuesday."

23

A S A LAST GASP attempt to find out what really was on the mind of America, I walked over to a middle-aged man with a pair of beautiful young girls on his arms.

"Sir," I inquired, "is it your belief that Vice-President Humphrey's presidential aspirations can withstand the onslaught of Lester Maddox?"

"If you're from the private detective agency, tell my wife she can have the divorce, but I get to keep the car. Now stop tailing me, already."

Discouraged, I went in to the nearest bar, where the bartender asked me how I thought the convention was going to go.

Sway
Away

CHICAGO, ILL.—I've spent a lot of my time the past few days trying to find out what makes the "uncommitted" delegate tick.

Such people have always fascinated me. Here they are, within hours of the voting at the national convention—after months of primaries, speeches and position papers—and these delegates haven't yet made up their minds about whom they want for president. What could they be waiting for?

I had heard reports of a legendary uncommitted delegate who waited until 1950 before coming out for Truman. I decided to look him up and found him having breakfast in the Conrad Hilton coffee shop. He was having two eggs, one up and one over.

"Excuse me, sir," I said, "but why do you veteran uncommitted delegates wait so long before making up your minds?"

"I don't see any reason to rush things. What good are campaigns if nobody pays any attention to them?"

"But surely you have enough information by now to reach a decision on whom you're going to support for the nomination."

"Having enough information isn't the point. Having ALL the information, that's the point. Do you think I should drink my coffee with or without cream?"

"With. Are you leaning toward any one candidate right now?"

"An experienced uncommitted delegate never leans, he sways. One day I'll be swaying toward one candidate, then I'll see something in another candidate that will make me sway toward him."

"WHAT ARE some of the major things you look for in a candidate you sway toward?"

"Free drinks."

"Besides that."

"It varies with the campaign. For example, earlier this year I was very definitely swaying in the direction of McCarthy."

"You admired his courage in speaking out on the issue of Vietnam, eh?"

"No, I don't know anything about Chinese food. What I liked about him was that his supporters used hand-lettered signs."

"Hand-lettered signs?"

"Yes, I think hand-lettered signs show a great deal of warmth and sincerity. Those machine-made signs Humphrey and Kennedy had just couldn't compete. I was a big McCarthy swayer until McGovern got into the race."

"You felt that the added element of McGovern's strong commitment to civil rights gave him an edge over the other candidates, right?"

"**Wrong. He not only had hand-lettered signs, he had them done in Crayola, which I considered a significant improvement over McCarthy's magic marker models. You couldn't even read them, they were so sincere.**"

"SO McGOVERN won the battle of the signs?"

"Not really. Lester Maddox took honors with hand-lettered Crayola signs on which all the words were misspelled. He made them himself. More sincere than that you cannot get."

"Does that mean you're a Maddox swayer now?"

"*I considered it briefly, but one of his supporters took me to lunch yesterday and suggested we flip for the check.*

A man with supporters like that doesn't have any charisma."

"Where does that leave you?"

"Uncommitted. I'm keeping my options open. I'm somewhat hampered by the lack of spontaneous demonstrations on the convention floor, however."

"You like demonstrations, do you?"

"**I put considerable stock in them. A candidate who can't organize a disciplined spontaneous demonstration can't heal the wounds that divide our nation.**"

"That's well put."

"Thank you. If you'll excuse me now, I have to go. I have an appointment to be wooed by a Humphrey supporter. And would you mind picking up my check? I came to this convention with a clean shirt and a $20 bill and I want to go home without changing either of them."

J. W. Inuendo
Speaks Up

CHICAGO, ILL.—It's been an exhausting week for everyone here, but no one has a better right to be weary than J. Walter Inuendo, the convention's official rumor-monger.

Inuendo is responsible for keeping the news media supplied with rumors and false reports and he's done a brilliant job.

Where would the convention have been had it not been for the stories that President Johnson was coming to the convention or that Ted Kennedy was coming to the convention or that the convention was going to Ted Ken-

nedy? It would have looked like an instant replay of Miami Beach.

I went up to Inuendo's command post yesterday, high atop the Conrad Hilton, and found him slumped over his rumor mill, hand on the crank. Asleep. I touched him on the shoulder and he awoke with a start.

"**Huh? What?**" he said. "**Betty Furness' name will be placed in nomination for the vice-presidency.**"

"Take it easy, sir," I said. "I'm not here for a rumor, I've come to learn about your art. How have things been going?"

"It's been brutal. Just brutal.

This is the toughest convention I've ever worked. I'm not sure I'll make it through the day."

"YOU mean it's been more strenuous than other conventions?"

"Definitely. They get rougher every time. When I started in this business a rumor-monger who knew his business could get by on two rumors a day. You allowed four hours for the rumor to get around the convention and another four hours for the reporters to prove it was without foundation."

"But things move more quickly now, eh?"

"You can say that again. Television's done it. I'll put out a perfectly good rumor—say, that Lyndon Johnson will make an appearance at the convention and that the California delegation will attempt to burn him at the stake. They put it on television and, blooey . . . in 15 minutes everybody knows about it and in another 15 it's a dead rumor and they're back clamoring for more material."

"How have you managed to keep up with this increased demand?"

"I've expanded my staff. Right now I have three men working on vice-presidential rumors alone and I've recently added a special section to turn out unconfirmed reports."

"What's the difference between a rumor and an unconfirmed report?"

"It's a rather technical matter. Generally speaking, an unconfirmed report is more specific.

"For example, if I were to put out the story that Hubert Humphrey was going to renounce the candidacy and attack the Chicago superintendent of police with a McCarthy button, that would be a rumor. If I said he was going to do it at 10:15 a.m., it would be an unconfirmed report."

"ARE there any rumors at this convention that you're particularly proud of?"

"I suppose you always have a soft spot in your heart for the runt of the litter. I put out a rumor the other day that Humphrey and McCarthy were joining forces in a stop-McGovern movement. It never got off the ground, but I liked it."

"Have you ever had the experience of putting out a rumor and having it turn out to be true?"

"Not often. I suppose the most famous one was back in 1960 when I issued the rumor that John Kennedy was going to pick Lyndon Johnson as his running mate."

"How did it make you feel when it actually happened?"

"Not too bad. After all, you can't win them all."

Law and Order Chicago Style

I GOT MY first real taste of Law and Order in Chicago last week, and I must say that, in retrospect, it was no worse than being tarred and feathered and ridden out of town on a rail.

Admittedly, Mayor Daley had a problem. Four or five thousand Yippies or hippies descended upon the city with the avowed intention of disrupting the business of the Democratic National Convention.

I have never been a great fan of the hippies and I was not particularly fond of these. They chanted obscenities. They waved Viet Cong flags. They littered the public parks.

Clearly they could not be allowed to have their way with the town, but Daley's response to the situation was altogether incredible. He turned Chicago into a police state—literally.

In most cases, the cops outnumbered the hippies by at least two to one, so that whenever the cops went headhunting, which was often, there simply weren't enough hippies to go around.

Lacking sufficient hippies, the cops made do with whatever was available—reporters, delegates, shop girls, lovers on strolls and Pulitzer Prize-winning cartoonists.

ON THE NIGHT before the convention I followed some raucous hippies down Michigan Avenue to the Chicago River where they were stopped by a police line. At this point, there were about 100 hippies, 50 cops. **The cops began to herd the demonstrators into the blind corner in front of the Wrigley Building when a scruffy, barefooted kid in a helmet yelled out: "Don't let them get you in there. It's a death trap."**

I thought that overstatement pretty funny and was still chuckling about it when four buses pulled up to within 10 feet of where I was standing.

"That's strange," I said to myself, "I thought the buses were on strike."

In the next two seconds 150 cops piled out of those buses, all with helmets, all with clubs—150 cops and I was afraid of every one of them.

As I sprinted down the street yelling "Press! Press!" I decided to get a haircut the next day. Chicago was not a good place to be mistaken for a hippie in a suit and tie, was the way I figured it.

SO THE NEXT day I got the haircut and went to Lincoln Park to watch the police clear it of its hippie squatters.

There must have been a thousand police there.

They warned the snarling, bottle-throwing h i p p i e s to leave the park and, upon being ignored, hit them with tear gas and sent in 200 cops to beat them up.

As the first wave of police advanced, their comrades standing in reserve began yelling: "Kill! Kill! Kill!" I began to have second thoughts about the death-trap remarks.

I managed to stay out of trouble throughout the long and bloody evening and on my way back to my hotel I was stopped by a police officer.

"Where do you think you're going, buddy?" he said. I showed my press credentials.

"Oh, one of the hippie press, eh?" he said. Right there I knew I hadn't gotten my hair cut short enough. He seemed about to bash me when two of his fellow police officers stopped him and told me to get the hell out of there. I got the hell out of there.

OTHER WELL-KNOWN hippie elements—John McCormally, editor of the Burlington Hawk-Eye, and The Register's cartoonist, Frank Miller—were tear-gassed.

Miller had a particularly rough convention. He was knocked down by a policeman during a hippie demonstration early in the week, he was tear-gassed and he was harassed.

One day he was sitting in the Conrad Hilton coffee shop, staring abstractedly into space as is his habit, when a cop walked over and said: "What are you staring at us for?"

Miller denied that he was and produced his credentials, which happened to be those of a news photographer.

"Where's your camera?"

"In my hotel room," Miller answered, not wanting to go into a lengthy explanation.

"If you know what's good for you, you'll keep it there," the cop said, and walked away.

On Scene at World Series

DETROIT, MICH.—Say what you will, covering a World Series game in the round certainly beats watching one at Ethel's Tavern in Van Meter.

There I was Saturday, standing right smack down on the field before the game, talking baseball with one of my sportswriting colleagues—Gene McCarthy.

We were discussing the merits of Orlando Cepeda as a fielder (low mediocre, we agreed) when a line drive came shooting in our direction from the bat of a Cardinal.

The senator ducked to his right to avoid being hit, which prompted me to say: "Good move, Senator. That's the first time you've gone to your right all year."

"Actually," he replied, "I've spent most of my time going backward."

It was good talk, man talk. The kind you're likely to hear when sportswriter meets sportswriter.

I happen to be one of the few newspaper men to cover both the 1968 Democratic National Convention and the 1968 World Series. But I don't know what that means.

ACTUALLY, though, my most memorable experience was Mike Galanovich.

I was standing on the sidelines during batting practice, listening to the other sportswriters interview each other, when this stray ball rolled through the crowd, followed by a stocky little gray-haired man in sports shirt and ripple-sole shoes.

The ball rolled against the stands and the little guy picked it up and began to yell, "I got it, I got it."

Then he ran to the edge of the infield and waved the ball high

Donald Kaul
Now a Sportswriter

over his head, still yelling, "I got it."

So I asked him what he was doing and, in a voice that was 85-proof, he replied:

"My name is Mike Galanovich and I'm showing this souvenir to my wife Lucille in the bleachers. She's up there with binoculars."

"Souvenir?" I asked.

"Yeah, this ball I just picked up. Gee, I'm really proud of it. Do you know where I can get it autographed?"

"Are you a sportswriter?" I asked.

"No," he replied. "My name is Mike Galanovich."

"Mike," I said, "it just might be that the Cardinals would object to signing one of their practice balls for you to carry away."

"You really think so?"

"I really do. If you want my

28

advice, put the ball in your pocket and go back to Lucille without saying anything to anyone else."

"Okay, pal," he said. "I'll do it. My name is Mike Galanovich." And so saying, he disappeared.

IT WAS all down hill after Mike, however. They chased all us sportswriters off the field and played an absolutely wretched game.

The Cardinals played badly, but not terribly, which is what differentiated them from the Tigers.

The quote of the day was uttered by a young man who, prior to the game, asked Senator McCarthy:

"Does anything you've seen in the Series so far lend itself to poetic thought?"

When you can think up questions like that, you're never going to be at a loss for words. The senator answered with a negative-sounding mutter.

McCarthy's never going to make it as a sportswriter, however. He gives too many interviews.

New York, Here I Come

I WAS SITTING at my desk, going through my collection of Italian gestures, when a secretary informed me that the boss wanted to see me.

"Sit down, O.T.," he said, as **I entered his office. "The smoking lamp is lit. O.T., I have an assignment that I'd very much like you to take."**

"Sure, Chief."

"But before you agree to do it, I want to make it perfectly clear that you're free to turn it down. If you don't want to do it just say the word and no more will be said about it and no one will think the worse of you for it."

"Chief, have I ever let you down? Have I? Your wish is my command, Chief. Just tell me what the job is and I'll do it."

"It could be dangerous."

"On the other hand, I've been having a lot of trouble with my back lately."

"We want you to go to New York City for us, O.T. We want you to go to plays and movies

and hang around cheap dives. We want you to immerse yourself in the life of the city."

"On an expense account?"

"Yes. Will you do it?"

"The way I figure it, you're either a newspaperman or you're not. I'll do it."

"Bless you, my son."

"Exactly what angle do you want me to work on?"

"ARE YOU AWARE that many persons on the east and west coasts consider Des Moines a hick town?"

"I've heard rumors to that effect, yes."

"Why do you suppose that is?"

"I've always thought it had something to do with the fact that Des Moines' jet setters use non-scheduled airlines and the late news comes on at 10 p.m."

"That's part of it, but that's not all of it. Have you ever stopped to consider why Des Moines is considered a hick town and New York isn't?"

29

"Now that you mention it, I don't think I have."

"Nobody around here has. That's just the trouble. We've allowed ourselves to become trapped by traditional thinking."

"You're right, Chief. Spats don't necessarily make the man."

The nice thing about going to New York City is that it feels so good when you stop.

"DON'T OVERPLAY your part, O.T. The day is coming when Des Moines will be a megalopolis stretching from Ankeny to Carlisle, from Adel to Pleasant Hills. We want to be prepared for that day."

"*I shouldn't wonder.*"

"Look upon your trip to New York as a fact-finding mission. We want you to find out what New York has that Des Moines doesn't."

"That's quite a challenge."

"**We want you to do the town; climb the Statue of Liberty, visit Grant's Tomb, get mugged in Central Park.**"

"Can I visit the Empire State Building?"

"Why not? Shoot the works. And hang the expense; the sky's the limit."

"It is?"

"**Up to $5 a day.**"

"You're all heart, Chief."

"Don't thank me, kid. You're worth every penny."

• • •

LAST WEEK an armed bandit, dressed in black, robbed a messenger of $5,000 in an elevator of a building in New York City's garment district.

His weapon? A three-foot long saber can disappear in a New York is probably the only city in the world where a guy dressed in black, carrying a bag full of money and a three-foot-*long saber.*
crowd.

• • •

Blood and Asphalt

NEW YORK, N.Y.—The people of New York are not a superficial people; they are deep.

They are informed by a profound sense of the duality of life —its beauty and brutality, its ecstasy and anguish.

One sees evidence of this exquisite sensibility on every hand but nowhere does it find more eloquent expression than in New York's gay, yet poignant, ritual of the streets.

They call it traffic.

Each morning, noon and evening, on street corners throughout the city, the festival of the traffic is carried on. It is here that the tragic soul of the true New Yorker is revealed.

Hoards of pedestrians gather at the curbs, taking final puffs on cigarettes . . . waiting. Then the green light flashes "walk" and the drama begins to unfold.

The crowds break from the sidewalk in a wave and flow across the intersection.

The cabs—moving slowly at first, then more rapidly—begin to execute their sweeping, graceful turns. Through the pedestrians.

For the aficionado this duel of death becomes the symbol of the human struggle, an intensification of life itself.

INITIALLY, the numero uno cab driver will make his way through the lines of people, dominating them with his fenders.

This part of the festival is called, "The Running of the Pedestrians."

First he chases the little old ladies back to the curb, then the mothers with small children.

Next he goes after the tourists,

then red-faced men with high mortgage payments and middle-aged women with charge accounts.

One by one they scurry back to safety, until only one is left —the brave New Yorker. The driver nods, acknowledging the worthiness of his opponent, and the battle is joined.

The pedestrian, who trains for his role in traffic by walking across the track at stock car races, affects not to notice the cab.

But the cab driver is not so easily fooled. He approaches the pedestrian slowly, cautiously until the cab is almost upon him. Then he sounds his horn and jumps on the accelerator pedal. *This is known as "The Moment of Truth."*

The pedestrian leaps to get out of the way but . . . if the driver has done his work properly . . . it is too late.

SOME drivers cheapen the spectacle by opening their doors to knock down pedestrians they have fairly missed with their fenders and bumpers. They are butchers and deserve no praise.

But when it is well done, the moment of contact—with the pedestrian flying high over the heads of the spectators, his eyes glazed, his mouth ajar— is a scene of breathtaking beauty.

The crowd shouts "ole" and surges forward to award the driver his trophies—the pedestrian's commuter ticket and attache case.

The brave New Yorker is dragged off for the ceremony known as "The Placing of the Bandages."

There are those who call it a cruel sport and even go so far as to demand its abolition. To the true New Yorker, this is unthinkable.

For him, traffic is not a sport. It is a way of life.

March? What March?

NEW YORK, N.Y.—This is a difficult town to impress; it's like trying to make a splash in a tidal wave.

If New York were to come under invasion by creatures from outer space, it wouldn't find out about it until the third day. New Yorkers would first try writing it off to the circus being in town.

They had a peace march here Saturday, the first mass anti-Vietnam demonstration of the Nixon administration. Estimates of attendance at the rally in Central Park ranged from 25,000 to 250,000.

Personally, I would have set the figure at 100,000, give or take 100,000. It was a bunch.

But New York didn't even notice them. There they were, tens of thousands of demonstrators, carrying signs and waving Viet Cong flags and shouting slogans, some of them not obscene, marching right up the heart of mid-Manhattan and nobody paid them any mind.

New York just swallowed the demonstration whole, without chewing.

It rained Saturday, lightly but steadily, and the procession to Central Park had a funereal atmosphere; which is perhaps appropriate for what must be the fourth or fifth annual mass protest of an ongoing war.

(It occurs that it might be cheaper to build a series of monuments across the nation in protest of the war in Vietnam. And, if the monuments were made of granite, they might outlast the war.)

AT ANY RATE, I was walking into the park with the

31

crowd, giving the "V" sign to hecklers, when this guy falls into step beside me. He is a thin, sallow-faced man with a Rex Harrison checked hat and bad teeth.

As he begins to talk to me I notice that he looks a little loony. Which figures. Sane people do not talk to strangers in New York.

(Two people had talked to me just the day before in New York. One of them believed the world was coming to an end within 10 years and that only the True Believers of Christ would be spared and the other attempted to involve me in a conversation he was having with an invisible companion.)

"I didn't really join this protest march," Checked Hat was saying. "I was just sort of walking down the street and fell in."

"Oh?" I say, moving a little faster. He increases his pace to stay abreast of me.

"Hey! I want you to hear something I just thought up. Are you listening?"

"Sure."

"*Nix Nixon, Dump Humphrey, Rock Rockefeller. How do you like that?*"

"It sounds derivative."

"What's that?"

"I love it."

"You do? I made it up myself. Nix Nixon, Dump Humphrey . . . what was the other thing?"

"**Rock Rockefeller.**"

"Yeah, Rock Rockefeller. I made it up. You think it's good, huh?"

"Terrific."

"LET ME TRY this on you. Tell me whether you like it. Be honest."

"I will."

"*You know how the tzar in Russia had his own troops to protect him? Well, would you say that the New York police here today are like the tzar's troops?*"

I thought about that a while. "No," I said, finally.

"Oh," he said, and began to move off. I broke into a half-run and heard Checked Hat accosting a marcher behind me. "Nix Nixon," he was saying.

My big moment of the demonstration came when a young black man waved a canister at me and said, "Support the H. Rap Brown Defense Fund."

"**I gave at the office,**" **I told him.**

He didn't seem much amused, but then he didn't look as though he had much of a sense of humor, either.

• • •

The older generation passes the torch of liberty to the older generation.

• • •

Vietnam Moratorium

ONCE UPON a time there was a president who came to us with heavy hurt. "Ma Fellamericans," he would say. "Yewr president comes to yew tonot with heavy hurt." He talked funny. His name was Lyndon the Lovely.

In many ways he was a very lucky man; he was rich and famous and powerful and he had a loving wife and two semi-beautiful daughters. And a heavy hurt.

"What makes your hurt so heavy, O Lovely One?" his subjects would ask.

"VEET NAM," he would answer. "Ah have waged war on poverty, Ah have laid the foundation of a Great Society, Ah have married off my two semi-beautiful daughters; but still people aren't satisfied. They want me to get out of Veet Nam."

"Uncle Dick Wants YOU."

"Then why don't you do it?" the people asked.

"And leave our supporters over there at the mercy of the majority? Yewr talkin' like Nervous Nellies. Besides, Dean Rusk believes in this war."

"But Dean Rusk believes in the tooth fairy."

"General Westmoreland believes in this war."

"General Westmoreland claps for Tinker Bell."

"And Ah believe in this war, Boy, and Ah'm gonna turn the corner over there and nail up a coonskin on the wall even if it costs me my job."

AND SO IT CAME to pass that Richard the Nixon became president.

He spoke not of Great Societies or of fighting poverty; he spoke of ending the war in Vietnam.

And he spoke not of turning corners or coonskins nailed to walls, but of negotiations.

"I have a plan," he said, and the people rejoiced.

"He has a plan, he has a plan," they shouted. "Pray, tell us what it is."

"Later," he said.

"He's just being careful," the people said. "A slip of the lip can sink a ship. We will go away and come back later."

IN SIX MONTHS, they were back. "What about your plan?" they asked.

"Wait," he said.

So they waited . . . and waited . . . and waited, until finally, they could wait no longer. So they went to their

33

leader and said, "The hour grows late. Tell us your plan."

"I shall," said Richard the Nixon. "I shall go on national television in living color and explain my plan to the free world and uncommitted nations of the earth and it shall be good. I want to make myself crystal clear on that point."

"Wonderful," the people said. And they went to their homes and gathered before their television sets to hear the Word.

The President appeared on their screen and he began to speak.

"Ma Fellamericans," he said. "Yewr president comes to yew tonot with heavy hurt. . . ."

The Mitchells
At Home . . .

IT'S TIME TO take another look into the private life of one of the men who make up the administration of Richard (The President) Nixon.

This week we turn our attention to Atty. Gen. John Mitchell and his wife, Martha. We look in on the Mitchells in their fortress flat, high above the Potomac, as the attorney general comes home from work.

"Hello, dear," Mrs. Mitchell says, greeting her husband with a kiss. "Have an exciting day at the office?"

"Not very. I spent the whole day going over the Bill of Rights, looking for loopholes."

"Find any?"

"I'm afraid not."

"I'm not surprised. You know, John, sooner or later this country is going to have to face up to the fact that the Constitution was written by wild-eyed revolutionaries and that if we don't want to be overrun by very liberal Communists, we'd better stop being soft on civil rights."

"That's a beautiful sentiment beautifully put, dear, but I wish you wouldn't say it so loud."

"Why not?"

"Walter Cronkite might be in the building and you know how he is on civil rights."

"Why should we care what Walter Cronkite thinks?"

"The President doesn't want to make him mad for fear that he won't do a good job on the next moon shot and the space program will be canceled because of low ratings."

"You certainly take care of the President, John. Why doesn't he give you a raise? Lord knows we could use it, what with the price of sable being what it is and all."

"He can't, dear. He can't pay one cabinet officer more than the others."

"BUT THAT'S not fair. The other cabinet officers don't have their wives helping them. That should be worth something."

"Martha—you haven't b e e n helping me again, have you?"

"Just a little interview with Joseph Alsop. It was hardly anything at all."

"You p r o m i s e d me you wouldn't give any more interviews."

"Yes, but you know how glum Joe Alsop looks when you refuse him an interview. I just couldn't let him down."

"What did you tell him?"

"Just the usual things . . . the war in Vietnam is a Communist conspiracy . . . we should unleash Madame Chiang Kai-shek . . ."

"That doesn't sound too bad."

". . . And I also told him that you feel that all members of Congress who disagree with

34

the President's war policy should be jailed."

"Jailed! I never said anything like that."

"I know, dear, but it makes a story so much better if you say it than if I do. Besides, it'll serve all those congressmen right. Their wives act so snippy."

"We can't go around threatening congressmen like that."

"Why not? We do it to everyone else."

"Because congressmen can fight back. Justice is blind, my dear, but it's not stupid."

"I keep forgetting."

"I'll get on the phone and see what I can do about killing the story. In the meantime, don't answer the door. It might be a reporter."

"I declare, John. You're such a grouch these days. Where is the happy, smiling man I married? On second thought, don't answer that."

The Dilemma
Of I.Q. Tests

THE LATEST crisis in Washington circles revolves around the revelation that Spiro Agnew has an I.Q. of 135. (In the Intelligence Quotient game, 100 is considered about average and 135 is very smart.)

Politicians, diplomats, bureaucrats and shop girls are living in fear that someone will find out that they don't have as high an I.Q. as Spiro Agnew and leak the news to the New York Times.

The Democratic National Committee is considering an anti-I.Q. campaign entitled: "You've Got To Have Heart."

But the persons really worried over Agnew's I.Q. test score are the guys who gave it to him, "V.I.P. Psychological Testing Services." Let us eavesdrop on a conversation between the two founders of the firm, Elmo Pisgah and Park Binet, after they heard the news.

"WE'RE RUINED, Elmo, ruined. All the years we put into building our reputations, down the drain in a single afternoon."

"I know Park. We should have stuck to teaching rats to run through mazes. It was a small buck, but a steady one."

"Spiro Agnew scoring 135 on one of our tests! How could it have happened? Who'll believe anything we say now?"

"Let's call in the young man who administered the test, Simon Durak."

The young man is summoned. *"Look here, Durak," Pisgah says. "Was there any hanky-panky when the vice-president took his test? What I mean to say is . . . did he cheat?"*

"No."

"Are you quite sure?"

"Absolutely."

"Then how in blazes do you explain his scoring 135 on a test where 100 is normal? If Agnew has an I.Q. of 135, my secretary has an I.Q. of 180."

"No," says Durak. "184."

"What?"

"I tested your secretary just the other day. She scored 184."

"Miss Dingaling scored 184! Durak, nobody with a body like Miss Dingaling can have an I.Q. of 184."

"Well, to tell you the truth, boss, I altered the score a little. I did it with Mr. Agnew and some others too."

"But why, Durak? Why?"

"I used to give honest I.Q.s, chief. People would come to me, their eyes wide with hope and

The rejection of G. Harrold Carswell's nomination to the Supreme Court is a landmark in United States history. It is the first time that the U.S. Senate has looked upon a court appointee and said: "Mediocrity and bigotry are not enough."

35

stupidity, and I'd test them. They would score 105, 98, 101, an occasional 110. You could see the hurt in their faces. We had doctors, lawyers, judges, vice-presidents of banks coming in here brimming with confidence, and we were sending them out broken men, burdened with the knowledge they were dummies."

"SO YOU falsified the tests?"

"Just a little, enough to give them a little help and encouragement. You should have seen them walking out of here with big smiles and a spring in their step. I felt as though I was bringing happiness into a chill, harsh world."

"But why Agnew?"

"**I didn't expect the vice-president of the United States to leak his I.Q. to the press. No politician ever has before.**"

"No politician had reason to, so long as the tests were honest.

How did you fix Agnew's score, anyway?"

"I simply totaled Agnew's I.Q. and the I.Q. of his speech writer and it came out to 135."

"**Well, there's some justification for that, I suppose. Maybe we can ride out this storm.**"

The phone rings.

"Hello, this is Elmo Pisgah . . . Why, yes: yes ma'am. I'm honored that you would call us . . . We'd be happy to test your intelligence Mrs. Mitchell . . . tomorrow will be fine. We have a Mr. Durak who'll be happy to administer the test . . . And Mrs. Mitchell, why don't you bring along your chauffeur? We may have use for him, it's part of a new group testing technique we've developed . . . Thank you. And be sure to tell your friends about us won't you? Goodbye." He turns to his colleague and says, "You know, Park, we just may have stumbled into something here."

The Outside

Agitator

THE THING you have to watch out for these days is radicals; long-haired bearded revolutionaries who would set themselves against the legitimately constituted forces of law and order.

Take this fellow I met the other day. You could tell what he was right away; he had the hair, the beard, the sandals. And he talked right straight down the party line, if you know what I mean.

"*If thou wilt be perfect,*" he said to me, "*go and sell that

thou hast, and give to the poor, and thou shalt have treasure in heaven: and come and follow me.*"

"No thank you," I told him, keeping my distance. "I'm doing just fine the way I am. And, if you want to know the truth, the trouble with this country is that the poor get too much for free as it is."

"*It is more blessed to give than to receive.*"

"I don't think you do a man a favor when you give him something for nothing. It takes away

36

his incentive to better himself through his own efforts."

"*What is a man profited if he shall gain the whole world, and lose his own soul, or what shall a man give in exchange for his soul?*"

"ABOUT NINE per cent per annum, at current rates. I won't stand for anyone criticizing the free enterprise system. Capitalism is what made this country great and it's jaspers like you, who never met a payroll in your life, who are dragging it down."

"*Verily I say unto you, that a rich man shall hardly enter into the kingdom of heaven.*"

"Marx's theory of class warfare, eh? There was a time when people looked up to men who had accomplished something in the community."

"*And again I say unto you, it is easier for a camel to go through the eye of a needle, than for a rich man to enter into the kingdom of God.*"

"It's television that's done it, you know. They ignore us members of the Great Silent Majority and spend their time building up characters like you."

"*A prophet is not without honour, save in his own country, and in his own house.*"

"You can say that again. Take Barry Goldwater, for instance."

"*Many are called, but few are chosen.*"

"Look pal, I could turn you in to the FBI, you know that, don't you? But it's Christmas. Infected by the spirit of the season, I am going to forget what I've heard here today. Why don't you behave yourself and mind your own business?"

"*Think not that I am come to send peace on earth: I came not to send peace, but a sword. For I am come to set man at variance against his father and the daughter against her mother, and the daughter-in-law against her mother-in-law.*"

"YOU OUTSIDE agitators won't let up for a minute, will you? For two cents I'd . . . never mind. You're not going to spoil my Christmas for me. I'm going to walk away from this like it never happened. It's just a good thing for you that I'm a Christian gentleman."

"*Blessed are the poor in spirit for theirs is the kingdom of heaven. Blessed are the meek, for they shall inherit the earth. Blessed are the merciful, for . . .*"

I didn't want to hear any more, so I put my hands over my ears and ran down the block. But before I turned the corner I looked back at the guy and gave him a parting shot.

"New Dealer!" I yelled at him. But it didn't seem to faze him. Those people have no shame.

Christmas, 1969

• • •

Whatever else his accomplishments, Richard (The President) Nixon seems destined to go down in history as the president with the most White Houses. He's got the D.C. house, of course, and the Florida White House and the California White House and, the other day, reporters were filing stories from something called "The Flying White House."

Next thing you know, he'll be making house calls.

• • •

Quite a Town

NEWARK, N.J., must be quite a town.

A friend had occasion to go there recently on business. He had bought an English car on a trip overseas and it was being delivered to Newark.

Having spent almost all of his money on the European trip and the car, he took a bus to the East Coast to pick it up.

He arrived at his destination at 4 a.m. At that time in the morning the bus station, like any typical, red-blooded American bus station in a big city, was populated mainly by hookers, pimps, homosexuals, lesbians and thugs.

Ignoring his surroundings as best he could, he approached a cab driver who was standing in the waiting room and asked the hack to take him to the docks.

"Okay," the cabbie said, "but you'd better not walk around with that camera case you're carrying." (In point of fact, the friend was carrying a change of clothes in the camera case, but it looked as though he were carrying an expensive camera.)

"Why shouldn't I walk around with a camera case?" the friend asked.

"Because you'll get rolled, that's why. Check the camera case."

"I won't get rolled," the friend said. "Just take me to the docks."

"Look, Buddy," said the cab driver, "I'm telling you—check the camera case. This ain't New York, you know."

That did it. The friend checked the camera case.

A Plea for Rationality

IT'S BEEN a tough week; the kind that makes a dedicated rationalist want to stick his head in the oven, turn on the gas and take a nap.

We seem to be a society dead set on self-destruction with each element set against its opposite number—young against old, black against white, North against South.

And now we sit arguing whether those four dead kids at Kent State deserved what they got and where we should draw the line on the home front.

There can be no real winner in this internecine warfare, but surely the biggest losers will be neither the militants of the right nor the left; it will be us—those of us in the middle who feel concern for the injustice that motivates much of the protesting, who have a stake in this society and a desire to make it live up to its traditional ideals.

It is a middle ground that is rapidly turning to quickstand beneath our feet.

ARE YOU for the Chicago 7 or are you for Judge Hoffman? Are you for the Black Panthers or are you for the cops? Are you for the students or are you for the National Guard?

These are the forms in which the issues of the day are presented to us. Yes or no, they ask. Are you with me or against me?

It's no good making a rational answer; that the issues are too complex for such simplistic analysis. You're branded a coward, or worse.

Logic and r e a s o n are drowned out by the clash of events. So we stand—we of the middle ground—impotent, frustrated, bathed in self-doubt.

It is difficult, at this distance, to know precisely what to think about the confrontation at Kent State: Buildings burned, students shot and killed, charges and countercharges.

It sounds like a story coming to us from a banana republic, rather than from a straight campus in the Middle West.

One feels sure that the National Guard cannot escape major responsibility for the disaster. Its track record at riots during the past several years is hardly enviable. Guardsmen have a well-established tendency to see phantom snipers and to begin banging away at whatever moves.

They simply are incompetent to operate effectively in the highly charged atmosphere of a large-scale demonstration.

HOWEVER strongly one feels about the burning and bombing of buildings and mass vandalism, there are ways to prevent it short of indiscriminate slaughter.

One of the unmourned casualties of the Kent State affair was Mr. Nixon's Bring Us Together Bandwagon. That bloated piece of campaign rhetoric was born in Ohio, handlettered on a sign at a whistle stop, and it died there, amid the shots and screams of an anti-war demonstration nightmare.

You don't bring a divided country together by sending your vice-president around to heap scorn on everyone who disagrees with you; you don't do it by ignoring what you don't want to hear.

It is time to reassert the value of rationality in our society. This does not mean a lowering of voices, which does nothing but serve the corrupt interests in power, but rather demanding that the voices talk sense.

The beginning of sense in our society would be the recognition of this fact, so self-evident to the protesters, so incomprehensible to those in office.

One cannot recoil in shock and horror at the burning of a campus building or the hurling of a rock and, at the same time, nod approvingly while we send armies throughout Southeast Asia burning villages in support of regimes that massacre whole communities of peasants.

If one does not protest the barbarism of the latter act, how can he expect his protest of the lesser barbarism of the former to carry moral force?

39

"The first state west of Illinois,

"... just under Minnesota"

An Odyssey Begins

I WAS SITTING at my desk last week, thinking of the good old days when Lyndon Johnson was president, when the phone rang. It was the boss's secretary.

"The boss wants you," she said. "Pronto."

I leaped up and jog-trotted to his office, pausing only to inform his secretary that my name wasn't Pronto and I would thank her to keep a civil tongue in her head. (I find racism, in all its forms, despicable.)

I presented myself, snapped to attention and clicked my heels as well as a man wearing Hush Puppies could. "Sir!" I said.

"Kid," he said, "we're sending you to northwest Iowa."

"Where, sir?"

"Northwest Iowa."

"That's fine. Er . . . where is it?"

"Curiously enough, O.T., it is both north and west of here. You'll be surprised to learn that the western and northern boundaries of the state come to a point somewhere north of Klondike."

"Klondike? Did you say Klondike?"

"Yes. Klondike, Ia. What's the matter? You don't seem very enthusiastic about this assignment."

"I'm enthusiastic. The only thing is, how come Gordon Gammack gets to go to Vietnam and I get to go to Klondike, Ia.?"

"Gordon Gammack doesn't get lost in revolving doors."

"THAT'S NOT fair. Admittedly, I've had some bad breaks on a few of my trips. I've run into some poorly marked highways, but . . ."

"Excuse me, O.T., but aren't you the one who once got lost traveling from Des Moines to Ames on the Interstate?"

"It was a simple matter of making a simple miscalculation."

"I suppose it is easy to make too much of a thing like that. I promise not to mention your getting lost on the freeway again."

"I'd appreciate it, chief. In the meantime, could I have an advance on my expenses? I want to lay in some supplies for the trip."

"What sort of supplies?"

"Oh, the usual—a little hardtack, signal flares, beads to trade with the natives."

"O.T. . . ."

"I wouldn't underestimate the value of the beads, chief—a few brightly colored necklaces to still the hostility of an angry Eskimo warrior."

"O.T. There is no such thing as an Eskimo warrior; if there were, you wouldn't find him in northwest Iowa. Go rent a car. Go west until you hit the Missouri River. Turn right and proceed until you see a sign that says 'Welcome to South Dakota.' Back up a hundred yards. You will be in northwest Iowa. Come back and tell me what you find."

"I will, chief. And you'll be proud of me, just you wait and see."

"Don't make a farewell address, just go."

So I went.

★ ★ ★

THREE DAYS later, I was back. The boss leaned back in his chair as I walked into his office and said:

"Well? How did you do?"

"Not bad. I didn't get lost until I hit Omaha."

"I thought you were going to take the Interstate west."

"I did."

43

"Got lost on the Interstate, again, eh!"

"Not exactly. I mean, as soon as I found out I wasn't where I thought I was, I knew where I really was."

"Where did you think you were?"

"On Interstate 29, a little north of Missouri Valley."

"And where were you really?"

"In a vacant lot in south Omaha."

"Uh . . . huh. You did finally make your way to northwestern Iowa, however?"

"I did, sir, and I had many adventures."

"Write them."

So I did.

(Listen in tomorrow, gang, for the next exciting episode in the northwest odyssey of our fun-loving columnist, entitled: "Lewis a n d Clark Strike Out.")

A Visit to the Biggies

AFTER BEING unsuccessful in my attempt to reach the Great Iowa Northwest by traveling south (thereby proving that Iowa was square) I went straightway to Sioux City, often called the Gateway to the Northwest.

(Of course, if you happen to live in northwest Iowa, Sioux City is the Gateway to the Southeast, but that's neither here nor there.)

I approached a likely looking citizen on the street and shook my beads in his face.

"You wantum pretty beads?" I asked him. "You have furs, make heap big trade?"

"I don't know about furs and beads, Baby, but they have some kicky flared slacks at Weatherwax."

Well, what can you expect of a place that doesn't allow angle parking?

I QUICKLY DECIDED I wasn't far enough north, so I jumped into my car and set out to find the *real* northwest Iowa. Chatsworth, Hawarden, Rock Rapids,

all the biggies. What follows is a blow-by-blow description, give or take a blow.

AKRON—Advertises itself as "Gateway to a peaceful valley of opportunity." Northwest Iowa has more gateways than a giant slalom course.

HUDSON, S.D. — I suppose you're wondering what an explorer of northwest Iowa is doing in South Dakota. That's what the explorer wondered too. Hudson is an environmental gas station.

INWOOD—A town of some 600 which, according to a thermometer tied to a lamppost, has raised $32,000 of the $40,-000 needed for a new swimming pool. It looks as though it needs a swimming pool, among other things.

KLONDIKE—Once a bustling rural slum, this bend in the road has seen better days. It makes Hudson, S.D., look like the Big Apple. The community consists of a half-dozen vacant houses, a couple of empty stores and some rusting autos. The population was

44

away the day I was there, probably visiting his mother. At the edge of town, on the bank of the Big Sioux River, stands a long-abandoned mill. About 40 per cent of it is gone altogether and the remaining wood has the consistency of a badly used sponge. It carries a sign that says: "This historic old mill is a priceless heritage and there is now a movement under way to repair and preserve it . . ." It's nice to know they haven't lost their sense of humor up there.

OCHEYDAN MOUND — The highest point in Iowa, the map said. I couldn't find it at first; the lady at the farmhouse said: "You passed it just back down the road. It's not very noticeable, but it *is* the highest point in Iowa." I drove back and located it. There's a sign. I climbed it in easy stages, putting on my sheepskin gloves for the final assault. From its snow-capped peak you can see about 300 yards in any direction — except d o w n, of course.

(To be absolutely truthful, there was no snow on its peak. On the slopes, yes, but the snow had melted off the peak. I just put that in for literary effect, making up for the exaggeration by undervaluing the view, which is breathtaking if you smoke a lot.)

OKOBOJI—Take a w a y the people in the snowmobiles and this area has a winter population the size of Klondike's. You see these lovely homes, whole blocks of them, all boarded up for the winter. Where do people get the money to own a big home they live in only a few months of the year? Okoboji is truly the Cannes of the Piper Cub set.

I LEFT NORTHWEST Iowa then, broader for the experience, and headed for home by way of Humboldt, home of State Representative Harold Knight, who thinks Des Moines is a jungle. More about that later.

(Tune in tomorrow, folks, for the further adventures of our death-defying columnist as he searches for sin in the episode entitled, "Is Humboldt Burning?")

Irresistible Sioux City

I DON'T want this to get out, so don't brag it around, but I rather LIKED northwest Iowa. Not as a place to live, perhaps, but certainly as a charming place to visit. It's got a sense of spaciousness that you don't get in teeming central Iowa.

I particularly liked Sioux City, which surprised me. I'd heard a lot of people badmouth Sioux City but for me it had a kind of vitality and dynamism that I associate with cities, good restaurants, nice shops, first-class movie theaters downtown.

I even had an interesting experience with a woman on the streets of downtown Sioux City.

It was about noon. I had been wandering around town all morning and I was hungry. Not spying a restaurant at close hand, I sought to ask a passerby to direct me to a nice downtown steakhouse.

I immediately spotted a woman who seemed perfect for my purposes. She was neither young nor pretty, which made it unlikely she would take me for a masher; yet she was wearing a red raincoat, which denoted an optimistic spirit of the type that knows where the good restaurants lurk.

"Excuse me, Madame," I said in my best non-masher tone, as she approached. She made no sign that she either heard or noticed me. "Madame?" I said. She was almost upon me now.

Finally, as she passed, her eyes staring fixedly ahead, she spoke. "No," she said in a tight, low voice. That was all.

"No, what?" I shouted after her. "I just wanted to ask you a question." She kept walking.

To have one's most innocent intentions completely misunderstood is the most frustrating of experiences. I was beside myself. "You . . . you . . . New Yorker!" I yelled at her as she disappeared into a bank.

Taking all things into consideration, I'd rather be mistaken for a masher than a panhandler.

A Day at the Office

WE HAD a pretty good fight here at the office the other day.

A reporter came into the newsroom and said, "Hey, they're painting out the wheat shocks on the inside of the Statehouse dome!"

And another man, an editor, said "They're not painting out the wheat shocks on the Statehouse dome." He didn't even look up when he said it.

"What do you mean they're not painting out the wheat shocks? What do you mean?" the reporter said, his voice squeaking a little.

"I've just come from the Statehouse and they're painting out the wheat shocks. I saw them with my own eyes."

THE EDITOR looked up and smiled a cruel smile. "They're not painting out the wheat shocks on the Statehouse dome because there are no wheat shocks on the Statehouse dome; they're wheat sheaves. Sheaves, not shocks."

Which inspired the reporter to come back with a devastating "Oh yeah?" and the battle was joined.

Those who do not believe that such a disagreement is enough to sustain a really good argument do not know the newspaper business.

It is not uncommon for reporters and editors to fight to exhaustion over the distinction between "flout" and "flaunt," and differences over "flounder" and "founder" have been known to end in death.

In any case, the wheat experts argued on volume for a while and various staff members began to choose up sides.

Eventually the dictionary was consulted. As it turned out, sheaves were bundles of grain while shocks were bundles of sheaves.

"THERE!" cried the reporter triumphantly. "I knew old man Webster would back me up."

"What do you mean, back YOU up?" the editor shouted. "It proves what I've been saying all along. Sheaves, not shocks."

Finally a neutral observer, a young man recently graduated from college, was dispatched to the Statehouse to judge whether the emblems were sheaves or shocks.

He returned shortly saying he thought they looked like fleurs-de-lis to him and was hooted out of the office for his trouble.

The Capitol's Sheaves
Fleur-de-Lis?

Toledo, Ohio, was a farm because that's where the Detroit Tigers farm c l u b played baseball, shocked a secretary and things pretty much deteriorated after that.

LATER that day the sheaves editor chastised a reporter for using the phrase "one of the foremost," arguing persuasively that you're either foremost or you're not, and whether "or not" is necessary after "whether," or not.

As night fell, two reporters stood at the water cooler discussing whether or not the terms "protagonist" and "antagonist" were mutually exclusive.

All in all it had been a fairly typical day in the newsroom.

[*Editor's note: The Sunday Register of a week ago told of the painting over of the Statehouse dome sheaves. Later, the Iowa Executive Council ordered the sheaves repainted.*]

Another man, who claimed to have been raised on a farm, said he'd always called the bundles "bundles" and a member of the sheaves camp responded with, "You must have sounded pretty silly singing 'Bringing in The Bundles.'"

Then a reporter from Detroit who had grown up thinking that

Oh, the Bridges of Des Moines

PEOPLE WRITE GAY songs about the bridges of Paris, London's bridges, bridges in San Francisco and bridges in New York.

They rhapsodize about long bridges, high bridges, old bridges and new bridges. There's probably even a song about the Holland Tunnel.

BUT DO THEY write songs about Des Moines' bridges?

No. And it's a great opportunity lost.

If Mother Goose were able to compose a timeless rhyme about

the London bridge falling down, think what she could have done after a gander at the bridges of Des Moines.

Des Moines' bridges make the old London bridge look as durable as the Pyramids. It's gotten so bad that pigeons that can't swim refuse to roost on them.

The recent high waters have thrown a spotlight on the spans across the Des Moines and Raccoon rivers and set the stage for some really good songs.

For example, a "Farewell to the Old Commerce Bridge," in honor of the stately structure

People often say: "But what does a column accomplish?" A week after I wrote this, one of the city's major bridges collapsed. Which proves that there either is or isn't a God.

47

that was swept away by the Raccoon a few days ago, is crying out to be written.

A LITTLE FARTHER downstream stands (just barely) the Sixty-third Street bridge—an ideal subject for a rock 'n' roll tune. Its road surface has the texture of a rumpled corduroy suit and a trip across is accompanied by snaps, pings, and sharp cracks that resemble the background noise on a Beach Boys' record.

For songwriters with a more classical interest, Des Moines offers the University Avenue bridge, a neo-Roman ruin.

It's got more holes in it per square foot than Irish lace. It used to carry a four-lane road but the city fathers, in their wisdom, have blocked off two lanes a n d posted a sign: "Structure Unsafe—Pedestrians Keep Off."

Those with a talent for syncopation will want to try their luck on the S.W. Ninth Street bridge over the Raccoon. This artery to the south jiggles and jumps whenever anything heavier than a bicycle built for two crosses it.

It has a posted load limit of three tons or about one and a half cars. This does not prevent many drivers, apparently owners of water-proof wrist watches, from lining up and going across three and four at a time.

A "Southwest Ninth Street Bridge Cha-cha-cha," might be a big seller.

The bridges over the Des Moines River in the downtown area—all in varying stages of senility—could be treated as a group.

IT IS AN awe-inspiring sight to see them at high water. The Des Moines River resembles the

Atlantic Ocean during the storm season as it boils over the Center Street Dam and rushes toward the forlorn structures at Grand, Locust, Walnut, and Court.

They look like captains going down with their ships. If they could talk they'd probably say "Help."

Or, perhaps, just "Goodby."

Should anyone want to write an over-all song about the area's bridges he could try "I'll Be Seeing You."

Or he could wait a few months and do "And Then There Were None."

The Bridges Revisited

A NUMBER OF persons have suggested that I had something to do with the collapse of the Sixth Avenue bridge. This is nonsense!

These p e r s o n s base their charges on the fact that I wrote something about the bridges just a few days before the Sixth Avenue structure surrendered to gravity.

This analysis ignores the fact I DID NOT MENTION the Sixth Avenue bridge in the article. At the time, I thought that the Sixth Avenue span was one of the safest in Des Moines.

As a matter of fact, I took another look at the remaining bridges the other day and I still think Sixth Avenue bridge is one of the safest in Des Moines.

★ ★ ★

It is an absolutely UN-FOUNDED rumor that the bridge fell down because a troop of girl scouts marched across without breaking step.

We're Over The Hump

THE OPENING of the bridges Friday in Des Moines was truly a gala occasion. A band played, men gave speeches, pretty girls held ribbons; old-timers said they'd seen nothing like it since the launching of the Titanic.

Mayor George Whitmer presided at each of the four dedication ceremonies and it can be reported that he was in top form.

At the opening of the Sixth Avenue bridge he said, "This is a great step forward . . . we're over the hump now."

At the University Avenue bridge opening he declared, "This is a great step forward . . . we're over the hump now."

PAUSING reflectively at the dedication of the Walnut Street bridge he stated, "This is a great step forward . . . We're over the hump now."

And, saving the best for last, he used the opening of the Seventh Street viaduct as an occasion to say, *"This is a great step forward . . . we're over the hump now."*

The enthusiastic response that greeted the mayor's speeches was all the more remarkable for the fact that they were delivered before essentially the same audience.

A horde of city officials and persons directly connected with the construction of the bridges was hauled by bus and caravan from dedication to dedication to mingle with the handful of interested citizens that showed up at each ceremony.

The over-all effect, after the

My favorite quote of the week, maybe of the year, came from Ted Johnson, president of a Cedar Rapids oceanographic firm.

Asked why Iowa was chosen as the location for a firm whose principal interest is the ocean, he replied:

"It's as close to both oceans as you can get." That's positive thinking.

Out of a conviction that every columnist should crusade for a worthwhile cause, I launched a campaign to make Des Moines a seaport by Christmas. Any Christmas. The only practical method I was able to come up with was to dredge out the median of Interstate 80 and limit traffic to ocean liners no more than 60 feet in length. Some people took the proposal to be ironic.

first bridge, was that of a television replay of the proceedings. The only significant difference between the four ceremonies was that speakers at the Sixth Avenue and Seventh Street structures tended to think of their bridges as links between the north and south, while Walnut Street and University Avenue speakers favored east and west.

ONE SPEAKER compared the opening of the Seventh Avenue viaduct to a wedding, since it meant that north and south Des Moines would be joined again.

Whereupon a woman in the crowd turned to a companion and said, "It'll never last."

Still and all, the bridges look as though they're built to last. They do not tremble when you walk out onto them and jump up and down; which is more than you can say for some of the older bridges.

As Mayor Whitmer pointed out, all we have to worry about now is the Locust Street bridge and S.W. Ninth Street bridge and proposed viaducts at Eighth and Ninth streets. That's all.

It was probably the first time since the reconstruction of Europe after World War II that a town in the Western hemisphere opened four major bridges in one day.

IT WORKED out so well, though, that they might open our next four on the same day. The beauty of the plan is that it gives each of the councilmen a bridge of his very own to open while the mayor can concern himself with over-all supervisory activities.

Opening the bridges one at a time would undoubtedly create dissension among the city fathers.

A number of persons commented privately on the refusal of the Des Moines School Board to provide four bands for the opening. Instead, one band—from North High—was furnished for one dedication, the first.

The absence of bands at the other openings took away from what was otherwise a heart-tugging occasion.

No longer can it be said that Des Moines is the only city in the United States with more fallen bridges than fallen women.

A Seaport?
Yes, Virginia!

DEAR Mr. Coffee:

I am eight years old.

Some of my little friends say there is no Des Moines Seaport.

Papa says there is, but he drinks a lot.

Please tell me the truth, is there a Des Moines Seaport?

Virginia O.

VIRGINIA, your little friends are wrong. They have been affected by the skepticism of a skeptical age. They do not believe except that which they see. The truth, so often elusive, evades them.

Yes, Virginia, there is a Des Moines Seaport. You may not be able to see it, but it's there.

It exists as certainly as all the other unbelievable phenomena of our society, like doctors who hate money, politicians who love controversy and aluminum siding salesmen who are shy.

It exists as certainly as peace

on earth, good will toward men, charity toward all, malice toward none and a chicken in every pot.

How dreary our world would be without these things.

There would be no childlike faith in real-life happy endings, no belief in the reward of virtue, no romance to make tolerable our existence. We would be forced to take refuge in shallow fantasy to shield ourselves from reality.

"The Sound of Music" would run forever.

WE WOULD have no appreciation of life except that which we could taste and touch, and the charming innocence of childhood would be extinguished before childhood ran its course.

Not believe in the Des Moines Seaport? You might as well not believe in the evils of liquor billboards.

It is true that, should you go to the banks of the Des Moines River, or to the median of the freeway, you would not find a seaport. But what does that prove?

Nobody ever sees members of the City Council argue with each other but that doesn't mean they don't. The realest things in the world are those that neither children nor men can see.

NOBODY CAN conceive or imagine all the wonders that are unseen and unseeable in this world.

There are those cynical men and women who would have you believe that generosity, devotion to ideals, brotherhood, tolerance, truth and beauty do not exist.

That's nonsense. Though unseen, they exist everywhere, in books, magazines, on records and in commencement speeches. As you grow older you will hear more and more about them.

No Seaport? Unthinkable. It exists, thank goodness, and it will continue to exist.

A thousand years from now; nay, ten times ten thousand years from now, it will exist—in the minds of men.

Just like the Sixth Avenue bridge.

Your friend,
O. T. Coffee

3-Day Weeks
For All

WHEN I first heard that the Iowa Legislature had had raised its pay to $5,500 a session, I was pleased. Five-and-a-half thousand dollars a year seems just and adequate compensation for that kind of work.

Then I found out that *each member* was to get that much!

That's appalling. I mean, I know we're living in an inflationary economy, but how much can sheer foolishness be worth when there's so much of it around?

The Iowa Legislature is funny, but it's not the Colgate Comedy Hour or anything — $5,500 for three or four months' work is a lot of money.

And as if that weren't enough, now they're talking about putting the Legislature on a three-day week. That's right — last week some legislators were in town to study "improvement of the legislative process" and came up with the idea of taking Mondays and Fridays off.

Fantastic. Cutting the work load of the Iowa Legislature is like giving a mattress tester a sabbatical.

51

The legislators, of course, didn't merely put forth the proposal in naked self-interest. Oh no, they argue that a three-day work week will measurably improve the legislative process. Here's how:

It would afford legislators a greater opportunity to go home every week and consult with their constituents.

It would give legislators more time to ponder the wisdom of proposed legislation.

By removing legislators from the Des Moines scene more often, it would make it more difficult for lobbyists to work their magic on the innocents occupying seats in the House and Senate.

It would encourage busy, competent people who, at present, cannot find the time to run for office. (As things now stand, most legislators are either competent and lazy or busy incompetents.)

WHICH IS all well and good, but you can make pretty much the same arguments for any field of endeavor. To test that theory I went out and interviewed a few random workers.

First I sought out a garbage collector and asked, "Do you think that going to a three-day work week would improve the garbage-collecting process?"

"Very definitely," he replied. "The major advantage would be in recruiting. You would be surprised at the number of competent, busy people who ignore garbage collecting as a career because they can't afford to devote full time to it."

I then found a police officer and asked him his opinion on the three-day week and the law enforcement process.

"I am a great believer in the four-day weekend as a tool for more effective law enforcement," he said. "This would give the officers more time to read psychology books and attend seminars on sociological behavior that would prove invaluable in their work. In addition, it would be that much less opportunity for bribery."

Thus informed, I called a teacher I know and asked her whether a reduction in the school week would have a beneficial effect on the educational process.

"It certainly would," she said. "It would give the good teachers more time to reflect on what they're doing and it would keep the bad teachers away from the kids two more days a week. And, in many schools, it would give slow-healers a much-needed chance to recover from a week's battle wounds."

On my way home I stopped in at a fire station and asked a firefighter, "How would you like to go on a three-day work week?"

"I wouldn't be for it unless we got a raise in pay to compensate for the extra time worked," he said.

Before you know it, the General Assembly will be meeting by mail. Hey! Maybe that's not such a bad idea.

• • •

Let's hope we never see the day when politicians tell the truth, the whole truth, and nothing but the truth.

That way lies anarchy.

• • •

Trouble With A Capital T

A FELLOW stood on a street corner the other day, making a speech. He was a good-looking fellow—checked s u i t, belt in the back, yellow shoes, all the latest in haberdashery—and he was talking and waving his arms and his listeners were nodding their heads and joining in on the chorus.

"**You've got Trouble, my friends,**" the man was saying, "**trouble right here in Bridgeless City. I said Trouble with a capital T and that rhymes with P and that stands for Pornography.**"

"Oh, we've got trouble," the crowd answers back.

"Friends, either you are closing your eyes to a situation you do not wish to acknowledge or you are not aware of the caliber of disaster that can be created by a single dirty book."

"*Smut, filth and corruption. Tell us more.*"

"Has your son been leafing through copies of Vogue lately? Has he taken out a subscription to Harper's Bazaar? Is he lingering over the lingerie ads in the Sunday Magazine of the New York Times?"

"Yes, yes," they all cry.

"**W**ELL THEN you're in a mess and that rhymes with S and that stands for Sex."

"No, no," they shout in unison. Two women faint and a strong man breaks down and cries like a baby.

"**I'm here to tell you that Bridgeless City is the home of some of the vilest pornography I've ever seen, and I make a living looking at the filthy stuff.**"

"Say it ain't so," a tall man in a stovepipe hat calls out.

"It is so," the man says. "And it just so happens I brought some of that pornography with me to show you honest, decent folk just how vile it really is."

"Show us, show us."

"*Let me thumb through this magazine here so you can see what I'm talking about. Look at this.*"

"Wow!"

"And this."

"Boy, oh boy!"

"And how about this?"

"You're turning the pages too fast," a man in a beard says.

"**N**OW FRIENDS," the man says, "you and I know that you and I can't be corrupted by this sort of thing. I doubt whether most of us present even have a prurient interest."

"**Of course not,**" the bearded man says. "**I could stand here and look at that stuff all day.**"

"It's the children who need protection."

"The children! The children!"

"*It is for their sake that we must drive the smutrakers from the marketplace. Surely no right-thinking person can defend hard-core pornography.*"

Cries of "That's right" and "You tell 'em" ring out.

"**A**ND WHEN the hard-core pornography is gone, we will start on soft-core pornography; books like 'Fanny Hill,' 'Candy' and 'Tom Swift and His Electric Flying Machine.'"

"**Hey, wait a minute!**" The guy with the stovepipe yells. "**I read that Tom Swift book and I didn't see nothing dirty about it.**"

"You read it?" the man says. "For pleasure? It wasn't to find out how dirty it was, or anything? You just read it?"

"Yes. I read a lot in my spare time."

"*Just as I thought. A reader trying to infiltrate our group. Brain him with your pocketbook, will you Madame? Thank you very much. That's the stuff. Drive him off down the street. Look at him run.*"

"Let a reader in a censorship group and you've got Trouble, my friends. Trouble with a capital T and that rhymes with . . ."

Iowa may or may not be the state that sin forgot; but Iowa is most assuredly not the state that forgot sin. Condemning pornography is the state's second largest industry, ranking right after animal husbandry.

53

Don't Walk on The Grass

DES MOINES schools have been taking their lumps lately.

They've been denounced on the floor of the Legislature for the alleged sheltering of lascivious acts, investigated by a grand jury kept under surveillance by Des Moines police.

As a matter of fact, from the rumors flying around town it's hard to tell whether Des Moines is running a school system or a pool hall.

I decided to make a personal investigation. I called a high school kid I know who plays lead guitar for a local rock group, "Euthanasia and the Unteachables."

"Hello, Gaston?" I said. "This is O.T. Look, Gas, haven't I always been like an uncle to you?"

"No."

"Well, maybe I have made fun of your haircut from time to time, but I never meant any harm. You've always considered me a friend though, haven't you?"

"No."

"Okay, so we're not close, but you do trust me, don't you?"

"Not particularly."

"Stop kidding around, Gaston. I need your help."

"YOU WANT to know about the sex orgies in the Des Moines high schools, right?"

"Yeah, how did you guess?"

"You're the fifth guy today who's called saying he's always been like an uncle to me."

"I can understand your cynicism, but let me assure you that I have absolutely no prurient interest in this matter. I'm just a newspaper man doing his job. Any enjoyment I get from this story will be strictly incidental."

"Well, as long as you put it that way . . ."

"Let's get down to business. What portion of the school day, on the average, is given over to orgies in your school?"

"Orgies! Heck, we don't even have a Coke machine."

"You mean there are no sex orgies in your school?"

"No. We had a butterscotch orgy once, but hardly anybody showed up."

"How about grass?"

"We try not to walk on it."

"Come on, kid. What do you take me for, a square? Tell it like it is. I know where it's at, baby."

"Would you mind not talking like that. You sound like my father."

"IS IT TRUE you can buy beer in the parking lot during the lunch hour?"

"You're lucky if you can find a parking place."

"Not even ginger beer?"

"Gee, if we teen-agers had as much fun as you adults give us credit for, there wouldn't be any time left for all-school assemblies."

"You must think adults are awfully dumb. We were young once ourselves, you know. You're not fooling us for a minute."

"You mean when you were a kid you were having sex orgies and drinking and gambling and staying out late at night."

"Well, we did stay out late from time to time."

"Boy, no wonder you senior citizens are always talking about the good old days. And, as long as we're on the subject, what about wife-swapping clubs?"

"Huh?"

"We kids are always hearing about adults swapping wives

54

in the suburbs and like that and we wonder about it."

"Well . . . uh . . . you HEAR about parties like that but you never get invited to them. I mean, it's certainly nothing you'd want to take your wife to. It's just not nice."

"Yeah. Well, that's the way most of us teen-agers feel about sex orgies."

Head 'Em Up, Root 'Em Out!

YOU LEARN a lot of things if you read the Congressional Record—particularly about congressmen.

Iowa Representative Fred Schwengel recently waxed lyrical about hogs for the benefit of his colleagues.

"I like pigs," he said on the floor of the House, "and I honestly believe that most pigs like me. Hogs are beautiful. Some of my best friends are hogs."

So saying, he launched into a lengthy discourse on the folkways of swine that included this information:

"I am sure you are aware that Iowa and other Midwestern states are famous for corn and hogs. But perhaps you are not aware that the area was also once famous for its great hog drives.

"In pre-Civil War days, the early settlers herded their pigs cross the countryside to eastern assembly points for shipment by rail or water.

"Madison, Ind., and Cincinnati, Ohio, were both known as 'porkopolis' about 100 years ago. In those days, hogs had different names, too. They were commonly called elm peelers, alligators, land-pikes, r a z o r b a c k s, and prairie rooters.

"They ran at large until two or three years old, living mostly on acorns, beechnuts, and whatever they could scrounge. But before the drives began, they were fattened out on corn.

"THE DRIVES often contained 2,000 to 3,000 hogs. They traveled hundreds of miles from Illinois, Kentucky, Indiana, and surrounding states.

"These hog drives were similar to the famous cattle drives of the early West. But the men were not called cowboys; they were called drovers.

"The trail boss was usually owner of the drove. He brought up the rear, seeing to it that his drovers—usually on horseback—kept the hogs moving. At night the crew would make camp in the beech forest and sit around the campfire, singing ballads and telling stories, just like in a western movie."

Can you imagine such a western movie? And the reaction of the actor who's told by his agent that he's been picked to play the lead?

"Hey Brock, I just signed you up for the part of your life. It's going to do for you what 'Maggio' did for Frank Sinatra."

"That's what you said when you got me the title role in 'Son of Rosemary's Baby,' Manny. You said it would make them forget about Rudolph Valentino. As it turned out, it made them forget about me."

"Forget the past, kid. Let the dead bury the dead. This new flick is going to be a smash. It's a western."

"A WESTERN, eh? That doesn't sound bad. I've always thought I resembled Clint Eastwood a little, right around

The State Department of Health has offered a number of suggestions related to the Big Clean-up. For example: "The Iowa State Department of Health strongly advises that where city sewage treatment plants have been out of operation, they should be restored as soon as possible." Good thinking.

my eyes. What part do I play?"

"A drover."

"Good. I've always had a kind of feeling for the life of a cowboy."

"That's fine, kid; but you're not exactly a cowboy in this, technically speaking. You're more of a swine drover."

"Huh?"

"Yeah, you're the head drover in a pig drive from Otter Creek, Ia., to Cincinnati. The last big pig drive of the Old West. The end of a way of life. It'll be bigger than 'Shane.' "

"Cincinnati?"

"The big climax comes when a farmer near Indianapolis tries to poison your mudhole and you fight it out with him."

"Well, at least I get to wear a gun, huh?"

"Not exactly. You face him armed only with a ham sandwich and he backs down."

"That's the climax? Gee Manny, I don't know . . ."

"Look Baby, you can't afford to be too picky. I had to talk pretty fast to get you this gig. They were thinking of Mickey Rooney for the part."

"How come they chose me over Mickey Rooney?"

"Mickey Rooney is too tall. They were afraid he'd dwarf the hogs."

It's BB Time Again

I HAD parked my car, made sure the license plates were firmly bolted into place and was on my way to the office the other day when I was stopped in my tracks by a familiar cry.

"Hey you, columnist!"

It was my old friend, the man in the plaid cap with the earflaps and the galoshes with the buckles, unbuckled.

"Long time no see, O.T.," he said. "How have you been?"

"Fine until now," I replied. "I hate to rush off but I have a rather full day ahead of me."

"Sure, I understand. I'll just walk along with you. I guess you just can't wait to start on those girls."

"Pardon me?"

"The girls' basketball tournament. You're going to write something about it, aren't you?"

"I hadn't planned on it, no."

"COME ON, O.T., you're putting me on. What are you going to say this year; that if girls' basketball were a car it would be an Edsel? That if it were a Broadway musical, they'd call it 'North Pacific?' "

"No, I think my views on girls' basketball are well known. I see no need to elaborate on them."

"What do you mean? You've got people counting on you, O.T. There's a hundred things you could say. You could say that the only good seats are the ones behind posts."

"That would be cruel."

"You prefer the subtle approach, huh? How about saying that you went to a girls' basketball game once but it was asleep. The crowd was delirious with apathy, you could say."

"I don't think I'm making myself clear."

"I GET YOU. You columnists like to think up your own stuff, right? I admire that. You don't have to write any of this down; I'm just trying to spark your imagination. Why don't you suggest that next year they time the games with an hour glass?"

"Look here . . ."

"*You've got to say something, O.T. You can't let your fans down. You could ask them why don't they sew pockets into the girls' uniforms so that the players will have something to do with their hands during games.*"

"Here is my office," I said.

"Tell them, why don't you, that if somebody hid the game ball, nobody would notice until the third quarter."

"It's been very interesting, but I really have to go now." I moved into the revolving door and heard his voice call after me.

"The least you can do is say that charging admission to girls' basketball is like making people pay to watch haircuts!"

He was still shouting as I began to climb the stairs.

1, 2, 3 or None
Of These

I once suggested that girls' basketball, as it is played in Iowa, was not so much a sport as a small town sociological phenomenon. A lady wrote in to the paper saying: "Small town sociological phenomenon! They play girls' basketball in Boone, Perry, West Des Moines! Do you call those small towns?" At which point I rested my case.

IT IS GIRLS' basketball tournament time again. *Tra-la.*

There are those who charge me with having been unfair to girls' basketball. They say that my commentaries on the sport over the years have been uninformed, bigoted, puerile, jejune and downright stupid. To which I can only answer—nobody's perfect.

Still, in keeping with O. T. Coffee's Bend-Over-Backwards Policy of Fairness, this year's girls' basketball column will be *completely objective.* Nowhere will my opinions on the game intrude upon the reader's consciousness.

It is, as a matter of fact, a multiple choice, do-it-yourself column designed to teach the neophyte something about the game and allow the fan to demonstrate his mastery of its subtleties.

FOLLOWING are nine typical situations one might witness during a girls' basketball game. Numbered below each situation are three interpretations of the action. The object of the test is to match the situation with its most likely interpretation. Here goes now, and may the best interpretation win:

The players of both teams are standing around on the court. This means:
1—*The game is about to start.*
2—*A time-out has been called.*
3—*One of the teams is staging a furious, come-from-behind rally.*

A girl is stationed at the foul line, shooting a ball at the basket. Therefore:

1—*You are watching the victim of a personal foul.*
2—*You are watching the beneficiary of a technical foul.*
3—*You are watching the most exciting part of the game.*

Players of both teams running downcourt is significant of:
1—*A fast break.*
2—*A slow break.*
3—*A mad dog at the other end of the floor.*

When a coach is seen with his team gathered around him during a timeout:
1—*He is telling his players how to break a zone-press.*
2—*He is telling his players how to install a zone-press.*
3—*He is telling his players, "This round thing here is what we call a basketball."*

Players are jumping high into the air:
1—*It is a jump ball.*
2—*It is a rebound.*
3—*It is a mouse.*

Two girls holding onto the same ball is a sure sign of:
1—*A jump ball.*
2—*A personal foul.*
3—*A heavy ball.*

When the stands rise up as one and begin to yell, you know that:
1—*A turning point in the game has been reached.*
2—*The cheerleaders are on the floor during a time-out.*
3—*The vendor has run out of hot dogs.*

A player is observed bouncing a ball:
1—*It is a bounce pass.*
2—*It is a dribble.*
3—*It is a mistake.*

Players crying means that:
1—*A team has just lost.*
2—*A team has just won.*
3—*A girl has just announced her engagement.*

Take a completed test form, put it in a stamped, self-addressed envelope and mail it. Those scoring under 135 will be drafted. Good Luck.

More About BB

A NOTHER HONOR has befallen your humble columnist. The Society for the Prevention of Cruelty to Girls' Basketball, in recognition of my long interest in the sport, has asked me to name an all-time girls' basketball all-star team.

Naturally, I agreed to do so.

So here, for the first time anywhere, are the O.T. Coffee All-Stars:

    Left forward—Sophia Loren
    Right forward—Alice B. Toklas

    Center—Evelyn and her magic violin

    Leftover—Lynda Bird Johnson

    Red guard—Mao Tse-tung

    Hungarian—Zsa Zsa Gabor

    Student manager—Albert Einstein

There's not a team in the country that could run with that one on a given day.

Real vs. Mock Injuries

I SAW DES MOINES' civil defense apparatus at close hand Sunday, as the city responded to a mock tornado. The drill was designed to determine the city's readiness to deal with a natural disaster.

Pray for nice weather.

It all began when my friend, Stephen Seplow, fell off the merry-go-round and hurt his arm. (No, he wasn't drunk. It's too long a story to tell. He fell off the merry-go-round; take my word for it.)

Seplow was staggering around, holding his arm, trying hard not to faint. We decided the thing to do was load him into a car and get him to a hospital.

W E HAD JUST gotten him to the car when a cop came up and said: "What's happening here?"

Thinking he might want to offer us a motorcycle escort, I said: "This man's been hurt and we're taking him to a hospital."

"You can't take him anywhere until I make out my accident report," the cop said.

Well, that touched off a debate as to whether we were going to take Seplow to the hospital right then or allow him to be interviewed.

I told the cop a few things you generally don't hear around merry-go-rounds and came an inch within being arrested for resisting a report. But we did get off to the hospital without any report nonsense.

A S IT TURNED out, we needn't have hurried.

We went to Broadlawns Polk County Hospital, on the theory that they were hip to emergencies.

They started off real fine, too. They took Seplow to an examining room, took his temperature and blood pressure and seemed to be moving ahead smartly.

Then the nurse came in and said: "You'll have to go into the waiting room now. We're having a disaster drill."

So Seplow, whose arm had stiffened into a right-angle bend by this time and who hurt like hell, had to go into the waiting room and sit while the hospital staff waited for the fake injured to be brought in from the mock tornado.

At one point an ambulance pulled up and the staff members ran to the door yelling "Is that a real one?" It wasn't, which meant that he got immediate treatment.

Seplow was taking a remarkably detached view of things. "Maybe if we told them I got hurt in the mock tornado, they'd give me a mock X-ray."

I finally found a guy in a suit. (When you're being given the run-around in a hospital, find a guy in a suit. Doctors and nurses can get away with treating people like germs, but the men in suits don't have so strong a union.)

The man in the suit arranged for Seplow's X-ray (nothing broken) and they managed to work in some bandaging in between "disaster" victims and we got out of there before the rescue helicopter arrived. (I don't know what that was about either, but it was due to arrive and the hospital staff was pretty excited about it. That was good enough for me.)

I̶T WAS AN experience out of Kafka, by Joe Heller. The only truly human being we encountered during the day was the hospital receptionist.

Two of us walked up, half-carrying Seplow. We were wearing our day-off clothes and looking grubby.

"How did he get hurt?" she asked.

"He fell off a merry-go-round," I said, looking sheepish.

She nodded knowingly. "It happens," she said.

They should put her in charge of disaster operations. She understands them.

A Cure for Medicare

I̶T SEEMS that Iowa doctors are being asked to contribute money to a fund that will be used to attempt to defeat congressmen who voted for Medicare and "other of the Great Society free-spending, power-centralizing schemes."

The asking reportedly is being done by the political arm of the State Medical Society, the Iowa Medical Political Action Committee.

There's nothing wrong with that. Physicians have as much right to pursue what they regard as their enlightened self-interest as do labor unions and farm organizations.

It would be surprising if medical organizations throughout the nation were not now making similar pleas to their members.

There is a danger, however, that the involvement of organized medicine in practical politics might continue to grow until it comes to interfere with the traditional and sacred doctor-patient relationship.

Then a visit to the doctor might be something like this:

A SLEEPY-LOOKING man walks into his doctor's office. The doctor asks:

"What seems to be the trouble?"

"I don't know, Doc. It's nothing you can put your finger on. I just seem to feel tired all of the time."

"Do you experience any difficulty sleeping?"

"No. I have trouble staying awake."

"*Does running up two flights of stairs leave you short of breath?*"

"Yes."

"Do you suffer a loss of appetite after a big meal?"

"Now that you mention it, yes I do."

"Now, tell me whether you feel any pain when I jab you right above the wallet—"

"AGHRRR!"

"Just as I suspected. Let me ask you one more question."

"Anything. Just don't hit me in the kidney again."

"Did your congressman vote for Medicare?"

"I think he did. Yes, I'm sure he did."

"And you voted for your congressman, didn't you?"

"Why, yes I did."

"That's what I was afraid of."

"What is it, Doc? What have I got?"

"Creeping socialism. One of the worst cases I've ever seen."

"Is it . . . serious?"

"Hmmmm."

"THAT BAD, huh? How long have I got? You can give it to me straight. I can take it."

"It's hard telling. I've seen people with cases as bad as yours hang on until they were 90. On the other hand, some of them just go to bed one night and . . . pfft."

"Pfft?"

"That's right. I wouldn't worry about it too much if I were you, though. I mean, your life insurance is paid up, isn't it?"

"Well, yeah, but are you sure of the diagnosis?"

"Definitely. You've got all the symptoms: Neo-Marxist fatigue syndrome, welfare state weakness, pie-in-the-sky lesions. There's no mistaking it."

"But why me, Doc? Why did it have to happen to me?"

"*You were a victim of circumstances. You see, in the old days man could look forward to a yawning abyss of poverty and privation upon retirement. This kept him in a constant state of nervous anxiety, worrying about the future. With the advent of cradle-to-the-grave security this fear has diminished and many persons, like yourself, are developing cases of creeping socialism. It starts with a loss of faith in the principle of survival of the richest and ends with a marked lessening of the will to live.*"

"It's hopeless, then?"

"THERE'S A slim chance for recovery if you're willing to do exactly as I say."

"Speak and it shall be done."

"I want you to change your party affiliation, burn your Social Security card on the Statehouse steps and take these little pills three times a day, after every meal."

"These sure are funny-looking pills. It looks as though they have a Latin inscription on them."

"They do. It's the motto of the American Medical Political Action Committee: *Our Fees We Prize and Our Price We Will Maintain.*"

61

The Campus Wasteland

THAT WAS an oddball protest they conducted at Coe College the other day.

A bunch of students got together to protest the school's treatment of custodians and dormitory maids. These people were paid too little and made to work too hard, the students said, and if things didn't change there were going to be some student demonstrations.

There's something refreshing about that. It's good to see the students and workers developing a common front.

The thing that precipitated the crisis was a report made by an efficiency expert the college had hired to streamline the school's operations.

The report suggested that the custodial and domestic staffs should be cut; which they were. That's an efficiency expert for you. His idea of saving money is to have one person do the work of two.

It would be interesting if colleges were to carry this process one step further. What if they turn the efficiency experts loose on the academic side of college life?

THIS IS what an efficiency expert might then sound like reporting back to a college president:

"Mr. President," he says, "I've completed my study."

"I suppose that you've found that we run a pretty tight ship here."

"Not really. I saw a good deal of waste in my studies around campus."

"You did? Where?"

"For example, I walked into a lecture hall and found one man lecturing to 300 students."

"You think 300 isn't enough?"

"Too many. It's an inefficient use of students. You could keep the lecturer just as busy with four or five students, releasing the others for other tasks."

"But . . ."

"And then there's the library."

"Was it empty?"

"No, full. Everybody was sitting around reading. How do you expect to get anything done around here when everybody reads all of the time? I suggest you limit attendance at the library to students on their coffee break."

"BUT IF we don't allow students to attend lectures or go to the library, how will we keep them busy?"

"Simple. Give them scholarships in custodial work, maid service and groundskeeping. That way, they'll stay out of your hair and you can cut down your overhead at the same time."

"Don't you think that will interfere with the achievement of the traditional goals of the university?"

"No. If you play your cards right you can bring it off without losing a single defense contract."

"I see. That's certainly an interesting theory. Do you have any other recommendations?"

"Yes. I visited the English department and met a professor who said he was a Chaucer specialist."

"You must mean Malcolm Foothfayer. He's one of the top men in his field. We're very lucky to have him."

"Yes, I'm sure he's fun at parties. The point is, it's inefficient to have one man for every author in the English language. So I told him that from now on he'd be a lunch

room monitor and take tickets at basketball games."

"Will that really save so much money?"

"What's his salary?"

"Eighteen thousand a year."

"It's saved you $18,000 already. He just quit."

"I'm not sure that you . . ."

"In addition, I've recommended that you combine the offices of the deans of men and women and do away with the office of student affairs altogether. If students want to have affairs they should rent their own office. Which leaves only one more thing to be decided."

"Yes?"

"Mr. President, just what do you do around here, anyway?"

Memo From
U. of I.

A NEWS RELEASE (handout) came into the office the other day informing the world that University of Iowa students were forming a "shadow State Department" to "solve national problems."

It seems that there's going to be an Action Studies Program next fall that will feature a class structured like the State Department.

Students will form a staff, complete with prestigious titles, and prepare papers supporting their foreign policy decisions. **Some of the papers, says the handout, will be sent to the real Department of State in Washington, D.C. (Disneyland Central) for consideration.**

It's a good idea, but a dangerous one. Suppose, for example, that student radicals manage to gain control of the university's State Department.

The fellows at the real State Department might be opening the mail one day and run across a position paper from Iowa City signed merely "Sec. of State."

"Oh, oh," one of them says. "Here's a note from the boss. I didn't know he was in Iowa City."

"He's probably there to take the water. He's been a little low on iron lately. What does he say?"

"Let's see . . . he says we should get out of Vietnam."

"Are you sure he cleared that with Mel Laird?"

"WOULD HE SAY it if he hadn't? He says that it has become obvious that our foreign policy has reached a dead end and that it's time to seek new solutions."

"Okay, I'll make out a memo to that effect and send it out to all of our embassies.

"And while you're at it, tell them to fire all of their CIA agents."

"What!"

"The secretary seems to think that having spies working out of our embassies destroys our credibility in the court of world opinion."

"The hell you say."

"Yeah. Right here it says, 'The United States must be ever-mindful of its position of world leadership and its responsibility to set an example of high moral standards.' "

"I think they're putting something besides iron in that Iowa City water."

"Ours not to reason why. Send out the memo."

"Does the secretary say anything else?"

"AS A MATTER of fact, he does. He says it's time we stopped supporting corrupt dictatorships in South America."

"But that's the only kind of dictatorships they have in South America."

"*Right. He says we should start supporting people's revolutions.*"

"Boy, I knew Rocky would make some recommendations but I didn't think we'd follow them."

"And, as evidence of our commitment to a society organized on democratic principles, says the secretary, we should hang a picture of Che Guevara in each of our South American offices."

"That won't be any problem. I'm sure we still have some of those 'wanted' posters around."

"I don't understand this next part of the chief's directive.

He says he's making non-negotiable demands for a black studies program in the department, greater student participation in the decision-making process and coeducational dormitories with unlimited visiting privileges."

"Maybe it's some kind of code."

"Could be. Just to be on the safe side though, I think I'll drop over to American University and ask some students what they think. That way we can say we involved them in the decision-making process."

"You're not going to take their suggestions seriously, are you?"

"*Of course not. Can you imagine the kind of suggestions students would make?*"

Abandoning a Railroad

THAT STORY about the Centerville man who pleaded guilty to criminal charges of abandoning a railroad w a s enough to blow your mind. *CRIMINAL CHARGES OF ABANDONING A RAILROAD!*

If it's a crime to abandon a railroad, then practically everybody should be in jail.

The real complaint was that the operator of Southern Industrial Railroad, Inc., which ran between Centerville and Moravia, abandoned the 15-mile line without telling the Interstate Commerce Commission (ICC).

(The ICC requires railroad operators to make a showing that the public will not be inconvenienced by the abandonment of a line before approving such abandonment.)

YOU WONDER how the ICC has time to fool with 15-mile railroads when it has all those other problems to worry about. Can you imagine the scene at the ICC offices? A top official is discussing policy with a top aide:

"Here, chief," the aide says. "Here are last month's railroad accident reports."

"How do they look?"

"Let's see, we had 342 derailments, 17 head-on collisions and one train that hit an iceberg and sank with all hands."

"Great! I knew we could improve rail safety if we put our minds to it. The only thing that puzzles me a little is that train hitting the iceberg. How did that happen?"

"We think the engineer had been drinking."

"When will they learn that alcohol and diesel oil don't mix. What other problems do we have?"

"WE HAVE several requests for special permits. They're all routine except one."

"What is that one?"

"The Army wants to move 900 tons of nitroglycerine across country in open vats, passing through the major cities along the way during rush hour."

"I thought you said this wasn't a routine request."

"I haven't gotten to the exceptional part yet. They want to disguise the train as an afghan so that it will be able to cross the country unnoticed."

"I don't see anything wrong with that; permission granted. What else?"

"We have a complaint from a passenger of an eastern line. She says she had to hire a private detective to find the local ticket agent in order to buy a ticket to Chicago. Her train was 32 hours late and the conductor made her stand the whole way because he didn't want her to wrinkle the seats."

"Yes, and what was her complaint?"

"The train wasn't going to Chicago."

"Boy, some people are really soreheads. I wouldn't even dignify her letter with an answer."

"We didn't. We just turned it over to the FBI for prosecution."

"FINE. Anything else?"

"Just one thing. There's this fellow in Iowa who abandoned a 15-mile line without telling us."

"That makes my blood boil. Who does he think he is, anyway, inconveniencing the public that way? Doesn't he realize he's a quasi-public institution?"

"Don't worry boss. We won't be easy with him."

"I should hope not. Throw the book at him. Abandoning 15-mile railroads is the first step along the road to anarchy."

"Gee, you're pretty when you're mad."

"I can't help it. It's men like that who give railroads a bad name."

So Much for Comic Relief

IT'S GOOD to have the Des Moines City Council around. Even with the Iowa Legislature on annual sessions, it would get pretty dull around here in the fall — silly-wise — without our council.

Take the recent flap over Dennis Fitzpatrick, the young man on the Human Rights Commission staff who is seeking a conscientious objector's status with his draft board.

The council has been all over that issue; they've had it surrounded at least twice. No one is entirely sure exactly where the council members stand on it now (they may be holding a meeting right this minute, for all we know) but one thing is clear—they've had an uproarious time getting there.

Councilman Jack Woods, who is developing into one of the really fine government comedians around, nearly broke the laugh meter with his comment that keeping Fitzpatrick on the city payroll would be "a slap in the face of every one of our men fighting now in Vietnam."

PICTURE THAT, will you? A group of U.S. troops are at the foot of Hamburger Hill, about to make yet another assault on the deeply entrenched enemy troops.

One thing you have to say for the Des Moines City Council—it manages to be funny without being vulgar.

"Excuse me, lieutenant, sir," says one of the men. "I was wondering—why are we trying to take this hill? It has no strategic value."

"I know that, son, but we're trying to show the dirty Commies that they can't hurt us by killing us."

"Oh. For a minute there I was afraid we didn't have a good reason?"

"Ha! Would the Army do something without a good reason?"

"I guess not. I'm afraid I haven't been thinking straight since I spent those three weeks under siege at Khe Sanh."

"Were you at Khe Sanh? You're in luck then. The colonel said that after we take this hill, he's going to give us a chance to retake Khe Sanh."

"The colonel is my kind of guy. Say, I notice you have a copy of The Des Moines Register there. What's the news from home?"

"Let's see . . . Goodness gracious!"

"What is it? Are they trying to oust the council-manager form of government again?"

"Worse than that."

"They're going to turn the Home Federal building into a parking ramp?"

"No. They're allowing a young man who claims conscientious objector status to remain on the staff of the Human Rights Commission."

"You're joking!"

"I wish I were."

"But don't they know that's a slap in the face to every fighting man in Vietnam?"

"With the possible exception of the Viet Cong."

"Right. Why doesn't he want to fight over here, anyway?"

"He thinks it's a stupid, immoral war."

"Picky, picky, picky. Hasn't anyone told him you have to ac-

cept the bitter with the sweet; that you can't expect the Battle of Britain every time out?"

"The trouble is, people were spoiled by World War II."

"Yeah. They don't make enemies like the Nazis anymore."

"Still, I wish the City Council would do something about that objector. It's guys like him who give war a bad name."

★ ★ ★

FRANK MILLER, the Register's cartoonist, dealt with the Fitzpatrick-council controversy by suggesting that "Joe McCarthy Is Alive and Living in Des Moines, Iowa."

The morning the cartoon appeared Miller was standing at one of the elevators in the building when a man approached him and said: "I didn't like that cartoon this morning."

Miller couldn't quite place the man's face. "Oh?" he responded. "I thought I was easy on 'em."

"If you didn't have freedom of the press behind you," the man said, "you wouldn't have gotten away with it."

• • •

A NUMBER of persons in Ankeny—in particular the members of an English class at the high school there—are upset over my giving their town away in the Over the Coffee Win Ankeny Contest.

They don't know the half of it. I have just received word that the winner of the contest never received his prize. Ankeny is lost in the mails.

ATTENTION ALL POST-MASTERS—If Ankeny turns up in your dead letter file, please return it to this address. Postage guaranteed.

• • •

I see by the city salary list that the lowest paid employees are the councilmen, who make $2,400 a year.
I hadn't realized the city was using the merit system.

Iowa's Remap Struggle
Gives Currier the Hives

SAM CURRIER, outlined against the Iowa Capitol in the distance, was standing in front of his favorite barbershop watching haircuts when his friend, Albatross Ives, walked up to him and said:

"Sam, what do you know about reapportionment?"

"It's a medium-sized country somewhere on the west coast of Africa," Sam replied like a shot.

"Of course it isn't," cried Al in exasperation. "What made you say a silly thing like that?"

"Just a stab in the dark. For the past year it seems like everything that I never heard of before turns out to be a medium-sized country on the west coast of Africa."

"Reapportionment," Al explained carefully, "is the rearranging of legislative districts so that each legislator represents about the same number of people."

SAM OPENED his eyes wide in surprise. "You mean there actually are states where some legislators represent more people than other legislators do?"

"Yes. In fact that situation exists in most states, Iowa among them."

"Why that's unfair," Sam declared. "Every legislator should be given just as many constituents as the next guy. How would you feel if you were a legislator with hardly anybody to represent?"

"I think you're missing the point here, Sam."

"No, I'm not. Each legislator, regardless of race, color or creed, has a constitutional right to his fair share of voters. Wipe out second-class legislatorship, that's what I say."

"Sam, forget about under-privileged legislators for a minute. Our main concern is not legislators but people. Do you believe in the principle of one man, one vote?"

"I don't know, is it legal?"

"Legal?" yelled Al, grabbing his friend by the lapels. "It's the cornerstone of Western civilization. It's the principle on which the ancient Greeks based their government. It's what the New England town meetings are all about. It's as American as apple pie and TV dinners."

SAM, VISIBLY MOVED, nodded. "Then I guess it can't be all bad. I'm for it."

"Our present system of representation violates that principle," explained Al. "The vote of people in sparsely populated counties, in effect, carries more weight than the vote of city people."

"Then I'm against the system and, furthermore, I think something should be done about it."

"Something has been done," said Al. "Reapportionment has come to Iowa. A special session of the Iowa Legislature has passed temporary and permanent plans for legislative redistricting."

"Good for the Iowa Legislature," shouted Sam, startling a

Many persons believe that the Iowa Legislature deserves a special citation at the conclusion of its 174-day session. They think it should be cited for leaving the scene of an accident.

67

passer-by who was wearing an Alf Landon button. "Quick, tell me about the temporary plan."

I T'S SORT OF Ben Hur with bifocals," replied Al. "Cast of thousands, two years in the making, that sort of thing. The legislators couldn't decide whether to give the cities or the rural areas more representatives so they compromised by giving both of them more legislators. The next session of the Legislature is going to be bigger than the Russian army."

"But surely the permanent plan must be an improvement. What's it like?" asked Sam.

"Like the partition of Germany," said Al. "It lumps the big counties together in one group and the little counties in another, then gives about one-third of the Senate seats to the big counties, who have half of the population. Some legislators wanted to build walls around the big counties but t h e y couldn't decide whether to make them of concrete or asphalt."

"And that's the permanent plan?"

"Yes, but don't worry about it. Unlike the temporary plan it's a constitutional amendment and needs approval by the next session of the Legislature and a vote of the people. That's like expecting the Kansas City Athletics to win the Olympic Games."

S AM SILENTLY MOVED his lips for a moment, then said, "Let me get this straight. You mean that the temporary plan is really more permanent than the permanent plan, which isn't even temporary."

"Sam, you are well on your way to becoming an expert on reapportionment."

"But there's still one thing I don't understand."

"What's that?"

"Why are the rural legislators so dead against putting representation on a pure population basis?"

"They're not, Sam. It's just that they believe that the pure population lives on farms."

Measure Mob Mentality

I OWA ATTY. GEN. Richard Turner keeps on in his quiet way, trying to improve the quality of life in America.

His most persistent effort in this direction has been the fight to overturn the U.S. Supreme Court's 1966 decision that law enforcement officers must inform an accused person of his rights before taking a statement from him.

Mr. Turner's chief objection to this ruling is that it takes away the lawman's traditional advantage over dumb crooks as opposed to smart ones.

"Merely because you can't force a smart fellow to talk doesn't mean you should encourage an ignorant man to clam up," Turner says.

If Turner is successful in his crusade, the most obvious result will be the raising of educational levels of criminals throughout the nation. The Mafia, unable to keep dumbheads out of jail, will begin screening job applicants for intelligence.

Can't you just hear a Mafia personnel director interviewing a prospect?

"So you want to join the Mob, eh, kid?"

"Yes, sir. Ever since I was a little kid and witnessed my first

Overheard in the Iowa Statehouse: "We've got too many bills before us this session. I'm plumb worn out from trying to read all of them." "Eyestrain?" "No, but my lips sure are tired."

68

mugging, all I've wanted to be is a professional hoodlum."

"YOU KIDS ARE all alike. You only see the glamorous side of the business. Crime isn't all shooting and beating and looting, you know. There's a lot of bookkeeping and drudgery."

"I realize that sir, but I'm not afraid of hard work and I'm willing to start small."

"That's the spirit we like to see. Tell me, have you had any amateur or semi-professional experience?"

"Some. I got my start slashing convertible tops and making obscene telephone calls. Then, when I got older, I did some purse snatching and robbing of church poor boxes."

"That sounds pretty good. I see by your application blank that you have a good academic record."

"Yes, sir. Valedictorian of my reform school class."

"Let me give you a little intelligence test to see what they learned you. We can't afford to have no dummies in the Mob anymore."

"I understand."

"Okay, here's the first question: If a guy is running 5 bookie joints and the cops knock over 2 of them, how many bookie joints has he got left?"

"Uh . . three?"

"That's close enough. Now here's a toughie. It's just after midnight, see, and you're breaking into a warehouse. A voice behind you says, 'This is the FBI. Throw up your hands or we'll shoot.' What do you do?"

"I TELL THEM that the warehouse is not engaged in interstate commerce and they have no jurisdiction in the case, and I keep trying to break into the warehouse."

"Right. Now what if they're local cops?"

"I read them the second, fourth and fifth amendments and Commandments two through seven, then I tell them to buzz off."

"Congratulations, kid, you passed with flying colors. You're going to make a great punk. This intelligence test is the best thing that ever happened to us. There's only one thing that could cause us trouble."

"What's that?"

"If they ever start making attorney generals pass intelligence tests, we'll have to step up our on-campus recruiting to meet the competition."

A Lug Behind The Nut

THERE IS a bill before the Iowa Legislature that would allow driver training instructors to sit BEHIND the driver while instructing him in the operation of a motorcycle. Present law requires that he sit beside the student—preferably in a sidecar.

While the bill seems innocent enough, it is one of the most significant pieces of legislation to come before the Legislature during this session.

Should it pass, it would mean an end to the driver training instructor as we know him. No longer would he be the quiet, conservative man with the calm, soothing voice.

Instead he would be . . .

Let's project ourselves about 10 years into the future and see what the new breed might sound like in a radio interview.

AN ANNOUNCER'S voice says:

"Good evening ladies and gen-

Rumor of the week—Atty. Gen. Richard Turner has been signed for a series of appearances on the Johnny Carson show. He will do comic readings from the Iowa Constitution.

tlemen, welcome to another radio edition of 'Nuts Make News,' the radio program that proves you don't have to be crazy to enjoy life, but it helps.

"We have as our guest today, Scar Crashley, a driver education instructor at a local high school. Would you like to say hello to all the folks out there in Radioland, Scar?"

"Sure. Ciao, all you folks out there in Radioland."

"Would you describe your dress for our listening audience."

"There's really nothing very unusual about it. It's just the normal work clothes of a driver education instructor, World War II German helmet with swastika, black leather jacket, high-jack boots and shoulder-to-wrist cast."

"SCAR, YOU'VE won recognition as one of the top driver education instructors in the country. What would you say is the greatest asset an instructor can possess?"

"A high tolerance to pain."

"Is teaching motorcyclists to drive as dangerous as they say, then?"

"Not really. We instructors like to kid about it a lot but actually it's no more hazardous than bullfighting or sky diving. Many top instructors live to be 35 or older."

"How did you happen to get started in this business, anyway?"

"When I was a kid I used to fall out of trees a lot. I got so I sort of enjoyed it. One thing led to another and before I knew it I was getting my kicks from falling off the backs of speeding motorcycles. I figured if I could get paid for doing it, so much the better, so I became a driver training instructor."

"WHAT ADVICE would you give youngsters who want to prepare for a career in driver education?"

"I think that the best possible preparation is to spend an hour each day jumping into the deep end of a swimming pool."

"Wouldn't that be more helpful for a swimmer than for a prospective driver education instructor?"

"Not if you drain the pool first."

"Do you agree with the classic statement of the legendary driver training instructor, Slam Bumper, who, when asked why driver training instructors taught, replied: 'Because we're not all there.' "

"No, I don't agree with that at all."

"Why do you teach motorcycling, then?"

"Because it feels so good when I stop."

● ● ●

RUMOR OF THE WEEK—The Des Moines City Council is being sent on a cross-country Sell-Iowa tour by a grateful state. The grateful state is Nebraska.

● ● ●

Legislative Laffs

THERE'S A new kind of joke going around these days; the Iowa Legislature it's called. It goes like this: "Why does it take three legislators to change a light bulb?" **"One to hold the bulb and two to turn the ladder."** You say that sounds familiar? Stick around, you ain't heard nothin' yet.

"HOW CAN THE Iowa Legislature raise its intellectual level?" **"By making Spiro Agnew an honorary member."**

"HOW CAN YOU tell when an Iowa legislator is on his way to a fancy dress ball?" **"He wears a cummerbund over his bib overalls."**

"HEAR ABOUT the legislator who broke his leg while raking leaves?" "No, how did it happen?" *"Fell out of the tree."*

"WHAT DOES the Iowa Legislature think about manual labor?" "Best president Mexico ever had."

"WHY DOES it take five legislators to pop corn?" "One to hold the skillet and four to shake the stove."

"WHY DON'T they have a self-service elevator at the Statehouse?" "They did, but the legislators kept stopping between floors to ask directions."

"Did you hear about the Iowa Legislature passing a resolution of condemnation against Roy Rogers' horse?" "You mean Trigger, the smartest horse in the movies? No, why did they do that?" *"Jealousy."*

"WHAT DO YOU get when you cross an Iowa legislator with a canary?" "A cross canary."

"WHY DO IOWA legislators like girls' basketball?" *"They can keep up with the action."*

* * *

That's the name of the game, folks. Why don't you send in YOUR favorite Iowa Legislature joke? The best entry will be awarded a long-playing record of key legislators reciting passages from the collected works of Edgar Guest.

71

"Have you ever noticed

bow seldom you see couples
necking at
hamber music concerts?"

A Poet's Tree

SOME PERSONS in New Brunswick, N.J., are talking about tearing down Joyce Kilmer's birthplace and some others are talking about trying to save it.

The only logical conclusion to be drawn is that there isn't much worth talking about in New Brunswick these days.

Joyce Kilmer, as you may remember, is the author of the poem "Trees," the one that starts out "I think that I shall never see, etc."

The first two lines of the work and the last two are probably as well known as any lines of poetry in the English language. Certainly the work has been called "the best loved American poem," more often than any other.

There is but one other thing that needs to be said about it. It is perfectly awful.

It is an extraordinarily bad poem; so bad, in fact, that it is ridiculous to compare it with real poetry. It does not even stand up well in its own class—sentimental verse. Certainly it has none of the charm of "The Cremation of Sam McGee," a classic of that category.

WHAT ACCOUNTS FOR the poem's apparent popularity? The only plausible explanation is that people don't really read it; they simply know about the beginning and the end and have a vague remembrance of hearing it read once in the fourth grade.

Let's take a close look at the thing:

"I think that I shall never see

A poem as lovely as a tree.

[What's been said here is that each and every tree on earth is lovelier than any poem. Overlooking the considerable difficulty of comparing the beauty of a poem with that of a tree, the statement ignores the fact that there are a great many ugly trees.]

"A tree whose hungry mouth is pressed

Against the earth's sweet flowing breast;

[Either this tree is all crouched down and bent over or it's standing on its head.]

A TREE that looks at God all day

And lifts her leafy arms to pray;

[Here's this remarkable tree, its mouth pressed to the ground, its eyes rolled back into its head trying to look at God yet still able to throw its arms up in prayer. It's not a tree, it's a contortionist.]

"A tree that may in summer wear

A nest of robins in her hair;

[Presumably the author is referring to the hair on the arms lifted in prayer.]

"Upon whose bosom snow has lain;

Who intimately lives with rain.

[Just a minute, a while ago this tree was a suckling babe and now, all of a sudden, she's got a bosom and is being intimate with some guy named Rain.]

"Poems are made by fools like me,

But only God can make a tree."

[Which is fine, because if it were the other way round, we'd have some pretty strange looking trees.]

One can feel a certain sympathy for Mr. Kilmer's memory. Most of us can write a bad poem and have it disappear into the recent past. Kilmer wrote one and got stuck with immortality.

We'd have been better off had the oak died as an acorn, before Mr. Kilmer had a chance to be inspired by it.

Ups and
Downs

STEPHEN POTTER died last week. It would be unseemly to allow the great One-Upman to go permanently One-Down without a word of farewell.

Mr. Potter was an Englishman and his fame rested on his development of the philosophy of "gamesmanship," which he defined as "the art of winning games without actually cheating."

He viewed the games, and indeed life itself, as a psychological warfare whose object was to unnerve the enemy and shatter its confidence.

Thus, when playing tennis with a superior opponent (particularly a younger man) he would choose a crucial moment, then declare: "Kindly say clearly, p l e a s e, whether the ball was in or out," thereby suggesting that the opponent's advantage was somehow unfairly achieved.

Or he would come to parties armed with one of the "seventeen genuine *Ballades* in Medieval French" which he had committed to memory and, at an opportune moment, say: "Of course, you know this," then begin . . .

"*Ah, vielle septance de melange*" and so on, making sure that he accented the silent "e." The effect, of course, was to make his audience feel like illiterate clods, the supreme achievement of the art.

"Gamesmanship," Potter once wrote, "is the moral equivalent of assault and battery."

IN HIS SEVERAL books— "Gamesmanship," "Lifemanship" and "One-Upmanship" being the best known—he covered virtually every conceivable situation.

Suppose, for example, a gamesman who happens to be a rotten shot is invited on a pheasant-hunting trip. Not wanting to admit he's a rotten shot (thereby going one-down) he says, according to Potter:

"*Not my cup of tea. Stupid old conscience at work. Don't like birds, but feel I wasn't created to take pot-shots at them. Besides, I think the creatures are rather beautiful.*"

It makes the hunters seem like a bunch of Nazis. Potter also referred to a favorite monograph of his: "Famous People and When Not to Recognize Them," a classic in its field.

When serving an especially bad wine to guests Potter would say:

"I drink this now for sentimental reasons only . . . just a pleasant residue, an essence of sugar and water—but still with a hint of former glories.

"Keep it in your mouth a minute or two . . . see what I mean?"

Potter said, "Under this treatment the definite flavor of carbolic which has been surprising your guest will seem to him to acquire an interest if not a grace."

POTTER, WHO was 69 at the time of his death, was a great influence on the postwar generation. His philosophy made each day a fresh challenge.

A classmate would burst into the room yelling, "Guess what? Old Hotchkiss gave me an 'A' in history!"

"Good for Hotchkiss!" you'd fire back. "I'll never again accuse him of not having a sense of humor."

Or, on meeting a friend you hadn't seen in some time, you would say: "I'd heard you'd been ill. I must say you're not looking bad, everything considered."

"But I haven't been ill," the friend would say.

"Oh?" you'd reply, elevating your eyebrows in obvious alarm at his appearance. It ruined the friend's day and made yours.

Of course, the gamesmanship sword cuts both ways. I once had an editor who was a master at it. He would wait until you'd written a particularly undistinguished, bland, trite piece, then summon you to his desk and say, solemnly:

"That's the best work you've ever done for us." It was devastating.

Even the young are on to the game. The other day a rookie reporter actually helped me on with my coat and cautioned me against the slippery streets lest I fall and break a hip. It made me feel 140 years old.

Particularly since the reporter was a girl.

'Allen, Take It Easy'

IN AN AGE when it is the fashion for literary biographies to be exhaustive, comprehensive and definitive (that is to say, junked up with irrelevant detail), it is a pleasure to come upon Jane Kramer's "Allen Ginsberg in America," a book that sacrifices the more leaden biographical virtues for charm and warmth.

Ginsberg is by all odds the most interesting lunatic on the contemporary scene, and there's a chance—just a chance, mind you—that *he* may be the sane one.

Ginsberg's popular reputation rests not so much on his poetry as on his position as a kind of elder statesman of the hippie movement—a Bernard Baruch of the beatniks.

He's been in the vanguard of every oddball movement that's come down the road during the past 20 years. The beat generation, drugs, flower power—he was there, and there first. He's been weird so long that society has accepted his weirdness as normal. He is America's House Kook.

He's had ample preparation for the role. As a young man, working as a market researcher of all things, he began hearing voices, among them that of William Blake, the Eighteenth Century poet and painter. Understandably disturbed, he called a psychiatrist.

"Look," he said, "I have to see you. William Blake is in my room."

"You must be crazy," the psychiatrist said, and hung up on him.

THINGS LIKE that are always happening to him. But while Miss Kramer reports the comic-strip anecdotes that decorate his life, she also gets beyond that to reveal Ginsberg as a gentle, tender human being with an uncritical, child-like curiosity about life and its possibilities.

The real Ginsberg appeared after an encounter with yet another psychiatrist. He was still working as a market researcher and being miserable. He told the psychiatrist:

"I really would like to stop working forever—never work again, never do anything like the kind of work I'm doing now—and do nothing but write poetry and have leisure to spend the day outdoors and go to museums and see friends.

"And I'd like to keep living with someone—maybe even a man—and explore relationships that way. And cultivate my perceptions, cultivate the visionary thing in me. Just a literary and quiet city-hermit existence."

And the psychiatrist said: "Well, why don't you?"

Just like that. Ginsberg followed the advice and, to all intents and purposes, has lived happily ever after. Good psychiatrists are born, not made.

Perhaps the most delightful character in the book is Ginsberg's father, Louis, a lovely Jewish mother of a man. The elder Ginsberg is an English teacher, a square poet and an atrocious punster ("I have no axiom to grind").

He obviously loves his son and is proud of him, yet he wishes he were just a little more of a straight arrow.

A T ONE POINT in the book, Allen, whose tastes in companions is wide-ranging to say the least, brings a girl to his father's home. He is, by this time, a famous poet and well into the hippie scene. The girl, Maretta, is appropriate to that scene—finger cymbals, beads, Buddhist chants, incense sticks.

"What's with this Maretta?" the elder Ginsberg asks. "Why can't you bring home a nice Jewish girl?"

The son, laughing, answers, "For the love of God, Louis. Here for years you've been saying you want me to bring home a *girl* for a change, and now that I do, you want a *Jewish* one?"

"You're such an *experimenter*, Allen," says the father. "Tibetan Buddhist girl friends. Swamis. Drugs. All this talk from you about pot—*'It's so elevating, Louis. So ecstatic. My soul is outside my body. I see ultimate reality.'*

"You know what I say? I say, 'Allen, take it easy.'"

Somehow, it is reassuring to know that even Allen Ginsberg gets advice like that. It's a nice book, published by Random House.

Donald's Smitten

D ON'T TELL my wife but I've fallen in love with another woman.

Her name is Judith Viorst and she writes poems; wry, witty, perceptive poems about the dandruff of married life, the imperfections that distinguish real marriages from those in women's magazines.

Mrs. Viorst's book (and the sole agent of our love affair, alas), called "It's Hard to Be Hip Over Thirty and Other Tragedies of Married Life," has just been published in paperback.

You really shouldn't get married or divorced without reading it.

She is the one poet who speaks for those of us who once believed

78

that a candle in a Chianti bottle was a necessary adjunct to Gracious Living and who now live in the Generation Gap, rather than on either side of it.

HERE'S AN excerpt from "The Honeymoon Is Over."
The honeymoon is over
And we find that dining by
candlelight makes us squint,
And that all the time
I was letting him borrow my
comb and hang up his wet
raincoat in my closet,
I was really waiting
To stop letting him.
And that all the time
He was saying how he loved
my chicken pot pie,
He was really waiting
To stop eating it.

(I guess they call this getting to
know each other.)

IT'S A SHAME to tear these delightful poems into bits and pieces but there's not room for full quotation.

Perhaps the favorite of the slim volume is the last, "True Love." It begins:
It's true love because
I put on eyeliner and a concerto
and make pungent observations
about the great issues of the
day
Even when there's no one here
but him,
And because
I do not resent watching the
Green Bay Packers
Even though I am
philosophically opposed to
football,
And because
When he is late for dinner and
I know he must be either
having an affair or lying dead
in the middle of the street,
I always hope he's dead.

Lovely stuff. The New American Library published the hardcover edition, Signet Books the paperback.

Rat Race to Incompetence

A MAN CALLED Peter has just made one of the great discoveries of the ages, ranking in importance with that time Archimedes found Eureka in his bathtub.

Dr. Laurance J. Peter, a professor of education at the University of Southern California, has come up with the reason everything always goes wrong.

It doesn't always go wrong, you say? Nonsense. How many times have you or your wife said: "Nothing in this house works."

Does your car work properly, can you mail a letter with confidence that it will be delivered to the correct address promptly?

Do you count on that battery-operated toy to last more than two weeks? Would you stake your life on the performance of your electric can-opener?

Of course not. Everything goes wrong. Always.

And Dr. Peter knows why.

IT'S SIMPLE, really. Like most great ideas the great wonder is that nobody ever thought of it before.

The reason everything always goes wrong is that nearly everybody is incompetent to do the job assigned them.

That's the Peter Principle in a nutshell: "In a Hierarchy Every Employee Tends to Rise to His Level of Incompetence."

He demonstrates it this way:

Suppose a man is a brilliant mechanic. His good work will attract the eye of his boss, who will promote him to foreman. If he is a bad foreman, he will remain a foreman. If he is a good

foreman, however, he will be rewarded with another promotion.

He will keep getting promotions until the organization finds a job he cannot do, then he will stay at that job for the rest of his days, not doing it. He will have reached his level of incompetence.

The corollary to the Peter Principle states: "In time, every post tends to be occupied by an employe who is incompetent to carry out its duties."

BUT HOW THEN, you might well ask, does anything EVER get done, if everyone is incompetent to do it?

Peter has the answer to that, too.

"Work," he says, **"is accomplished by those employes who have not yet reached their level of incompetence."**

All of this is set down in a book Dr. Peter wrote in collaboration with Raymond Hull, "The Peter Principle," published by William Morrow and Company, Inc.

Life's great challenge, in Peter's view, is to avoid reaching one's level of incompetence.

He points out a number of ways of doing this, the least satisfactory being the refusal of promotions.

Refusing a promotion might work for a person relatively free of responsibilities, he says, but for one encumbered by family, it is virtually impossible.

Such a person's wife attacks his action because all her friends' husbands are getting ahead and hers isn't; his children feel that their birthright has been devalued and neighbors gaze upon him with scornful eyes.

DR. PETER does not foreclose hope for the family man, however. He holds out to him: Creative Incompetence.

This is the ability to do your job well, without seeming to.

It is the efficient office worker who tricks his superiors into thinking he's operating at the level of his incompetence by maintaining an incredibly littered desk.

Or the secretary who masks her competence by filing her

nails in the presence of her boss's boss.

In some organizations something as simple as bringing your lunch in a brown paper bag is enough to ward off potentially destructive promotions.

If you should be seduced by the challenge of a new job and find yourself operating at the level of your incompetence, Dr. Peter advises narrowing your specialty until it becomes manageable again.

As the most outstanding example of this technique, he points to the historian who became an expert on the first 30 minutes of the Reformation. Go thou and do likewise.

The Erotic Reservoir

I WAS SITTING at my desk, perfecting my a r t—finger-painting—when the phone rang. It was an old friend who was now in the book publishing business in New York.

"O. T.," *he said, "we want you to do a book for us, a sociological, semi-documentary novel."*

"Great," I replied. "As a matter of fact, I'm working on one now. I'm thinking of calling it 'Station Master.' It'll do for railroads what 'Airport' did for the airline industry."

"Oh, that kind of sociology."

"It tells the story of a typical railroad station master; the lonely hours he spends waiting for a train to come in. It deals with the psychological stress of a man cut off from human contact. On another level the train

becomes a symbol of God in our modern society, with the station master's alienation representative of . . ."

"Hold it right there, O. T., 'Station Master' isn't going to make it."

"But I haven't told you about the dream sequence."

"FORGET it. What we're interested in is something more along the lines of a Harold Robbins or Jacqueline Susann book."

"Oh, that kind of sociology."

"Right. You read about that new book, 'Naked Came the Stranger'"?

"You mean the hoax?"

"Hoax Schmoax. It's selling like crazy. We want you to do a Midwest version. All the big sex novels so far have been about the East or West coast. We feel there's a vast reservoir of erotic fantasy in the Midwest. We'd like you to tap it for us."

"Gee, I don't know. I'm a family man. What would my kids say if I wrote a book like that?"

"They'd probably say, 'Can I have the keys to the Jaguar tonight, Dad?' 'Portnoy's Complaint' has grossed more than $2 million so far."

"I'll do it."

"FINE. The book doesn't necessarily have to be autobiographical, but feel free to draw upon your personal experiences. I mean, after all, we're all men of the world, right?"

"Oh, yeah, I can throw in a few personal things."

"Could you give me an example or two, just to help me decide how big a first printing I should order?"

"Well, there's this thing I do every once in a while after work."

"Yeah?"

"I go over to the telephone company and watch the girls get off work."

"Yeah, go on. What then?"

"That's all; I just watch them get off work."

"*That's it?*"

"After all, I am a married man."

"LOOK, O. T. Why don't you forget your personal experiences altogether? Write about other people. I think that'll give you esthetic distance. You know any s w i n g e r s around Des Moines?"

"Do I? I happen to be a very close friend of the president of the local La Dolce Vita Club."

"Now, that's more like it."

"Yes, sir, he's seen the movie 18 times."

"What movie?"

" 'La Dolce Vita,' of course. Why do you think they call it the La Dolce Vita Club? There's an active Sound of Music Club in town too, but I don't see how I can work them into the book."

"Say, O. T., I've had a second thought on this. Your station master idea doesn't sound so bad after all. Why don't you keep working on that. Funk and Wagnall's is looking for a property like it. In the meantime, can you put me in contact with someone on the paper who knows about sex?"

"Well, our farm department is said to be very knowledgeable."

The operator must have cut us off just then. He must have been calling from a pay phone too, because when I tried to call him back, his secretary said he was out of town.

Perelmans

Of Wisdom

ONE OF THE nation's great unnatural resources reached full maturity last week. Sidney Joseph Perelman became 65.

For those of you recovering from a bout with amnesia (and there's been a lot of it going around lately), S. J. Perelman is a writer; a satirist. As a matter of fact, he is to American satire what Elizabeth Taylor is to sex —the greatest living exponent of the art.

Of course, he's not to everyone's taste. Take this lunatic sentence from one of his stories:

"The following morning the 'Maid of Hull,' a frigate of the line mounting 36 guns, out of Bath and into bed in a twinkling, dropped downstream on the tide, bound for Bombay, object matrimony."

There undoubtedly are persons who don't find that funny. I hope I owe them money.

Not the least of Mr. Perelman's talents is a genius for titles. His stories are found under titles like: "Gather Ye Rosebuds, But Watch Ye Step;" "Monomania, You and Me is Quits;" "Baby, I Will Enchant Thine Ear—Maybe," and "Rent Me and I'll Come to You." Actually, you'll find them under those very titles.

ONE OF PERELMAN'S few peers, R o b e r t Benchley, once said: "In the dementia praecox field Perelman is in a class by himself. He has driven the rest of us to writing articles on economics."

I was first won over to Mr. Perelman by a story called "To Sleep, Perchance to Steam." Written in 1942, it explores the potentialities of an electric blanket, which was then in the thinking stage.

"Set me down as a dusty old eccentric," he wrote, "but frankly, there would seem to be some more ideal haven nowadays than a skein of copper wire, no matter how fine or flexible.

"Nor is it any more reassuring to learn that 'six rubber molded safety thermostats are placed at intervals in this web of insulated wire (you can feel these thermostats with your fingers beneath the cover of the Comforter).'

"It needs no vivid imagination to imagine oneself lying in the dark with eyes protruding, endlessly tallying the thermostats and expecting at any moment to be converted into roast Long Island duckling."

A man who can write that shares my vision of life, or rather, I share his. We also see eye to eye on the subject of humor. Interviewed recently by William Zinsser in the New York Times magazine he said:

"Generally speaking, I don't believe in kindly humor. I don't think it exists. One of the most shameful utterances to stem from the human mouth is Will Rogers's 'I never met a man I didn't like.'

"**T**HE ABSOLUTE antithesis is Oscar Wilde on the foxhunting Englishman: 'The unspeakable in full pursuit of the uneatable.'

"The two examples sum up, for me, the distinction. Wilde's remark contains, in the briefest span, the truth; whereas Rogers's is pure flatulence, crowd-pleasing, and fake humility . . ."

"Humor is purely a point of view, and only the pedants try to classify it. For me its chief merit is the use of the unexpected, the glancing allusion, the deflation of pomposity, and the constant repetition of one's helplessness in a majority of situations.

"One doesn't consciously start out wanting to be a social satirist. You find something absurd enough to make you want to push a couple of antipersonnel bombs under it.

"If it then seems to have another element of meaning, that's lagniappe. But the main obligation is to amuse yourself."

So who am I to argue with S. J. Perelman?

A Dark Odyssey

IF I TOLD YOU I had just read a book that dealt almost exclusively with rape, murder, incest, war, bestiality (in its most explicit form) and other of the more baroque styles of sexual encounter, you would probably think I was some kind of creep, right?

But, if I then informed you that the book had just won the [1969] National Book Award for fiction, would you still think so?

It would depend on how you felt about the National Book Awards, I suppose, but the point is that I've just read "Steps," by Jerzy Kosinski, and it's a great book.

Kosinski, author of "The Painted Bird," is one of those people—like Conrad and Nabokov—who writes in a second language; that is to say, he is a native Pole who writes in English. And for us who struggle to write in our own

83

tongue, it is heartbreaking to see him do it so superbly.

"STEPS" IS A SERIES of related vignettes dealing with the experiences of a young man during World War II and after—a dark odyssey of the Twentieth Century.

Scene after scene of savagery and brutality are set down in unornamented prose, beautiful in its precision.

Here, for example, is a partial account of a revenge executed by a young boy who is reviled and spat upon by the members of a village somewhere in Eastern Europe. The boy kneads fish-hooks and ground glass into tiny balls of bread and feeds them to the villagers' children.

"There were no doctors or hospitals in the area," Kosinski's narrator writes, "the nearest railway only carried an occasional freight train.

"*At dawn crying parents carried their gasping children to the church so the priest could purify them with holy water. But at dusk, in a more desperate mood, they took the dying to the distant huts of the local witches who practiced sorcery and healing.*

"But death continued to levy its toll, and children went on dying. Some of the peasants blasphemed God, whispering it was He Himself who had dispatched His only son, Jesus, to inevitable crucifixion, in order to redeem His own sin of creating so cruel a world.

"Others insisted that Death had come to dwell in the villages to avoid the bombed cities, and the war, and the camps where furnaces smoked."

THE CONCENTRATION camp is a central image of the book. A woman is talking to the narrator about a friend, an architect who designed the camps:

"You could look at it from many points of view," she said. "In a maternity hospital for instance, more people leave than arrive; in a concentration camp the reverse is true. Its main purpose is hygiene."

"What do you mean?"

"Have you ever seen rats being exterminated? Or, better—do you like animals?"

"Of course."

"Well, rats are animals."

"*Not really. I mean they're not domestic animals. They're dangerous, and therefore they have to be exterminated.*"

"Exactly: they have to be exterminated; it's a problem of hygiene. Rats have to be removed. We exterminate them, but this has nothing to do with our attitudes toward cats, dogs, or any other animal. Rats aren't murdered—we get rid of them; or, to use a better word, they are eliminated; this act of elimination is empty of all meaning. There's no ritual in it, no symbolism; the right of the executioner is never questioned. That's why in the concentration camps my friend designed, the victims never remained individuals. They existed only to be killed."

KOSINSKI DESCRIBES the feelings of a young man about to behead a prisoner:

"I saw myself as someone else who felt nothing, who stood calm and c o m p o s e d, determined enough to stiffen his arms to grasp and raise the weapon.

"*I knew I was strong enough to do it. I could recall the precision with which I had felled young trees: I could hear their moaning and creaking, and see their trembling, and I knew I could jump aside as they cracked and fell.*"

One gets the impression that Mr. Kosinski is trying to tell us that we do not live in the best of all possible worlds. It is a harrowing book.

12 Gs for Algren

IOWA CITY, IA.—Nelsen Algren is one of the foremost exponents of the tough guy tradition of American letters; he is not a man to call a lady a prostitute when she's really a whore.

Ask him what a confirmed Chicago roughneck like him is doing as an instructor at the University of Iowa's Writers' Workshop this year and he says:

"That's a very easy question to answer, my friend. I'm here for the money. I can make more in a month here than I can in a year of writing."

Such candor is enough to make an old school board reporter weep for joy.

Still, the answer surprises as well as shocks. Algren is a major American novelist who has written a number of successful books; notably "The Man With the Golden Arm" which won the prestigious National Book Award in 1949.

THAT BOOK and a later one, "A Walk On the Wild Side," were made into successful movies, and an earlier work, the very fine "Never Come Morning," has had a substantial paperback sale. **With all of this apparent financial success, why should Algren be concerned about money? What happened to his loot?**

"The people around the edges of the business got it," he says. "The publishing business is a racket; the publishers don't have any more ethics than loan sharks.

"A writer's got to have protection. An unprotected writer has about as much chance of getting and keeping his royalties as a guy does of making it by opening a pizza house on Chicago's south side and just selling pizza."

Why no protection?

"Bad agenting. I happened to have an agent who hung a very low price tag on herself—which was appropriate for herself—but she wrapped me into her crackerjack box. I'm the tin whistle of American letters.

"It's not just the money, though. Both 'The Man With the Golden Arm' and 'A Walk On the Wild Side' were supposed to have been plays. I didn't want a movie.

"WHAT HAPPENS after I put a work on the stage doesn't concern me. I don't care how they degrade it, I don't have to see it.

"But I lost control of my books. I saw 'The Man With the Golden Arm' once; it was terrible."

One might expect Algren to have become embittered by his experience, but he's not. He seems to be able to accept adversity with a what-the-hell shrug.

Algren's latest book is a collection of essays, "Notes of a Sea Diver." He's currently at work on a racetrack novel, "Moon of the Arfy-Darfy."

HE ADMITS, however, that the racetrack work is not "a big book." He has said that he probably won't attempt another big book.

"One reason is that you've got to believe in a big book before you try it. And then, how would I live for five years while I'm writing it?

"You can't teach class for five years and write a big book on the side, at least I can't.

"You've got to stick with it for two or three years, work on it all the time. You have to keep pushing it along like a snowball. If you stop it'll roll back on you."

AS MIGHT be expected, Algren's preference among contemporary writers is for those "out in the scene."

Joseph Heller ("Catch 22"), Terry Southern ("The Magic Christian," "Candy") and J. P. Donleavy ("The Ginger Man") are among his favorites. He says he finds Saul Bellow ("Herzog") "a very small writer."

He calls "In Cold Blood" by Truman Capote "a little masterpiece."

"Capote is going to make a lot of money on that book, but he didn't do it for the money.

"He got away from that New York literary crowd and took a six-year risk. It was a long chance and he made it.

"The chief fault of American writers is that they won't take that chance."

Algren is off for Cahokia Downs, a racetrack in Illinois, when his tour of duty here ends this summer.

While the Iowa salary ("about 12 Gs") has been pleasant, the academic life ("passive") is not for him.

● ● ●

HAVE YOU ever noticed that, in a civil war, the losing side almost always has the best songs?

● ● ●

Fear Without Love

AS A SOCIETY we seem to be far more tolerant of violence than we are of sex.

If a married woman is publicly revealed to be sexually promiscuous, she very likely will be ostracized by her middle-class friends.

If she merely caves in the head of her husband with an iron, however, she can count on her friends to stand by her in her time of trial.

This same point was made by Lenny Bruce, the comedian. Bruce, throughout his career, was plagued by the charge that his act was obscene.

Although many registered, bona fide intellectuals testified that his material, far from being obscene, was highly moral, the police of our great cities repeatedly protected the morals of nightclub-goers by jailing Bruce.

In arguing the hypocrisy of the society that judged him obscene, Bruce would point to the case of Kitty Genovese in New York. She was the girl who was loudly murdered while dozens of apartment dwellers watched and listened but failed to call the police.

He said that the same people would have been quick to interfere and notify authorities had they spotted a couple making love in front of their building.

And finally, the point is made again by Dr. Fredric Wertham in his recently published book, "A Sign for Cain: An Exploration in Human Violence."

He says that we consistently show a preference for violence

over sex. In comics and films, for example, an obviously lewd encounter is often resolved by revealing that the motives of the male are destructive rather than erotic. The doctor states:

'A producer of horror films said with pride over the radio:
" 'Our pictures are absolutely clean. The monster might abduct the young bride, but only to kill her.' "

Meanwhile,
In the Ring

I WAS READING an article on bullfighting recently — it was by Kenneth Tynan, who is best known as a drama critic—when I came across a startling statement.

Tynan, in writing about a torero named Jaime Ostos, described him as "the exuberantly handsome young Andalusian who received, in 1963, a wound that brought him nearer death than any matador of the front rank since Manolete's fatal goring 16 years earlier."

THE PART I found shocking was that only one top-grade bullfighter had lost his life in those 16 years.

I had long ago come to the conclusion that the danger of bullfighting—at least to the bullfighter—was overrated, but I hadn't realized that it was less risky than jaywalking.

IT BECOMES obvious that the aficionados of the world are the victims of a high pressure snow job. They've been sold a bill of goods through the use of market-tested nomenclature; moment of truth, blood and sand, brave bulls and the rest of it.

If it is possible to capture the imagination with a profession that is only slightly more hazardous than clamdigging, think of what could be done with a really dangerous occupation—process serving, for example.

In an effort to lift the art of process serving to its rightful place in the public's affection, the following handbook is presented:

There are three classic passes that a server of legal papers must master before he can lay claim to the noble title of Servero.

FIRST THERE IS the Natural, which is the basic pass of the paperos, or legal papers as they are known to Gringos.

To execute this properly the Servero approaches with stately grace the home of the person on whom the papers are to be served (the Serveree). He mounts the front steps with heavy footfalls and pounds loudly on the door.

When the door opens the Servero must stand straight and fix his prey with a long stare, letting him sense his mastery. Then, with a deep bow, the Servero gently places

87

the paperos in the hand of the Serveree, performs a slow turn and walks slowly away, taking great care not to look back.

This is considered the greatest of the classic passes and is the most dangerous, for obvious reasons.

The legendary Numero Uno Servero, Morton D. Arthur of Los Angeles, lost his life in a 1953 corridora while executing a Natural. A woman on whom he had just served a court summons threw a flatiron through the back of his skull.

THE SECOND of the classic passes is the Harmonica. In this test of guile and agility the Servero silently sneaks up on the front porch and flattens himself against a wall, just to the side of the door. He then plays four bars of "On the Street Where You Live," on a harmonica. When the person inside, who can see no one at his door, comes out to investigate the noise, the Servero spins out from his hiding place and, as he twirls by, slaps the paperos into his victim's hand.

He continues the pass by leaping over the porch railing and executing a volapie (flying feet) down the street.

Speedy Gonzales, the greatest exponent of the Harmonica, cashed in his chips in Philly in 1958 while doing it. He forgot that the guy on whom he'd just served papers lived on the third floor.

THE LAST of the classic passes is, of course, the Escaptada, the supreme moment of spectacle (la hora de verdad) of the corridora.

To perform this the Servero must wait until the Serveree leaves his home. The Servero then enters the home and hides, preferably in a closet.

When the Serveree returns

the Servero leaps from his hiding place, shouting "Ole." As the Serveree's jaw drops in amazement, the Servero stuffs the paperos into his prey's mouth and does a volapie out of the house.

These, it must be remembered are only the classic passes. There are many variations that help make process serving the mystical and symbolic thing that it is.

The Spanish, however, have never been able to appreciate the drama and beauty of the spectacle. They live, like flies, on the surface of life.

Unbearable, But Brilliant

PETER De VRIES is one of my favorite writers, but for a number of years I had avoided reading his novel, "The Blood of the Lamb," for the rather ignoble reason that I was afraid to.

I knew what the book was about, you see.

Eight years ago one of De Vries' daughters, a girl of 10 or 12, died of leukemia. It was shortly thereafter that he published "The Blood of the Lamb," the story of a man whose pre-teenage daughter dies of leukemia.

That's writing pretty close to the nerve; closer, I feared, than I wanted to get.

A friend finally convinced me that not reading the book was an act of moral cowardice and so I read it.

I HAD BEEN right. The reading of it was an almost unbearable experience. But my friend had been right, too—it is a brilliant book and not to be avoided for any reason.

The book is more than the story of his child's death, for De Vries is a novelist rather than a journalist. It is the story of a man's search for the answer to the central question of life: Why? *And it is a funny book—as all De Vries' books are. A funny book touched by death.*

The hero is a man who, as a boy, loses whatever faith his Dutch Calvinist heritage had bequeathed him as he watches his older brother, himself a boy, die of pneumonia.

His subsequent life is a study in personal disaster.

He contracts tuberculosis and enters a sanatorium. He falls in love with a girl there, shortly before she dies.

His father goes mad and he leaves the sanatorium to support his mother. He marries, has a daughter, and enjoys a few years of happiness before his wife succumbs to insanity. She eventually commits suicide.

YET, THROUGH all of this, he maintains his faith in reason.

His college paper asks him for a brief statement on his philosophy of life and he replies:

"I believe that man must learn to live without those consolations called religious, which his own intelligence must by now have told him belong to the childhood of the race.

"Philosophy can really give us nothing permanent to believe either; it is too rich in answers, each canceling out the rest. The quest for Meaning is foredoomed. Human life 'means' nothing. But that is not to say that it is not worth living.

"What does a Debussy Arabesque 'mean,' or a rainbow or a rose? A man delights in all of these, knowing himself to be no more—a wisp of music and a haze of dreams dissolving against the Sun.

"Man has only his own two feet to stand on, his own human trinity to see him through; Reason, Courage, and Grace. And the first plus the second equals the third."

THEN HIS daughter, a delightful child, contracts leukemia and begins to die. As the ordeal wears on, he finds himself drawn back toward the church. He wraps himself in the cloak of religious faith to shield himself from the pain of his loss.

Months after her death, while cleaning out the house preparatory to moving, he flips on a tape recorder and hears his daughter's voice.

She tells him that his efforts to keep knowledge of her fate from her had been in vain. She was comforted, she tells him, by his statement on the need for reason, courage and grace. It helped her tolerate her pain and face her death.

And so he finds himself undone by his own glib, facile words. While he can no longer embrace the philosophy with his previous smugness, neither can he repudiate it for to do so would mean, in a sense, the repudiation of his daughter's life.

But the major thrust of the book is not metaphysical. It's theme is simply this: Life is a gift to be savored daily, its meaning is a meaning to be explored daily.

Neglect an opportunity to enrich it and you may find you've neglected an opportunity you'll never have again.

Then again, perhaps that is metaphysical.

• • •

SIGNS OF THE TIMES—A recent book sale in Des Moines had "The Sex Life of the Animals" selling for $1.98, while "How to Stop Killing Yourself" went for $.99.

• • •

89

Hey, All You
In Jr. High

A NUMBER OF junior high English teachers in Des Moines have assigned their students a list of words with instructions for the students to find the words in the newspaper.

It's a real humdinger of a list. You could read the London Times for five years without finding all of them.

You don't believe me? Here's the list:

Anagram, alloy, alpha, armada, addict, august, abandoned, accessible, acclamation, antiphony, abject, askance, aghast, avid, anoint, apiary, annihilate, avest.

Benign, behoove, botany, belfry, belie, bigamy.

Cache, chaos, covet, canopy, cudgel, cower, curry, cistern, cherub, copious, cataract, chaplet, chagrin, creche, candid, chassis, clarity, convoy, candor, chaparral, coquette.

Demirep (slang), dogma, demise, dubious, dormant, dregs, deity, digress, drastic, dissemble, diligence, dissect, diadem, damsel.

Edible, epic, erosion, excavate, eavesdrop, epaulet, escarpment, encore, edict.

Facade, fiat, flora, frankincense, finale, fascinate, fanatic.

Ghetto, geology, ghoul, gazelle.

Hostel, hermitage, hamlet, Hanukkah, hostage.

Imbue, indigo, igloo, implant.

Jargon.

Longitude, lagoon, lieu, lunar, lethal, lenient, lyric, lineage.

Mesa, morbid, manege, moraine, monogram, moonstruck, menorah, myrrh, mistletoe, menagerie, mutilate, Morpheus, morose.

Notorious, negotiate.

Organic, omega, ogre, orgy.

Pegasus, petrel, petrify, parquet, primate, pinata, profane, pastorate, pastel, placid, plaintiff, pathos, perforate, pigment, prithee.

Quibble.

Rector, rabid, regent, rotary, registrar, remiss, remedial.

Statuette, solace, servile, squelch, synod, sojourn, stanza, shofar, seraph, sarcasm, somber, souvenir, scavenger, skeptic, sapling, shanghai, swarthy.

Tact.

H OW ABOUT that?

It seems only fitting that Over the Coffee, friend to those who have no friends, should come to the aid of the kids who have to find all of those oddball words. The following tale uses as many of those words as can be contained in a story of high literary quality.

O NCE UPON a time, in the month of August, a brave knight, Frankincense Finale, while on his way to a brief sojourn at a hermitage, stopped off at an inn, where he met a colleague, Anagram Moraine.

"What ho, Anagram, you old scavenger you," said Finale. "Prithee, how goes things with you?"

"Not well, Frank," his friend replied. "I am most morose. Somebody stole my ghoul."

"You mean Flora Demirep, the vampire's daughter? How came you to be mixed up with that dubious damsel?"

"It was scarcely a lunar year ago when I first spied her washing her glass eye in a cataract."

"And she shanghaied your heart?"

"Without a quibble."

"Surely a skeptic like yourself must have known your epic could never be. You come from two different pathos."

"Myrrh."

"Pardon me?"

"I WAS JUST clearing my throat—but I digress. We were young, avid, candid, drastic, lyric, morbid, rabid and swarthy. How could we know it wouldn't work? What cared we for lineage? By the way, what's that you're wearing under your coat?"

"**Avest. You mean you did not recognize that she was a coquette and a phony?**"

"But she wasn't a phony; as a matter of fact she was an antiphony and I loved her for it."

"How benign. Still, with all of this love, I don't understand why she abandoned you."

"*Imbued you asked me that question. She left me for the Egyptian movie star, Omega Seraph.*"

"That somber fanatic? I'm aghast."

"She looked at him askance at first but his facade fascinated her. Imagine my chagrin when she fell for him bats over belfry."

"I SUPPOSE that made a mesa things."

"Sheer chaos. They were married by a lenient rector in an accessible hamlet and spent their honeymoon in an igloo."

"What a cache!"

"**So she thought, until their first fight, when he said, 'Get thee to an apiary' and, so saying, threw her chassis out into the snow, leaving her with a single ice cube as a souvenir of their love.**"

"Synod."

"Here, use my handkerchief."

"I'm sorry to break down this way, but this is such a plaintiff story."

"She died shortly thereafter, her demise witnessed only by her brothers, Pegasus and Morpheus. They buried her near a lagoon, under a canopy of mistletoe, at the foot of a giant statuette of a cherub."

"Synod, synod."

"**And I, my friend, I live out the dregs of my life attempting to drown my sorrow in drink.**"

"How are you doing?"

"Shofar, shogood."

Designed for People

L UDWIG MIES van der Rohe died last week at the age of 83. I wouldn't bring it up except for the fact that, if you live in Des Moines, you owe him something.

Mies was one of the three giants of modern architecture (the others being Le Corbusier and Frank Lloyd Wright) and the only one represented by a building in downtown Des Moines—the Home Federal Savings and Loan Association building.

That's what you owe him; gratitude for the Home Federal building.

In that sea of ugliness we call downtown Des Moines, the Home Federal building offers one of the few, one of the very few, touches of class.

It stands there at Sixth and Grand, with its trees and benches, saying "Welcome" to the tired passerby. It is a delight to the eye and a refreshment to the spirit; the very antithesis of a parking ramp.

Mies did not believe in flamboyant architecture.

"Architecture has little or nothing to do with the invention of interesting forms or with personal inclinations," he would say. "Nor is it necessary to invent a new architecture every Monday morning. It is better to be good than to be original."

STATEMENTS like that and his "less is more" dictum might lead one to suspect that Mies' architecture was cold and dehumanized. There was more to him than that.

Mies was a master of subtlety and proportion and his masterworks—like the Seagram building in New York or the 860 Lakeshore Towers in Chicago—were elegant structures of exquisite taste.

The Home Federal building (like Des Moines' other Mies building, Meredith Hall at Drake) is not up to those, but it's still very good. It approaches Mies' architectural goal of "giving the spirit the opportunity for existence."

It would be nice if all buildings strove for that goal, but you can't sell the people who run things on an intangible like that. Not in Des Moines, not anywhere.

"Human spirit?" they ask. "How much does it cost per front-foot? Can you depreciate it?"

You see, city fathers seem unable to grasp the fact that downtown areas that aren't good for people, aren't good for anything.

And furthermore, that people and cars cannot co-exist on the same thoroughfares. One or the other has to go.

This misunderstanding has led to the fiction that downtown business districts are losing trade to shopping centers because of a lack of parking spaces. Nonsense.

People don't go to shopping centers because it's easy to park there. When you stop to think about it, it *isn't* all that easy to park there.

They go because once they've parked, they can forget about cars; their own and other people's. They can go about their business in an atmosphere designed for people.

That's why we should be grateful to Mies.

In one small corner of downtown Des Moines he created an atmosphere designed for people.

Soul
Music

I WAS SITTING at home the other night, listening to my lo-fi, when it occurred to me that it would be a wonderful Cosmic Joke if people, having lived out their lives on this planet, could come back as an appropriate piece of music.

It would serve the same function as Heaven and Hell and the overhead would be a lot lower. Imagine how the president of a chamber of commerce, smug in his self-importance, would feel returning to consciousness as an accordion solo? Or the agony of a poor, white, southern tenant farmer who learned he was to spend the rest of eternity as a Negro spiritual?

The only trouble with making a suggestion like that is that you never know whether your advice has been followed until it's too late to brag to your friends about it.

Personally, if I had my choice, I'd like to come back as a Rossini overture. That's a preference, not a prediction.

But it is entertaining to speculate on what musical forms the great figures of our time would return as.

Charles de Gaulle could be nothing less than the triumphal march from "Aida."

George Wallace would be a tune from the Grand Ole Opry.

Billy Graham would be the soundtrack from "Elmer Gantry."

George Romney would be the score of a musical comedy that closed in Philadelphia.

Eugene McCarthy—the Unfinished Symphony.

Lyndon Johnson—the Cowboy's Lament.

Hubert Humphrey—"Flight of the Bumblebee."

Spiro Agnew—"Chopsticks."

And Richard Nixon? Richard Nixon would be reincarnated as Muzak—what else?

Footprints in the Sand

THE ALEXANDER Calder retrospective exhibition now at the Des Moines Art Center is utterly delightful but its charm has grown rather thin for Frank Benge.

Benge is a guard at the Art Center. It's his job to see that visitors don't disturb the exhibits.

"I've been here five years and this show has caused me more work than all the other shows put together," he says.

The visitors to the Calder show tend to handle the exhibits, then?

"**They do everything to them,**" Benge states. "**There's an area of sand under the larger pieces and it's one of my jobs to keep it raked.**

"Well the kids write their initials in the sand a lot and some of them walk in it. And then they have a way of moving their hands around in the sand so that it leaves a mark like a bare footprint.

"That was funny at first but it gets old after a while."

Nor are children the only offenders.

"One woman walked right through a sand area," he says. "She said she thought it was linoleum.

"Another woman was wearing an old felt hat and she took it off and began fanning a mobile, trying to make it go around. Another one stood underneath a mobile hanging from the ceiling and kept opening and closing her umbrella, trying to make the mobile move. She wasn't even supposed to have an umbrella in the room.

"Some of the adults are really worse than the kids. You can tell the kids to leave things alone and they will, but the adults just keep on."

THE EXHIBITION has proved immensely popular with both the children and adults who have come to see it.

93

"They keep coming back to see it," he says. "Some people have come back two to three times in a week. Kids too.

"One little boy saw that "Sandy's Butterfly" o v e r there and said the sand around it was water and called the work a boat with a helicopter on it.

"He didn't touch it, though. He was afraid of the water."

Calder's witty motorized mobiles have proved to be particular favorites. These curious machines are powered by electricity and swing, rock, or revolve in an amusing manner.

"Some of those things get so hot on a Saturday or Sunday that I have to go turn them off," Benge says.

"A few of them aren't wired up and the people twist them around trying to make them go. You have to watch that. Ac-

tually though, these things can take a lot more punishment than you'd think."

Benge says that many of the youngsters come away from the exhibit saying that they're going to "make something like this" themselves.

OTHERS ARE MORE attracted by extraneous matters.

"One of them came up to me the other day and asked to shake my hand. He said he'd never been up close to a policeman before."

The 59-year-old guard says that he liked the Calder exhibit when he first saw it and he likes it now.

"But it sure gets tiresome trying to keep people off of it.

"I work six days here and Mondays I'm ready to go out to a state park somewhere."

Now that they have a kiddies' room and an adult room at the Des Moines Art Center, they should give some thought to a geriatrics wing. That way the Des Moines City Council could have a private entrance.

Getting 'Op'
On Art

A DES MOINES man was at the opening of the Art Center's op art show, intently studying a seven-foot chrome bar that seemed to be jumping up and down in a little pan of water, when he became aware that the man at his side was staring at him.

An elaborately casual glance to his right revealed a face that was not so much old as world-weary. The starer spoke.

"Well," he said with a nod that managed to encompass the whole show, the entire blizzard of twisting, leaping, screaming lines, "what do you think of it?"

"Oh, I like it," the Des Moines

man said. "I think it's a very nice show."

A look of contempt came over the other man's face. "You like it," he mimicked. "A very nice show." He made "very nice" sound dirty.

"What's wrong?"

"YOUNG man, I am a veteran of many occasions such as this, one might even call me an expert in such matters. And, let me hasten to assure you, 'like' and 'very nice' do not belong in the vocabulary of a true patron of the arts."

"Why not?"

"They're not very expressive, they don't have any pizzaz, for

94

one thing. For another they're too definite. If you say that you like something, someone is apt to ask you why, and then where are you? If you say it's very nice some expert is sure to say it stinks and you've lost face."

"*Then I suppose it's best simply to keep your mouth shut?*"

"Not at all. Beginners at avant garde art shows can get by with no more than three phrases. 'It works.' 'Exciting.' And 'very interesting.' It helps if you drag out the very."

"That's all? Just those three phrases?"

"Certainly. Then if you say 'exciting' and some expert says it stinks you can respond with 'Of course I agree that ultimately it lacks artistic validity, still one cannot reject it out of hand.'"

"I'M NOT sure I have the confidence to do that."

"Develop it. Practice at home in front of a mirror. When you gain control over the three basic phrases you can branch out. For an op or pop show you can make a tour of the gallery with a sardonic little smile on your lips, and, as you leave, announce 'It's fun.'"

"Masterful."

"**When you get so that you really know what you're doing you can attempt variations. For example, you say it's exciting, then you add a 'but' and leave the sentence hanging in air as you roll your eyes toward the ceiling. That generally gets everyone nodding in agreement.**"

"And if it doesn't?"

"You simply say after the 'but,' in a low voice, 'Is it art?' By the time the others are finished arguing that one you can be in a nice little bar."

"You're opening up a new world of art appreciation for me."

"*Don't mention it. You can also use terms like 'baroque' and 'monolithic,' but never for-*get *that you run the risk saying them to someone who knows what they mean. At most shows it's not a big risk, but it's there.*"

"I'll remember."

"And, when all else fails, there is one comment that will fit any work of art, from the Mona Lisa to that orange and green thing over there that makes you dizzy when you look at it."

"What?"

"It's a nice painting to visit, but I wouldn't want to live with it."

Radio Is Not Up His Alley

ONE LISTENS to the radio these days and thinks of Fred Allen, even as one thinks of the sun on a gray, winter day.

What do you think would happen if the young Fred Allen—the genius of radio's "Golden Age"— were to walk into a radio station today and apply for a job?

"**So you want to be a disc jockey, eh kid?**" the station manager says. "**Platter chatter, sock it to me, that sort of thing.**"

"Not exactly," says Allen.

"Well, I'll give you an audition. Here, read this."

"You mean like this, 'And now let's hear the Raspberry Electric Drill doing Let It All Hang Out, but first—Do you have pimples?'"

"No, no. You've got to read it faster, much faster; and louder. You have to remember that your audience is made up primarily of kids with bad mufflers."

"ACTUALLY, I don't think I'm the disc jockey type. I have an idea for a show . . . "

"Don't tell me; it's a giveaway show, right? You want to run our Cash on the Line feature. Do you think you have a talent for giving away money on the telephone?"

"I don't know. I generally give it away by mail. How does the show work?"

"You call someone up and ask them a question they can't answer unless they're listening to the station. It's a great incentive for them to listen to your show."

"Do you mean people actually listen to the radio on the odd chance that you'll pick their name out of the phone book?"

"Sure, why else would anyone listen to the radio?"

"Well, I have an idea for a show . . ."

"IF GIVEAWAYS don't appeal to you, how would you like a crack at a telephone show?"

"Pardon me?"

"A telephone show. People call in and ask on-the-air questions?"

"What kind of on-the-air questions?"

"Every kind. No holds barred. Why are we in Vietnam? Are you in favor of birth control? What are the hours at the Children's Zoo?"

"What was that noise?"

"What noise?"

"Either someone turned on a fan or I just heard Marconi whirling in his grave."

"YOU DON'T want to run a telephone show?"

"Not unless you give me an unlisted number. What I'd really like to do is . . ."

"About the only thing we have left is our trading center."

"What is that, a green stamp program for shut-ins?"

"No. People with things to buy or trade call in to the station and announce their phone numbers over the air."

"That's it?"

"What more do you want? It's only radio, you know."

"No it's not. It's a busy signal with call letters. Now I have an idea for a show that will introduce a whole new concept into the medium."

"What concept?"

"Entertainment."

"WELL, I'LL try anything once. What's your idea?"

"I have in mind a half-hour comedy show."

"That's a risky business. There aren't enough good comedy records to do a daily show.

"I wouldn't use records. I'd use real actors and I'd do the show once a week. We'd do little skits with a stock company of characters."

"Once a week?"

"Right. And each of the characters would have an accent—a New England accent, a Yiddish accent, a Southern accent—which would let us get in some dialect humor."

"Whoa! Stop right there."

"What's wrong?"

"You just lost me. This station is a subscriber to the National Code of Near-Perfect Broadcasting and we don't allow dialect humor. We don't want to do anything in bad taste."

● ● ●

No rock group has come up with any name so classy as the group "Steppenwolf," a name taken from Hermann Hesse's 1927 novel, "Der Steppenwolf," literally "The Wolf of the Steppes." It is the story of a man whose alienation from a philistine, technologically oriented society produces the image of himself as a "steppenwolf." You've got to admit it's a lot swifter than "Guy Lombardo and his Royal Canadians."

● ● ●

Magnificent Junk Shows

DID YOU ever spend an afternoon in the closet watching your Lone Ranger belt glow in the dark?

Or slip into your bedroom to decipher a secret message with your Captain Midnight Key-o-matic Code-o-graph?

Or throw away a full box of Wheaties after tearing off the boxtop?

If not, "The Great Radio Heroes," a new book by Jim Harmon, probably won't mean much to you. But if you did, if you, too, fought through the frozen wastes of the Yukon with Sergeant Preston and the opium-scented dens of the Orient with Terry and the Pirates, then, Kemo Sabay, you're in for a treat.

Harmon's exclusive concern is with the Magnificent Junk shows of radio's Golden Age; not Fred Allen and Jack Benny but the adventure and detective stories, the soap operas.

He offers little bits of radio history (like the fact that Orson Welles once played "The Shadow" for a year and a half) and scraps of dialogue from the dozens of shows.

You turn a page and are confronted by a line that brings the memories of a hundred wonderfully wasted afternoons and evenings flooding back.

THERE IS, for example, the introduction to "Grand Central Station," perhaps the best of the classic radio openings.

"GRAND CENTRAL STATION! As a bullet seeks its target, shining rails in every part of our great country are aimed at Grand Central Station, heart of the nation's greatest city.

"Drawn by the magnetic force of the fantastic metropolis, day and night, great trains rush toward the Hudson River, sweep down its eastern bank for 140 miles, flash briefly past the long red row of tenement houses south of 125th street, dive with a roar into the 2½-mile tunnel that burrows beneath the glitter and swank of Park Avenue . . . and then. . . .

"GRAND CENTRAL STA- **TION . . . crossroads of a million private lives, gigantic stage on which are played a thousand dramas daily!"**

For a young boy listening to a Gothic radio in Detroit, that summed up the excitement and grandeur of New York in a way that nothing else could.

OR CONSIDER the effect on a youngster hearing Tom Mix vanquish an Indian, then say:

"Now hear me! Your treachery, whatever the reason for it, will bring about your own downfall, Bear Claw! You seek to lead Gray Eagle's clan into war, when you know there can only be one result, death or imprisonment for them all!

"And like the jackal, you will stand aside, waiting for the kill, that you may feed! Be warned. Even the wind changes its course. Change yours before it is too late!"

No wonder we believed that Straight Shooters always won. How could we fail to in the face of examples like Tom Mix, the

Lone Ranger, Jack Armstrong, Buck Rogers, Captain Midnight, Sergeant Preston, Dick Tracy, and Superman?

(There has not been nearly enough research done on the role of radio melodrama in the shaping of the national character. One suspects there were as many battles won on the airwaves of the 1930s and 1940s as ever there were on the playing fields of Eton.)

THE SOAP OPERAS, of course were a different thing altogether. They were something you listened to when you were home sick from school or when it was too rainy out to play ball.

They and their various agonies were directed primarily at the American housewife. Harmon quotes the chief creator of this genre, Anne Hummert, in her revelation of the secret of the shows' success:

"The silence throbs . . . the empty hours are endless . . . then a friend in need is brought into the room by the turning of a dial. . . . Misery loves company. . . . Worry, for women, is entertainment."

There was a changeless quality to those serials. They didn't go off the air after two or three seasons like television shows; they played seemingly forever, spanning an entire childhood.

WHAT Harmon's book is, essentially, is a call to return with him to those thrilling days of yesteryear when, from out of the past, came the thundering hoofbeats of the great horse Silver, and the bark of the great dog King, and the roar of the great airplane Sky King.

It is a call that does not go unheeded.

The Taste of Television

CBS CANCELED the "Smothers Brothers Comedy Hour" the other day, ostensibly because the boys were unwilling to meet the network's "standards of taste." That's a giggle.

A television network being worried about taste is like the Boston Strangler being worried about having bad breath.

Television is a medium that uses sex to make lung cancer seem attractive.

It is a medium that looks at Nazi prison camps and sees situation comedies.

It is a medium that treats serious events as though they were sports, and sports as though they were serious events.

It is a medium whose idea of social significance does not extend beyond showing someone getting hit on the head with a rock.

Television? Taste? They've got to be kidding.

The Smothers show was not a great one. It wasn't even what it had been the previous season; but then it couldn't be. Dick and Tom Smothers are satirists by profession and satirists cannot function with someone constantly standing over their shoulders saying: "That's a no-no."

The point is, the show was the only big one on television that was TRYING to make satiric statements relevant to the times in which we live. ("Laugh-In" has some good gags but, as satire, it's pretty innocuous and thin.)

What, then, did the brothers do to offend the delicate sensibilities of the network biggies?

They made some people mad.

They attacked some sacred cows. They said nasty things about the President and the war in Vietnam.

That's why they were dumped.

Television's idea of bad taste is making somebody—anybody —mad.

The networks are dedicated to feeding the American public gruel, and a thin gruel at that. If it isn't perfectly bland, if it isn't simple-minded, if it isn't inane— it's a no-no.

T e l e v i s i o n is entertainment produced for dum-dums, by dum-dums. If you call that entertainment.

A Revolution
In Baseball

WITH THE FOOTBALL season safely behind us, it is not too soon to begin thinking in terms of baseball and, happily, the New York Yankees have announced plans for modernizing the television coverage of their games.

In an effort to attract a larger TV audience next season, the Yanks are going to use such football coverage techniques as isolated camera pickups, instant tape replays, superimposed statistics and directional microphones.

Of all the gimmicks, the directional microphones hold the most promise. Imagine, now the home viewer will be able to listen in on arguments with the umpires and on pitching mound conferences. It'll revolutionize the game.

An umpire and a manager who know they're on Candid Microphone will probably sound something like this discussing a called third strike:

"Pardon me, sir," says the manager. "I don't mean to impugn your judgment, but it seems to me that there's been some sort of error here."

"Well, I'm always open to constructive criticism," says the umpire. "What's the trouble?"

"That last ball thrown by their pitcher—from where I sat it seemed to be a bit wide of the plate."

"YOUR CONFUSION is understandable," s a y s the ump. "From your position in the dugout it might well have looked wide but I assure you, from my position directly behind the plate it was quite apparent that it was well within the strike zone."

"It was an optical illusion then; that explains it. Thank you for your time."

"**That's quite all right, that's what I'm here for. By the way, that's a handsome ring you're wearing. May I have a closer look at it?**"

"Certainly. It's a World Series ring. See how it catches the sunlight when I shake my fist?"

See My Ring?

"My! Doesn't it s p a r k l e though? Well, we'd better get on with the game. I wish you continued success in your career."

"Same to you."

AND A MANAGER yanking a pitcher will sound like this: "Excuse me, Lefty," says the manager, "but it seems to me that the trajectory on your curve ball has become somewhat flat."

"Do you really think so?" says the pitcher. "I hadn't noticed."

"Yes, as a matter of fact I would place it high on the list of contributing factors to the five consecutive hits they've gotten off of you."

"I would be more inclined to place blame, if blame there be, on the left fielder," says the pitcher. "He's a willing lad but rather uncoordinated. Correct me if I'm wrong but I believe he's unable to walk and chew gum at the same time. Had he but caught a few of the fly balls hit in his direction I would not now be left naked to mine enemies."

THERE'S A GREAT deal of truth in what you say, Lefty; still, I think a personnel change is indicated. Would you mind if I brought in Bullets?"

"Certainly not. You know I wouldn't want to remain in the game if you feel it would be detrimental to the team's welfare."

"Good boy! Why don't you go in and take a nice whirlpool bath?"

"I think I'll stick to a shower. I haven't enjoyed a whirlpool bath since the left fielder hid my rubber duck."

In Praise of the Tube

JUST when you begin to lose faith in the caliber of men appointed to high federal office, along comes someone like Lee Loevinger.

Mr. Loevinger, in case you haven't been paying attention, is the F e d e r a l Communications Commissioner who thinks the television networks are doing a good job.

Clearly this stamps the commissioner as an original thinker. Such an idea would not occur to your average man.

It is Loevinger's contention that critics who say that television is not meeting its responsibility to educate the public don't know what they're talking about.

There's a lot of education on television, he says. Where? You might ask.

In the commercials, of course. Commercials teach have-nots to aspire to the Good Life. Here's what he says:

"The one inescapable message of all commercials is: Here is a world that is attractive and that you should live in.

"The improbable heroes and heroines of programs can be dismissed as fictional and their environments can be regarded as fragments of a dream world. But not so the commercials. Instantly they say, this is real, this is available, this is for sale, and you should have it."

LOEVINGER goes on to say that this process — which might be called the candy store theory of educational television— probably had a great deal to do with triggering the civil rights revolution.

The implications of that remark are enormous. It could very well be that we are wasting our time and money supporting organizations like the United S t a t e s Information Agency and Voice of America.

If we really want to tell our story, we should flood the underdeveloped nations with television commercials. Imagine two peasants in a Latin American country that has been inundated by our commercials.

"Hey Pedro," says one, "it is such a nice day. Why don't we go downtown and stone the American Embassy?"

"No, Manuel. I am too busy studying."

"Study, study. That's all you ever do anymore; ever since the gringos brought you that television set you sit on your hacienda and watch commercials. Have you not heard that all work and no play make Juan a dull boy?"

"I can't help it, Manuel. I have this terrible thirst for knowledge."

"What have you learned from this television so far?"

THAT my mother has bad breath."

"Jumping frijoles!"

"And also that she knows the terrible heartbreak of psoriasis."

"I did not even know she drank."

"There are many things to be found out by watching the commercials, Manuel. The other day a television gringo told me to put a tiger in my tank and so I started to save my pesos."

"To buy a tiger?"

"No. To buy a tank."

"But Pedro, do you not miss the good old days when you went to school and the Peace Corps senorita taught you how to write your name with a piece of chalk?"

"Si, but what good did it do me? She had the only blackboard in the province. No, Manuel, there comes a time in a man's life when he must turn his back on playthings and get down to serious study. For myself, I have chosen the path of revolution."

"You mean you have taken up with Fidel?"

"No. I have joined the Dodge rebellion."

New
Lit. Crit.

LAURENCE OLIVIER'S "Othello" had just ended and the audience was filing out of the Galaxy Theater.

One well-dressed woman was overheard to say to friends:

"This may be an oversimplification, but that certainly goes to show that crime doesn't pay."

Eureka! The door is opened on an entirely new world of literary criticism, a world so pristine in character as to merit the term, virginal.

Why no university scholar ever thought of reducing the world's literature to aphorisms is beyond the imagination.

If "Othello" can be scaled down to "Crime doesn't pay," think how some of the other works of literature could be interpreted:

Joan of Arc—A woman's place is in the home.

Macbeth—Behind every great man stands a devoted wife.

101

Romeo and Juliet—Verona is a lousy place to raise kids.

Cleopatra—Two's c o m p a n y, three's a crowd.

Gone with the Wind—Where there's smoke, there's fire.

Faust—Don't accept candy from strangers.

The Odyssey—A rolling stone gathers no moss.

Medea—Children should b e seen and not heard.

The Greatest Story Ever Told—Every cloud has a silver lining.

Death of a Salesman—You've got to know the territory.

Oedipus Rex—Those May-December marriages never work out.

High Schools:
A Grim Saga

IOWA CITY, IA.—One of the great unseen movies got a showing at the Refocus Film Festival here this week; a documentary dealing with one of the most oppressive, stultifying institutions of our society—the high school.

"High School," produced and directed by Frederick Wiseman, is a look at Northeast High School in Philadelphia, Pa., a nice middle-class school not unlike the one most of our kids attend, or will attend, before they go on to college.

And that, of course, is the horror of the film: that this nice, middle-class school—superior to so many of our schools—should be so bad, so very bad.

One had thought, one had hoped, that high schools had gotten better in the 20 years since one's graduation. There was Sputnik, after all. Didn't that

cause a lot of talk about improving things, about making education relevant to contemporary needs?

Yet in this film we see the s a m e repressive, stupifying routines of our youth still grinding away at our children's minds—hall passes, deadening lectures, moralistic platitudes, dress codes. Ennui and frustration served in equal portions.

The great wonder is not that young people don't learn anything in high school, but that some few escape with their ability to function as human beings intact.

WISEMAN, a reformed lawyer, filmed "High School" during a 22-day period in the spring of 1968. The word is that when he showed the film to the school's staff, they liked it. But then it was shown to the students and, after observing the kids' reaction to it, the staff decided the film was unfair.

The incredible feature of the movie is the way the people fit into their roles, as though they've come from Central Casting.

The counselor, with the ruined face, advising a student to scale down her ambitions to a more realistic, lack-luster level.

The lumpy, empty-eyes teacher addressing her class as "boys and girls" and reciting "Casey at the Bat" to them without embarrassment. The sleazy gynecologist delivering an absolutely obscene lecture on sex education to a group of boys. It's all there, just as you remembered it.

THERE ARE poignant scenes of youngsters trying to confront the system and being overwhelmed by it.

A student is protesting an unjust punishment. The counselor admits the injustice of it but says, "We are out to establish

102

that you can be a man and that you can take orders."

A girl wants to wear a short dress to the formal prom. A school official tells her, "It's nice to be individualistic, but there are certain places to be individualistic."

The system is designed to beat down the individual, to close, not open the possibilities of life to them.

Its message is this: Existence is bleak. Don't color outside the lines and maybe you won't get in trouble.

The film ends with a teacher reading a letter from a recent graduate to a staff meeting. The ex-student is in Vietnam, about to embark on a dangerous mission.

"PLEASE DON'T say anything to Mrs. C. She would only worry over me," he writes. "I am not worth it. I am only a body doing a job."

And the teacher says "Now, when you get a letter like this, to me it means that we are very successful at this high school.

Yes. Successful at turning out bodies to do jobs. Is that what we want?

An Oscar for Astaire

THE ANNUAL Academy Awards television show has come and gone and—except for bow-legged Julie Christie's decision to wear a miniskirt — no grave errors of judgment were in evidence.

The picture that got the top award is undoubtedly a distinguished one; the winning actors were persons of proven ability. Nobody appeared on camera falling-down drunk—not quite.

A little of the excitement was drained from the proceedings by the absence of the major acting winners, but still the event came off rather well.

But for me the high point of the entire evening came when Fred Astaire glided onto the stage, whirled Ginger Rogers around and then stood there smiling at the audience, tugging his right ear.

There is no one, absolutely no one, who can whirl Ginger Rogers around and then stand there

Fred Astaire
An Ear-Tugger

tugging at his right ear like Fred Astaire can.

I MIGHT as well confess it. Fred Astaire was a boyhood hero of mine. I used to spend a lot of my time in school whirling girls around, then standing there, tugging at my right ear while they slapped my face.

I was constantly practicing, perfecting my art. I'd bound into the kitchen, go into a quick chorus of "The Continental" and bang my head against a door jamb as I finished with a spin.

"You're a regular Fred Astaire," my mother would say.

When my dad got home from work, I'd do my act for him, perhaps knocking over a lamp or chair in the process.

"You're a regular Red Skelton," he would say.

The thing about Fred Astaire was that he was suave. He was urbane. He was cosmopolitan. One of the very few men around who could wear a tuxedo without looking like a waiter.

And he was graceful, so graceful. He made things look easy, as though anyone could do them. That's what kept getting me in trouble.

I'll never forget the first time I saw him do the chair trick; the one where he dances around and jumps up on a chair and tips it over in slow motion. It was a very elegant move and I could hardly wait until I got home to try it.

Seventeen stitches.

Anyway, it was nice seeing Fred again. And when he whirled Ginger around, it really rolled back the years.

The doctor tells me that my knee will be as good as new in a few weeks and that my wife's back suffered no permanent damage.

That's Why!

L ONG AGO, when I was a much younger man, people would come up to me at parties and say:

"Tell the truth now, you don't really hate 'The Sound of Music' as much as you pretend, do you?"

And I would tell a little white lie. After all, they seemed to be decent folk, they obviously liked the movie; I had no desire to hurt their feelings.

So I would say: *"Oh, I suppose it's not all that bad, what with beauty being in the eye of the beholder and all."*

At which point the decent folk would say: "I thought so, you ratfink. You're just a smart aleck without convictions. I'll never believe another thing you write."

CONFRONTATIONS LIKE that seemed to indicate a change in strategy and, against my better judgment, I tried the honesty-is-the-best-policy approach. It was a miserable failure.

When I would tell persons that yes, indeed, I thought "The Sound of Music" was pretty awful, that it was, in fact, only slightly preferable to the German measles, they would say:

"Oh yeah? I suppose you think them foreign movies like 'Jules and Jim' are such a big deal. Filth and smut, that's all you've got on your mind. I've got a good notion to punch you in the nose."

It was a bad scene.

I finally hit upon diversion as a saving tactic.

Whenever someone approaches me now and asks the Big Question, I say, "Have you ever tried to say 'Toy Boat' three times, quickly?"

Then, while they're struggling with that, I move off to a quieter corner of the room.

BUT PEOPLE still stop me with, "Why do you hate 'The Sound of Music' so much?" These people, I think, deserve an answer.

This is why I hate "The Sound of Music" so much.

Take a typical two-car accident. A woman driver fails to signal as she slows to make a left turn and the man in back of her, following too closely, runs into the rear of her car.

He gets out and says, "Of all the stupid broads I've ever seen, you take the cake," and she says, "You wouldn't talk that way to me if my husband were here, you creep," and she hits him over the head with her pocketbook.

They exchange insults, threaten to sue each other and drive off in their separate directions.

Now, view that same accident through the eyes of the makers of "The Sound of Music." Imagine it as a technicolor musical directed by Robert Wise, scripted by Ernest Lehman, starring Julie Andrews, with music by Rodgers and Hammerstein.

Julie Andrews is driving along a tree-lined street when a small puppy runs in front of her car. She slams on the brakes and the car in back of her, although following at a reasonable distance, is unable to stop in time. The autos collide.

THE DRIVER of the second car, a handsome young man, jumps out singing "Some Enchanted Whiplash" and Miss Andrews responds with "I've Loved You Ever Since I Saw You In My Rear View Mirror."

It turns out that she is a girls' basketball referee who is the sole support of her 15 brothers and sisters and is saving her money so that she can get her mother's teeth capped for Christmas.

He is a poor but honest concert triangle player who is trying to peddle his unfinished symphony.

The pair enjoy one brief moment of happiness exchanging the names of their insurance agents, then drive off, saddened by the knowledge of a love that could never be.

On the way home, however, the young man remembers the sound the cars made as they collided. It inspires him to write a finish for his unfinished symphony and a Hollywood producer buys the movie rights to it for $100,000.

He calls up Julie Andrews and proposes to her with the delightful romantic ballad, "Your Mother Will Be Eating Corn on the Cob by Christmas." She accepts and they live happily ever after.

That's why.

105

"Love, death, marriage, and

"...ther viable alternatives"

Secret of My Success

WHEN I AM asked the question, "To what do you attribute your great success?" I often lock myself in the nearest closet and stay there until friends come to lure me out with candy. I'm funny that way.

(The question, incidentally, is most generally asked by high school students, a class of social critics who believe that success consists of not being a high school student.)

On the few occasions that a questioner has managed to break through my natural reserve and modesty, however, I have answered candidly.

"Shakespeare," I tell him. "William Shakespeare is the secret of my success."

At which point the questioner usually says, "Huh?" And I tell him this story:

I WAS BORN in a little mining town in Colorado, the son of a wealthy English lord. Until the age of 16 I was completely non-verbal. I communicated with my parents through the medium of the ocarina, on which I played Morse code.

Even when I learned to speak, however, writing did not come easily to me. As recently as 10 years ago I could not print my name without having someone spell the hard words for me.

Naturally, I consulted our family physician about my problem. "Live," he told me. "Writers need to have something to write about before they can write. So live!"

So I went out and lived; I lived a lot. I later learned that had I lived just a bit more, I would have been deported as an undesirable alien. But it didn't do my writing any good.

I gave up living and sought the advice of my pastor. "Suffer," he told me. "Writers have to suffer before they have anything to write about. So suffer!"

So I suffered; I really did. After a while I really got good at it, I could suffer for 20 and 30 hours at a stretch. Things got so bad that oppressed minority groups began sending me CARE packages. But my writing still came out like an unalphabetized dictionary.

I gave up suffering and consulted a Go-Go girl whom I had met while I was living. "Read Shakespeare," she told me. "Writers write from the soul and Shakespeare makes souls grow like weeds."

So I tried Shakespeare and it worked. Within weeks after reading "Troilus and Cressida" I was writing complete sentences. Soon after that my friends stopped laughing when I sat down to play the typewriter.

AFTER SIX short months of reading Shakespeare's plays I was able to write at the level of a 12-year-old, a level, I might add, that I have seldom fallen below since.

People to whom I tell this story often ask which Shakespearean passages have influenced me most. After some consideration I have come up with a list of the quotations that seem most meaningful to me.

HERE ARE THE words that changed my life. May they do the same for you:

"What ho!"—Richard III; Act III, scene 2.

"It is well."—Henry V; Act III, scene 6.

" 'Zounds?"—Henry V, part I; Act IV, scene 1.

"Ha!"—Julius Caesar; Act I, scene 2.

"Worse and worse."—Othello; Act I, scene 3.

"No, Madam," — Antony and Cleopatra; Act I, scene 2.

"Rogue, rogue, rogue!"—Timon of Athens; Act IV, scene 3.

"No, no, no, no, no."—Coriolanus; Act IV, scene 3.

"Not so hot, good sir."—The Winter's Tale; Act II, scene 2.

"Farewell." — Hamlet; Act II, scene 1.

The Roots Take Hold

YOU RENT AND YOU rent and one day your wife says, let's buy a house.

So you smile indulgently and say, sure, and you forget about it and keep renting and she keeps talking about buying and you keep smiling and renting until one day you find yourself actively looking for a house—to buy.

At first, it isn't so bad. The houses you like you can't afford and the houses you can afford, you don't like. There seems little likelihood that you'll ever match your elevated taste with your depressed pocketbook.

But you do. Almost by accident you run into a reasonably priced home that reaches out and gathers you to its brick veneer bosom.

And your wife says, let's buy the house.

And you say, but I'm too young to buy a house.

And she says, you're 30 years old.

And you say, that sounds older than it feels.

And you buy the house.

THIS PURCHASE—the first time a man buys a house—represents an awesome milestone in his life. It is not the fact that he is spending more money than he has ever seen that terrifies him. That has little to do with its importance.

Rather it is that the purchase of a house symbolizes the putting down of roots, the surrender of youthful dreams of glory.

Young men tend to have rather elaborate ideas about their futures. The dwelling places of their fantasy lives run to jungle mud huts or Paris garrets or New York town houses.

They proceed through early manhood prepared to execute these dreams at a moment's notice and imagine themselves to be free and loose and mobile.

They get married and the fantasy shrinks a little—their wives don't like snakes so the jungle is out—but only a little. They still feel ready to move on short notice; to confront the future where they find it.

THEY HAVE CHILDREN and the dream shrinks a little more—garrets are so drafty and, besides, the children need a yard to play in—but it remains a possibility.

Actually, at this point, the dream is all but dead but the no-longer-young man refuses to admit it.

Until he buys a house.

A free spirit cannot live with a 25-year mortgage. It cannot concern itself with leaky plumbing, peeling paint and cracked plaster.

A man who buys a house finds himself faced with the reality that he's never going to be a foreign correspondent in Tanganyika. You can't get there from here.

Employers are happy to see their employes buy homes. A heavily mortgaged employe is the business equivalent of a barefoot, pregnant wife.

Women are happy to see the husbands of their friends buy homes. It means one less bad example before the eyes of their own husbands.

AND THE HUSBANDS, the friends of the man; they're happy too. They know what's happening and profess sympathy, but they are reassured by their comrade's fall from freedom. After all, it happened to them, they put down roots; why shouldn't he do the same?

There are those who tell you that you aren't really tied down, that you can always sell the house.

Certainly you can, but will you?

The point is you no longer want to go to Tanganyika. You don't want to put up with snakes and drafts and the rest of it. You like being comfortable.

While this doesn't make you unhappy, it is not so shining a dream as you once had, nor so heroic, and you regret the old dream's departure.

The purchase of the house is simply a dramatic demonstration of lost youth.

You sign the final papers and notice that your hair is beginning to fall out.

Her Dream House

YOU BUY a home and you willingly sacrifice youth for size. None of these new efficiency crackerboxes for me, you say. You want space. You want charm.

You get an older home.

And, to tell the truth, it's not a bad looking place. A little beat-up, maybe, but it has size and charm. As the jovial realtor tells you, a coat of paint will work wonders.

What really sells you on the house, however, is your wife's reaction to it. It is her dream house. She's never seen anything she's liked so well. It is perfect and if she doesn't get it she'll expire.

After the final papers are signed, however, an astonishing transformation takes place.

A man's wife walks into her new home and says:

"Well, the first thing to do is to get that horrid wallpaper down. The whole house, every room, every inch of it has to go."

And the man replies, "But I thought you said it was darling. Besides, you don't just peel wallpaper off the wall. It is hard, expensive work getting it down."

SHE DOESN'T hear him. "And then we'll have to knock out the wall between the living room and den."

"You've gone insane."

"And I think we should move the dining room door over six inches."

"You're sick," he shouts at her, but she's already in the kitchen,

111

deciding where she's going to move the sink.

He catches up to her and says, "I thought you liked the house the way it is. That's why I bought it."

She stops and fixes him with an open-eyed stare. "I loved the house that I saw in my mind's eye. You have to use your imagination."

"Imagination we've got, but where are we going to get the money to convert this place into a miniature replica of Versailles?"

"I suppose we don't really have to tear down all those walls and things. I'll settle for new wallpaper."

"That costs money, too," he shouts.

"No, dear. You can do it yourself. It'll cost hardly anything at all."

"Me, wallpaper? I have trouble licking envelopes, let alone getting paper to stay up on a wall. Cutting and pasting was my worst subject when I took journalism in college. I don't know how to put up wallpaper."

Her eyes narrowed considerably. "You'll learn," she said.

And you do.

YOU ALSO learn that the down payment on your house is merely an entry fee, like buying a stack of chips at a poker game or a seat on the New York Stock Exchange.

It allows you to begin to spend your money, really spend money. There are many who would help you in your task.

Screen men: "Just passing by and I noticed that your screens are in bad shape. . . ."

Tree men: "Happened to see you've got a dead tree there. . . ."

Gutter men: "Need new gutters. . . ."

Brick men: "I wouldn't want to be responsible if that wall fell and killed somebody. . . ."

Kindly men all of them. Kindly, sharp-eyed men who just happened to be passing by.

And every time you try to call the landlord, you get a busy signal.

Generation

Gap

THERE is much written today day—perhaps too much—of the "generation gap," that gulf of understanding that exists, at any given moment, between the young and their elders.

Yet a gulf does exist; it is real. **For example, although I consider myself of liberal temperament—a live-and-let-live sort of person—every time I see a young man with flowing hair walking barefoot in a public street, twirling his Iron Cross, I have to resist an impulse to walk up to him and smash him in the mouth.**

Admittedly, it is not a difficult impulse to resist—the young man is invariably bigger than I—but it's there.

At first I thought this was a sign that I was getting old but, on mature consideration, I realized that, faced with a similar situation 15 years ago, I would have felt the same impulse.

THE problem is not one of growing old and conservative but of being a product of an entirely different environment, an environment hostile to present modes of dealing with generation gaps.

In the neighborhood where I grew up, on the near west side of Detroit, I was known as a sharp dresser. This was largely because of the fact that my white socks were of wool rather than cotton.

The wardrobes of me and my colleagues consisted almost exclusively of Levis and wash pants, worn with T-shirts. Occasionally a dandy in the group would wear a shirt with buttons, but it was a rare occurrence.

One of the local heroes was a young man named Sonny Kanarsky, famed because of a feat he performed while being savagely beaten by an older, much bigger boy.

The big boy, his name was Stiburski as I remember it, was sitting astride Sonny's chest, using his knees to pin the younger boy's arms to the ground, all the while pummeling Sonny about the head.

WE were all standing around, making bets on how much more of this treatment Sonny would take before crying "Uncle," when Sonny twisted his head around, scooped up a mouthful of dust and spat it into the face of his assailant.

Stiburski's hands went instinctively to his eyes and Sonny took the opportunity to get up and beat the hell out of the bigger boy.

Nobody in the neighborhood messed around much with Sonny after that.

The point is that it could be said that a generation gap of sorts existed between Stiburski the elder and Kanarsky the younger. But Kanarsky did not cry out that Stiburski didn't understand him, he did not complain about being born into a world he never made. He did not take off his shoes.

NO. WHAT Kanarsky did was to make an attempt to understand the problems of the older generation, in this case represented by Stiburski.

And what he finally understood, lying there in a vacant lot being hit on the head, was that Stiburski was the kind of fellow who would find dust being spat into his face a disquieting experience.

Stiburski, on the other hand, being less of an intellectual than Kanarsky, did not take the trouble to try and understand his opponent. He underestimated the displeasure Sonny would feel at being hit in the head repeatedly.

The lesson to be learned from the incident is clear.

It is only through mutual efforts at understanding, rather than through meaningless symbolic gestures, that the generation gap can be bridged.

•   •   •

A FRIEND at Iowa State University sent me the results of a "news identification quiz" given 19 students in a beginning reporting class there.

Sixteen knew who Mick Jagger of the Rolling Stones was, 12 correctly identified Ralph Nader, 11 got Donald Kaul, 10 knew William Calley, jr., and Neal Smith, and 9 had Golda Meir right.

Eight dunces in a class of 19 isn't bad for a journalism school.

•   •   •

113

The Legend
Of Bernie

WHEN ADULTS take over a kids' game, the first thing they do is draw up a set of complex rules to insure against the danger of accidental fun.

Little League baseball is a case in point. The conduct of the game has been turned over to adults—coaches, managers, umpires—with the result that most of its educational value has been lost, and much of its fun as well.

An incident at a recent Little League game in Des Moines is illustrative.

It is the last half of the last inning with the score tied 22–22, give or take a run. Two outs, winning run on third.

At the plate is a helmeted youngster whose baseball cap is hanging out of his back pocket. As the pitcher prepares to throw the ball, the hat falls out of the pocket of the batter.

The catcher yells "Time" and bends to pick up the hat, but the pitcher—lost in concentration—cuts loose anyway, zipping the ball past the catcher's ear and allowing the winning run to score.

The umpire, an adult, says the run counts because catchers can't call time outs, only umpires can. The game ends on that note.

NOW I ASK you—would kids, left to their own devices, foul up an exciting game with an idiotic technicality like that?

Of course not. Children have an innate sense of fairness that transcends a r b i t r a r y rules. They would have understood that the catcher was doing an entirely decent and commendable thing and should not be penalized and that, in any case, it was a lousy way to end a ball game.

We understood those things when I was a kid. We played most of our baseball in a small vacant lot in the neighborhood. We neither had umpires, nor needed them.

Balls and strikes were a matter of relative indifference to us and the fairness or foulness of a batted ball, we felt, could best be judged by whatever player happened to have the best angle on it, even if that player happened to be the batter.

Close plays at the bases were decided by voice vote, with the team yelling loudest presumed to have justice on its side.

We argued, certainly we argued; it was part of the game. But we settled the arguments without outside interference and without a rule book. If we needed a rule, we made one up on the spot.

WE PLAYED the game with integrity and we played it with style. Like the day Bernie Kaniewski became a legend in his own time.

Bernie was playing right field for us that day, and it was the last inning of a tight ball game. We needed one more out for the win.

Well, the batter really tagged one, long and deep to right field. It looked as though it were headed right for the front porch of the Kaniewski home across the street.

Bernie, who had been playing the batter deep—in the gutter—took out after the ball. He raced across the street, deftly dodging a slow-moving 1946 Chevrolet. His back to the infield, he crossed his lawn, his sidewalk and took two steps up his porch steps before turning and catching the ball above his head.

Then, while the rest of us were still immobilized by the

brilliance of this stunning play, he continued up the steps, through his front door and was gone. DiMaggio couldn't have done it better.

We stood there dumb with admiration for a few seconds more, sensing somehow that we had witnessed one of the all-time great moments of unorganized baseball.

An adult would have found a way to disallow it.

Davy Had A Stocking

EACH CHRISTMAS, when I look at my children's stockings hanging on the fireplace, I think of Davy.

Davy, was, I suppose, about eight years old when I knew him. He was a patient at a hospital for emotionally disturbed children, where I worked for a time.

People tend to get the wrong idea when you say "hospital for emotionally disturbed children." They conjure visions of pathetic, demented youngsters aimlessly wandering the halls. It wasn't a bit like that.

It was, in fact, a cheerful place at which to work. The inmates were a boisterous, rowdy bunch who, despite their various problems, did not seem to differ markedly from normal children. It made you wonder about normal children.

The majority of the children were entirely likable; some were adorable and the hospital attendants became quite attached to them.

Davy was at the other end of the scale. He was convinced that nobody loved him and, as it happened, he was right.

Many of us tried to love, tried hard—but without success.

It wasn't that he was aggressively obnoxious, it was simply that he was a cipher. There was nothing to like or dislike about him. He seemed destined to be one of those persons who moved through life leaving no wake.

I SAID THE HOSPITAL was a cheerful place at which to work. That's not entirely true. On Christmas Eve, it was a depressing place to work.

The hospital let almost all of the children go home for the holidays; about the only ones left were those whose parents could not be trusted with custody even for a short time or those whose parents wouldn't have them.

The hospital staff, then would spend Christmas Eve trying to lend false cheer to what was essentially a joyless occasion for the children left at the hospital. It wasn't duty one volunteered for.

Davy's parents, as I remember, had beaten him like a gong from the time he was an infant and either couldn't or wouldn't have him at home for the holidays. At any rate, he was one of the two or three kids there to greet me as I walked into the ward on Christmas Eve.

He seemed happy enough and continued to seem so throughout the evening. He entered into the games and songs with great enthusiasm.

Then it was bedtime and I was assigned the task of reading him his bedtime story.

AT THIS POINT let me digress a moment in order to explain the nature of the hospital's socks.

Most of the children wore white, cotton socks of hospital issue, and the hospital, although it was by any standards ex-

115

tremely well-equipped, possessed no children's socks.

Youngsters were forced to make do with oversized adult stockings, sometimes having to fold over the ends as much as five inches. The socks were all the same and had "Property of University Hospitals" stenciled on them in black letters.

Well, when I walked into Davy's room at bedtime that night he was crouched in a corner working on something. As I moved closer I could see it was a cardboard box, painted red with black lines drawn on it, crudely cut to resemble a fireplace.

He had been fastening one of the long, white hospital stockings to it when I came in.

He smiled brightly at me and said, with a certain pride, "I made it myself."

Then he jumped into bed and waited for his story, confident that Santa Claus was going to slide down an imaginary chimney sometime during the night, climb out of that cardboard fireplace and stuff toys into the stocking marked "Property of University Hospitals."

Such innocence did not go entirely unrewarded. He awoke the next morning to a full stocking and he accepted the miracle w i t h o u t a second thought.

And a Christmas never goes by but that I think of him.

Sadism Through the Ages

W HEN I WAS a youngster I knew what caused juvenile delinquency.

Comic books.

I knew it as surely as I knew that smoking would stunt my growth or that I would be hit by a truck if I didn't look both ways before crossing the street.

A ND, to make certain I didn't forget it, my parents would periodically call to my attention a newspaper account of a youthful ax-murderer who told police he committed his deed after reading a gangster comic.

"See!" my mother w o u l d scream, tearing a comic from in front of my moving lips. "See what reading junk like this leads to? Why don't you read good books like the other kids?"

In point of fact, all the other kids read comic books too, but I never felt it wise to point this out to my mother at times like that.

As it turned out, I never did kill anybody with an ax, nor did I ever steal any hubcaps, which was another thing reading comics was supposed to lead to.

The admonitions of my parents were not entirely lost upon me, however. Upon reaching adulthood, I realized my previous folly and determined that my children would have a better break in life than I did.

T HEIR MINDS would be molded by good books, the classics preferably, rather than trashy comic books.

To that end I have, of late, been reading aloud to my children from a book of Greek mythology, which is about as classic as you can get.

It is my preliminary impression that for sex, sadism and

bad *examples of deportment,*
there is no comic book ever
written that can match Greek
myths.

The book of myths opens with
Uranus, lord of the universe,
marrying Mother Earth and having 12 children—six boys and six
girls. So far so good, but things
immediately begin to get sticky.
The boys marry the girls.

URANUS and Mother Earth
have six more sons, three of
whom are immediately recogniz-
able by the single eye in the
middle of their foreheads and
three of whom have 50 heads and
100 arms each.

Uranus decides that's too much
of a good thing so he throws his
hideous offspring into a deep,
dark pit.

Mother Earth, for some rea-
son or another, finds this an
unsatisfactory arrangement so
she gets one of her good-look-
ing sons to chase his father out
of town with a sickle.

The son, Cronus, then takes
over as lord of the universe.

You'd think he'd know enough
to quit while he was ahead, but
no. Fearing that one of his sons
will do him in, Cronus takes to
swallowing his newborn sons.

(Say what you will about Batman, at least he was always nice
to Robin.)

CRONUS' wife (and sister) understandably has reserva-
tions about this kind of infant
care. She hides out her sixth-
born, Zeus, and he grows up in
secret.

As soon as he gets big enough,
he sends his father packing in the
same direction his grandfather,
Uranus, disappeared. He then becomes lord of the universe.

It goes on like that for pages
and pages. About as close as
anyone gets to middle-class re-
spectability is when Zeus mar-
ries his cousin.

Comics may have had an occasional confession produced by a
white-hot poker, but Superman
always kept a tight lid on his Id.

Yet no young ax-murderer in
memory has confessed to police
that his anti-social behavior was
induced by reading a Greek
myth.

I SUPPOSE I'll continue to further my childrens' classical
education. I've always believed
that it's not what you read that
hurts you, it's what you don't
read.

Besides, there's one thing you
have to give to those Greek
gods. They never stole hub-
caps.

She Outwits
Dad, But Not
Her Brother

STEW CAN be a good thing,
tasty and nourishing. That's
the first day.

The second day it's mainly
nourishing. By the third day, it's
good for filling cracks in cement
floors.

A Des Moines man recently
was chiseling his way through a
plate of fried, three-day-old
stew when he noticed that his
daughter was ignoring her por-
tion.

"Eat your stew," he said sternly.

"No," she replied.

His daughter was six years old,
considerably smaller than her
father and, besides, he paid the
rent. He felt that his will should
prevail.

EAT your stew," he said even
more sternly.

A 4-year-old child of lively intelligence interrupted her mother's rest period with the question: "Are tricycles supposed to squeak?" The mother, not wanting to move, thought it over for a moment, then answered, "Yes." And the girl said, "Well, mine doesn't squeak. Fix it."

"No," she said. "I don't like it. It doesn't taste good."

"Indigestion is bad enough," he said, throwing a quick glance at the little girl's mother, *"but insubordination is something I won't put up with, young lady."*

He pointed his finger at her and, this time in a voice that would have made John Wayne wince, said:

"Eat your stew."

The little girl bored her blue-eyed stare into her father's stony face, jutted out her toothless jaw and said:

"I wouldn't eat that stew if it was dessert."

Well, it's pretty difficult to maintain discipline in the face of a crack like that. The father fled the table in tears and had to be coaxed back into the dining room to finish his meal.

The incident aroused fears in the man about the future of his son, then four years old.

A N OLDER SISTER is always a trial for a young man, but when she possesses a razor-sharp tongue she can cause permanent injury to a little brother.

The boy shortly gave an indication that he would be able to take care of himself, however.

He and his sister were sitting in the back seat of the family car on the way home from the library.

"Ha, ha," she said mirthlessly. "I've got five books and you've only got four. Ha ha."

The boy stopped his cheerful humming, thought a moment, and said, "Yes, I've got four books and I'm four years old."

"And I've got five books and I'm five years old," she said.

"No, you're not. You're six," he said, and began humming again.

It ruined her whole day. You've got to admire him.

TV Dinner
A La Box

A FAMILY man whose wife is in the hospital is a man who knows something of the darker side of life.

He is awakened at dawn with the cry: "Why didn't you wake us up on time? We're going to be late for school."

"How could you be late for anything," he says, trying to get his eyes unstuck. "It's dark out."

"We're hungry. Fix us breakfast."

"You mean you actually eat at this time in the morning?"

"Mom always fixes us hot cereal."

"Stop, you're making me sick to my stomach. How would you like a little bowl of Wheaties, Breakfast of Champions, just for a change of pace?"

"Our teacher says kids need a good, hot meal to get the day started off right."

"Then let your teacher fix it for you. Besides, you don't start a day right by getting up at daybreak."

H E STAGGERS downstairs and fixes breakfast.

"Blaah!" says his eldest child. "This cereal tastes funny. It looks funny, too."

"Well, I left the milk out last night and it spoiled so I made the cereal with orange juice. That way you can get your Vitamin C and protein at the same time."

"When's Mom coming home from the hospital?"

"As soon as I can coax her back. Now shut up and eat."

"Have you fixed our lunches yet?"

"What lunches? You haven't even finished breakfast yet."

"Mom gives us peanut butter and jelly sandwiches and bananas in our lunch."

"No wonder she had to go to the hospital."

"Where are our galoshes?"

"What do I look like, a shoe salesman? I don't know where your galoshes are."

"But it's snowing out."

"Wrap tin foil around your feet. That's what I did when I was a kid."

"I thought you said they didn't have tin foil when you were a kid."

"So maybe we used wax paper, what's the difference? Hurry up or you'll be late."

"**G**OT THE lunches?"

"Yeah, here."

"These sandwiches aren't peanut butter and jelly."

"No, they're plastic cheese on cotton bread; the kind I ate when I was your age."

"They taste like you *made* them when you were our age."

"Tell me this, does your mother ever strike you across the head with a broom handle before school? If not, you're in for a new experience."

"I can't find my mittens."

"Don't walk on your hands on the way to school and nobody will know the difference. Now get out."

The children leave, and by the time he's had his coffee, read the paper, watched the Dick Cavett Show, washed the dishes, vacuumed the house and made the beds, it is early afternoon and they're back.

"**W**E'RE HUNGRY. What's for supper?"

"TV dinners."

"We had that yesterday."

"I know but this time I'm going to read the directions before putting them in the oven

and the cardboard boxes won't catch fire. How's that for a treat?"

"It's something."

"Anything happen in school today?"

"Yeah, my teacher asked me why my socks didn't match."

"What did you tell her?"

"That my mother was in the hospital and you were taking care of us."

"That's not much of an answer."

"It made sense to my teacher. She's coming over tomorrow morning to fix us some hot cereal."

Like Father, Like Fun

IN DAYS of old, when kids were allowed to wear knickers to school but didn't want to, instead of the other way around, the first report card of the year was a pretty important thing for many a student.

It not only told him how he was doing in class, it also told his parents, thereby setting the tone of his relationship with his mother and father for some weeks to come.

If the report card was good, everything was coming up roses. If it was bad, each request for extra privilege would be met with a deadening reply of "HAVE YOU DONE YOUR HOMEWORK?"

Things have changed considerably in the last few years.

This is the way things are in a typical American household on report card day:

THE FATHER comes home from a hard day at the of-

119

fice, sits down to the supper table and his son says, "I got our report card today."

"Look chief," the father says. "I'll make a deal with you. I won't say anything about it if you won't. I'll just sign it without looking at it and that'll be that, right?"

"Ignoring it won't make it go away, Dad. I think we'd best face up to it."

"**All right, but must we talk unpleasantness at the supper table?**"

"We got a U in math. U—that stands for unsatisfactory."

"I know what it stands for."

"Herbie Smith and his dad got an E—for excellent."

"Big deal. Herbie's father is an accountant."

"*My teacher says you shouldn't have to be an accountant to do third-grade math. She said any adult of normal intelligence should be able to do it.*"

"Yeah? Well I'd like to see her try to do new math problems when all you know are old math answers. Besides, Herbie's old man couldn't write his name if he lost his Social Security card. The man is all numbers.

"Herbie's mother helps him with language skills."

"*Oh. Well, look at it this way. You've got room for improvement and Herbie has no place to go but down.*"

"That's very comforting. I also have room for improvement in reading. We got a U."

"A U! But reading's our best subject. I thought you told me that our book report was a big hit."

"**With the kids, it was a big hit. With the teacher, it was a bomb. She thought that a synopsis of "The Naked and the Dead" was a little advanced for third graders.**"

"It's a World War II classic."

"She said we were lucky we didn't get thrown out of school."

"Book burner."

"She said that if we didn't start doing better they were going to put us in basic track."

"I can't understand it. I got such good grades in college."

"T HAT WAS in the old days. Things were easier back then. The four-minute mile was a big deal."

"Your teacher hates me, that's what it is. I could see it in her eyes at the open house. She took an immediate dislike to me."

"I don't think so, Dad. She always speaks highly of you."

"She does?"

"Sure. She says a lot of parents are late bloomers. They don't start getting good grades until their kids are in junior high, or senior high school even. She says she thinks you're one of those."

"*Gee, tell her thanks for me, will you. At a time like this it's a nice feeling to know that someone has confidence in you.*"

A Ride to the Cleaners

M OST CLEANING establishments treat stored clothing the way Fort Knox treats gold. This is what makes a customer's loss of a storage receipt so hazardous.

The collection of one's winter clothes from storage without a receipt often demands the nerve of a riverboat gambler and the tenacity of a gila monster.

Consider the case of a Des Moines man who, a few years ago, lost his receipt.

He searched his house top to bottom, inside and out, but two old theater ticket stubs were as close as he could get to the receipt.

So he shrugged and drove to the drive-in cleaning shop that was keeping his clothes. The shop was housed in a converted auto dealer garage; the advantage being that a customer could drive through a tunnel to pick up his clothes without leaving his car.

The man nosed his car into the tunnel, pausing before an electrically amplified m e g a p h o n e hung under a sign that read, "Call Out Your Receipt Number Here."

"No Number," he called out cheerfully and drove on to the window, where a thin, harried looking woman waited for him.

"WHAT DID YOU SAY your number was?" she asked. "I didn't say," he answered. "I don't have a number."

"Did you leave any clothes here to be cleaned?"

"Yes."

"Then you must have a number," she said. "It's on the receipt you got when you left the clothes here."

"I don't have a receipt. I lost it," he confessed.

"Have you looked everywhere for it? We can't give you any clothes without a receipt," she said, watching him carefully. "It's a rule."

"I don't have a receipt," he replied. "It's a fact."

Cars were beginning to line up behind him. "Would you like to see the manager?" she asked.

"Not particularly."

"Oh, Mr. Hotchkiss," she called over her shoulder. "Would you come here for a moment?"

A round, red-faced man appeared at the window. The woman quickly explained the situation to him.

"So you think that you've lost your receipt?" he said.

"No. I know I've lost it."

"Are you sure that you've looked everywhere for it? Sometimes if you go back. . . ."

"Yes, everywhere. I'm sure."

"This places us in quite a difficult position, sir." The line of cars was now overflowing the tunnel into the street. "Our rule is never to give out orders without a receipt."

"I GATHERED that."

The two men stared at each other for a moment. Then, with a studied casualness, the man said, "If you aren't going to give me my clothes, what are you going to do with them?"

The manager bit his lip nervously.

"I'd like to visit them on weekends if I may."

The manager looked as if he were going to cry. "You appreciate our position on this, of course. If we did it for you we'd wind up giving out clothes to everyone who asked for them. That's hardly a way to run a railroad, is it?"

"Indeed not." The line of cars was now half-way down the block and the driver immediately to the rear seemed to be having a heart attack.

"Would you park your car out front and come into my office?" the manager asked.

"No."

"It's a rule," the manager said. "We seldom make exceptions to rules."

"I believe it," the man said. The blare of a horn echoed through the tunnel.

"But I suppose we'll have to in your case. Miss Higgins, get the gentleman's name and get him his clothes."

It was done. As the woman handed over the winter clothes, she said:

"Next time, sir, please be sure to keep your receipt."

"What next time?" the man said as he drove off.

121

How to Fix
The Toilet

INDOOR PLUMBING, the symbol of man's control over his environment, is rapidly becoming one of the chief causes of mental illness.

It already has passed sharp blows on the head as a cause of insanity and is gaining rapidly on television commercials.

There is nothing surprising about this. The Chinese discovered the maddening potential of plumbing even before they discovered plumbing. The Chinese water torture is nothing more than an adaptation of the principle of a leaky faucet.

There is some question whether the faucet ever would have been invented had it not been possible to make it leak.

Yet a faucet that goes drip in the night is merely a minor irritant compared to some of the first class horrors that a truly modern bathroom can boast of.

There is the toilet that whines for prolonged periods after flushing, the shower that changes from very hot to very cold and back again without warning or reason, the ruthless mirror that gives back such a ghastly reflection each morning and, of course, the toilet seat.

SOME MIGHT argue that mirrors and toilet seats aren't really plumbing but that's a quibble. In the broad sense of the word, everything in a modern bathroom is plumbing, including towel racks that drop towels into tubs of bath water.

A Des Moines man recently had occasion to pit his strength, skill and imagination against his bathroom—with predictable results.

His wife came home one afternoon with a rather large, flat package under her arm.

"What's that?" he asked her.

"A toilet seat," she replied. "As you know the one upstairs is broken and has been for a week. I'm hoping you'll be able to install this new one.

"Sure, no trouble at all," he replied, hunching himself a little closer to the book he was reading. "Just put it in the closet and I'll get around to it the first chance I get."

She laid the package in the middle of the floor. *"I'm going to fix you steak for supper tonight."*

This put him in a spot. Only the most experienced of husbands could accept a thick juicy steak from his wife while continuing to ignore a household chore.

HE WASN'T UP to it. He went next door and borrowed the tools he needed.

For the next half-hour the entire upper floor and much of the lower floor were filled with passionate cursing, screams of pain and groans of despair.

He came stomping downstairs. *"Did you get it fixed, Dear?"* his wife called out.

He came into the kitchen, pointed a finger at her and said: "Do you know that old toilet seat is fastened to the toilet with bolts that could secure a jet plane to the deck of an aircraft carrier?"

Without waiting for an answer he plunged into the basement, to return a few moments later with a hack saw, a steel chisel and a hammer.

For the next half hour the curses, screams and groans were accompanied by the rasp of a saw cutting through metal and the clang of hammer on chisel.

Finally, suddenly, it stopped. After a few moments of silence the woman heard her five-year-old son hurrying downstairs.

HE RAN INTO THE kitchen wide-eyed. "You'll never guess what happened," he said.

"Your father broke the toilet," she replied.

"Daddy broke the toilet."

She went upstairs to the bathroom. The toilet was indeed broken, split in twain. It looked as if it had been attacked by a madman armed with a hacksaw, chisel and hammer.

She found her husband lying on the bedroom floor, his head under the bed.

"You shouldn't feel too badly about it, Dear," she said.

"Go away," he said.

"I really didn't like that toilet anyway."

"Go away," he said again. So she did.

• • •

A DES MOINES man lost a member of his family the other day. *His 1954 Pontiac died.*

Its life was gentle and the elements so mixed in it that General Motors might stand up and say to all the world, 'This was a car!' Surely the noblest straight eight of them all.

The man thought of burying the beast under a favorite tree in the back yard, but decided against it in favor of giving it to a found-object sculptor. He thought that the Pontiac would have wanted it that way.

• • •

123

How to Light
A Water Heater

THERE ARE DAYS when disaster stalks you, when it sets little traps for you and watches your every move, waiting its chance to strike.

On such days it is wise to be lucky.

It started, characteristically enough, with a noise in the furnace. Ka-chunk, ka-chunk, ka-chunk.

"The furnace is making noise," my wife said.

"I can't hear you," I replied, "the furnace is making too much noise."

So my wife called the furnace man, who came out and oiled the fan motor, silencing it. Fifteen dollars.

ON THE following night the furnace started making noise again. KA-CHUNK, KA-CHUNK, SQUEEK-SQUEEK-SQUEEK. This time I oiled it and felt pretty good about saving myself the $15.

That's the way disasters operate. They grant you small successes to set you up for the kill.

The next day the furnace began making noises too elaborate for phonetic reproduction and started giving off an ominous odor.

This time the furnace man diagnosed it as a burned-out bearing and said he'd be back the next day to fix it, which he was.

I left him at his work and arrived at the office to be greeted by Gordon Gammack, who looked up from his typewriter and said:

"*Call home, your house is on fire.*" Nice guy, Gammack.

As it turned out, the house wasn't burning but the fire department had been there. The furnace man had detected smoke in the basement and there was a burning smell in the house.

MY WIFE said the firemen had checked the house thoroughly and finding nothing, had left, telling her to call them if she saw any flames. My wife, a reasonable woman, was reasonably hysterical.

I called the fire chief and made irate citizen noises and he sent some men back to the house and they satisfied themselves (and my wife) that the cause of the trouble was the bad bearing; that there was no fire nor any danger of one.

Anyway, when I got home that night the new bearing was installed, the smoke was gone and I congratulated myself on having outwitted this particular disaster.

Then my wife said: "I smell something."

I went down to the basement to find that the gas pipe leading to our elderly hot water heater had become disconnected and was spewing raw gas into the basement.

I reconnected it, waited for the collected gas to dispel and attempted to relight the pilot light on the heater. It wouldn't light.

So I jerked the burner around to try and get more gas to the pilot valve.

The next instant my head was enveloped by flame. The disaster had finally made its big move.

It didn't hurt. The only clear sensation was the smell of

burning hair; a most un-pleasant smell, particularly when it's your hair.

I lunged to a nearby table and wrapped my head in a blanket.

It's funny, the things that go through your mind at a time like that.

I WONDERED what the Register would say about the accident: "Donald Kaul is dead. Today's column is by Jack Smith of the Los Angeles Times."

And would Variety pick up the obituary? "Movie Critic Lays Fried Egg in Stix."

Finding myself alive, however, I turned my attention to other matters. Like putting out the fire, for example.

My wife then drove me to the the hospital where the nurse looked at me and said: "What were you doing, writing a hot column?"

Right there, I figured I was going to make it.

The doctor said the damage was minimal, mostly hair, and that I was very lucky.

Which only proves that God takes care of everybody, even agnostics.

Leaky Tap
Fixits

I'VE FINALLY found a guy who can give me the kind of do-it-yourself advice I need.

For example, he says that if you see an electric cord around the house and it has three wires in it, you should leave it alone. That's my kind of fellow.

His name is Michael Kernan and he writes for the Washington Post.

He has prepared a list of repairs that can be made by people who don't know what they are doing.

This is the way he tells you to fix a leaky faucet:

"First, tell your wife you are going to turn off all the water in the house. Second, turn off all the water in the house. (There will be a wheel-shaped hand valve on the pipe in the cellar by the water meter. You will have to turn it for a long time, but by all means do turn it the whole way.)

"Take your s c r e w d r i v e r, wrench and pliers (which you should keep, along with your saw, in your bureau drawer, assuming you have small children), and remove the little screw on the hot-water handle—it is usually the hot water that leaks because hot water is more expensive—and pry off the handle.

"If you flake off a bit of chromium, don't worry. You can keep a washcloth draped over the handle in the future.

"Now you will see the seamy side of your tap, a businesslike protuberance. Near the base will be a hexagonal section and you should turn this with your wrench or pliers.

"Pretty soon the whole thing will come loose in your hand, followed by some water. Do not lose your nerve, for the water will stop welling in a moment. (Did you turn that valve in all the way?)

"Look at the bottom of the thing you have got loose. There will be a brass screw holding a small black rubber washer in place. Unscrew the screw and pry out the washer, which will be flattened with a ring deeply incised in it.

"YOU FORGOT to get washers, didn't you? Drive down to the hardware store and buy a box of assorted sizes. Tell your wife not to turn the valve in the cellar while you are gone.

"Find a washer that fits, noting that it is not flat like the worn one but is slightly cone-shaped, and screw in the brass screw. Put everything back and turn on the water.

"This exercise will introduce you to the world of plumbing, an alluring world in which logic reigns and everything fits.

"And if you are tempted to try more ambitious projects, the main thing to remember is that if something doesn't fit, it is you that is wrong and not the plumbing.

"Pipe threads do not make mistakes."

That, I submit, is nothing short of brilliant.

No cold, technical instructions that make you feel like an idiot for being unable to understand them; rather a warm, sympathetic word of advice by a human being who's faced the problems you face.

It's really the do-it-yourself equivalent of Dr. Spock. Here's Kernan's advice on retrieving a diamond ring from a toilet:

"You can't," he says. "Neither can you install a new hot water heater. You should know that."

The man should write a book on home repairs. And if he does, you'll read about it here.

If a Marriage Needs Anything, It's Warmth

THE WOMAN blotted her face with her soggy handkerchief, uttered a sigh of misery and frustration, and said:

"It's unbearable."

Her husband, who was sweating happily while reading a book, looked up and responded with:

"What's unbearable?"

"The heat," she answered, barely keeping control of her voice. "How can you sit down there and read that stupid book when it's 100 degrees in the shade?"

He put the book aside. "It's not a 100 degrees in the shade. It's 100 degrees in the sun. Why don't you take a cool bath or something? "It'll make you feel better."

"I don't want a bath," she said grimly. "I want an air conditioner."

"No," he told her.

"Why?"

"We can't afford an air conditioner."

Her shiny face became hard. "Then I want a divorce."

"They're more expensive than air conditioners," he replied calmly. "You can't have one."

"It's tough being married to a failure," she said. "All you get are the things that money can't buy."

"It's really too early in the game to call me a failure," he said. "Besides, I believe that when we got married you promised to stick with me through thick and thin. Have you forgotten so soon?"

"So when is it going to get thick?"

IF YOU wanted to live like a Rockefeller, you should have married a Rockefeller."

"You don't have to be a Rockefeller to have an air conditioner," she said. "In this day and age it's not a luxury, it's a necessity. It's something that goes along with being part of our affluent society."

"Two thirds of the world's people go to bed hungry every night and you're crying about a little heat," he said. "Shame."

"On my diet, I go to bed hungry every night too, and I'm hot besides."

"Being hot is largely psychological in nature. If you just ignore the temperature you don't notice it. Think cool."

"Ha," she replied. "It's easy for you to talk. You go down to your air-conditioned office every day and leave me here with two sweaty kids. As a matter of fact you've gone to work early every day this week."

He cleared his throat. "It so happened that I had a lot of work to catch up on this past week."

"How come you never have any work to catch up on when the weather is cool?"

"I won't dignify that comment with a reply," he said. He picked up his book again. "You're obviously suffering from heat madness and I'm not going to talk to you until you're rational again."

She stood up. "See me in September," she said, then went to draw herself a cool bath.

Newton

Knew

EVEN BEFORE the machinists' strike, there were a number of us who had reservations about air travel.

There are certain things about defying the laws of gravity that the average coward finds disquieting.

Like the way his life flashes before his eyes as he boards the plane.

Or the thought that strikes him as the plane is hurtling down the runway for a takeoff: "We're not going to make it."

Or the one that occurs to him during the landing approach: "I wonder if they let the wheels down."

The true Nervous Nellie knows but one moment of reassurance on a plane trip; the one that comes after the plane is safely in the air and the ground looks like an aerial photo.

A LOW, SLIGHTLY rough voice comes over the intercom and says:

"Good afternoon, ladies and gentlemen, this is your pilot, Capt. Rock Mason. Welcome to Flight 707. We will be flying non-stop to New York City today. Our altitude will be 20,000 feet, our air speed 550 miles an hour. Flying time will be approximately three hours. Reports from Kennedy Airport in New York are that the weather there is ideal.

"Lunch will be served in 20 minutes, after which a movie

will be shown. There will be shuffleboard and dancing on the afterdeck for those so inclined. Enjoy your flight."

Right then, just for a moment, the air passenger feels that there is hope for his survival. Why would the pilot sound so confident if his chances weren't at least 50-50?

But, during a strike at a number of major airlines, things change. Schedules become goals rather than realities. Nonstop flights become nonexistent. Tempers flare.

A ND THAT moment of inflight reassurance disappears. The plane takes off and the pilot's voice comes over the intercom:

"Good afternoon, ladies and gentlemen, this is your pilot, Lt. Sparky Nosedive. Welcome to Flight 6½. We will be flying to New York City today, God willing. Our altitude will be 200 to 5,000 feet and our airspeed will not exceed posted limits.

"We will be making our first stop in Colfax for refueling and then press on to Gary, Ind., where there will be a three-hour layover. From there we fly to Columbus, Ohio, and take a bus to Lancaster, Pa.

"We will be met there by Justice William O. Douglas and his bride, who will lead our Yak caravan across the Alleghenies. Our flight will be resumed in Poughkeepsie and we expect to touch down at Kennedy Airport no later than Tuesday. That's the Sol Kennedy airport in Atlantic City. We'll hitch-hike to New York from there. Flying time will be approximately 3½ days.

" A S YOU MAY have noticed, our plane today is a Ford tri-motor, the very same one that Admiral Byrd used to fly over the North Pole in 1926. Try not to lean back against the seats as we promised the Smithsonian Institution that we would not get them dirty.

"I must remind the children on board to refrain from sticking their heads out of the windows while we are passing through tunnels. The stewardess will pass out parachutes in 20 minutes. Have an exciting flight."

A Shallow

Plunge

A DEDICATED plunger scanned the stock page recently, then threw the paper aside and announced:

"I'm going downtown to take a look at the big board."

His wife was instantly alert. "What big broad?" she said.

"Not broad; board. The stock exchange board. The market's been doing funny things lately and I want to study it at the scene of action."

"What for?"

" I DON'T KNOW. The market's down, it might be a good time to buy in."

"With what?"

"You can never tell. One of my ships might come in."

"If it does, our creditors would appreciate knowing about it. I've been getting calls about our unpaid bills again."

"I never haggle with tradesmen," the man said. "Don't expect me for lunch."

"But you don't know anything about stocks," the wife said.

"Nonsense. I took economics in college; several courses as a matter of fact."

"Yes, and you flunked them all."

"The instructors didn't like me. Don't worry, I won't do anything rash. I'm just going to look."

He was out of the door when he heard his wife call: "Don't forget, you're the guy who wanted to buy Ford when you heard they were coming out with the Edsel."

He pretended he hadn't heard.

THE MAN got to the broker's office well before noon and settled into a chair to watch the big board. He stared intently at the ever-changing numbers and the endless tape for about an hour before realizing that he wasn't understanding it; not any of it.

Particularly confusing were the stock symbols, like GBW, PCX and SOO. Obviously they were abbreviations of names of firms; but which ones? As nearly as he could make out, the United Kingdom (UK) was slipping, while Standing Room Only (SRO) was holding its own. He looked around for help.

His eye fell on a woman seated next to him. A dignified, intelligent-looking woman, she was studying the board with fierce concentration, her lips moving. At frequent intervals she would write something down in a notebook.

The man leaned closer to her and said, "Pardon me, but could you explain to me what all those letters and numbers mean?"

Without even glancing at him she said: "Don't bug me, sonny. I'm busy."

HE PULLED away from her, hurt. In a few minutes, however, she evidently reconsidered.

"All right," she said. "What do you want to know?"

"What's happening to the market today?" he said.

"Blue chips are holding steady but the glamors are taking a dive."

"Huh?"

"You do know what glamor stocks are?"

"Revlon?" he said, weakly.

"No, honey; electronics, airlines, those are the glamors. Say, have you ever bought any stock?"

"No."

"That's what I thought. Look, the smartest thing you can do right now is get out of here. If you've got some money you want to blow, find a horse to bet it on. This market is no place for economic illiterates and you don't know a liquidity preference from the Johnstown flood."

"I GUESS you're right," he said. "Thank you for your help, anyway." He got up to leave but she stopped him.

"Say, before you go, maybe you can help me out on one thing."

"If I can, I will."

"Which is bigger, one-quarter or three-eighths? I can never remember."

• • •

I PLAYED GOLF again the other day and set a course record. Five putts on the sixteenth green.

It's not as bad as it sounds, though. They were long putts.

• • •

129

A Heady
Resolution

A number of persons have wondered what I look like in my Snoopy helmet. So I went to Frank Miller and asked him what I looked like. And this is what he said. But what does he know?

I'M NOT much for New Year's resolutions; as a matter of fact, I'm not anything at all for them.

January 1 has always seemed an arbitrary breaking of the year, an artificial ending and beginning. If you want to change your life, you ought to do it in the spring, at the start of a new life cycle.

However, I have a resolution to make that will not wait until spring. I make it now.

I resolve not to be intimidated by the gawks, sneers and giggles of strangers w h e n wearing my Snoopy flying helmet.

I got the helmet from a friend who got it from an attic which got it from a World War II veteran. It's a beautiful helmet, worthy of Lindbergh.

The original idea was that it would come in handy for riding a bicycle in cold weather. It's the perfect garment for bike riding. It's warm, offers no wind resistance and does not interfere with visibility. Neither does it fall off.

Its only drawback is that people seem to find it silly to see a grown man riding down the street wearing a flying helmet. They laugh, they point, they shout rude sayings. "Hey, where's t h e Red Baron?" That's one of the nicer ones.

But the taunts of strangers are not the only problem; there are often one's children, the arch-conservatives of the family.

You buckle the helmet on in preparation for a little ride and your son says, solemnly: "You're making a fool of yourself. You realize that, don't you?"

It makes you feel like a character in a Grace Metalious novel. Or your daughter looks at you and says, "Gross!"

It is a word that, in contemporary usage, conveys the combined feelings of contempt, disgust and loathing.

I wore the helmet to a movie once and I had to show my I.D.

130

to get in. They thought I was a 12-year-old with a mustache.

And, as I walked through the lobby, I heard a woman say, "Imagine how ashamed his children must be."

IT REALLY hit home. So I stopped wearing the helmet. I wanted my kids to be proud of me.

Until a few weeks ago when I found myself walking to the bus stop, bare-headed, on a cold morning.

I was getting a headache, it was so cold, and my ears had gone through the painful stage and were beginning to feel sleepy.

I was near death by the time the bus came and, as I got on and walked to my seat, it occurred to me that nobody was laughing at me.

I had come out in cold weather without a hat and undoubtedly had done my sinuses permanent injury and no one thought it silly. Neither would they have thought it silly had I worn a standard man's hat which covers just the top of the head, leaving the ears and back of the neck exposed.

But had I worn my flying helmet, and consequently, been perfectly warm, the bus passengers would have done double takes and stared and whispered.

And so it was revealed to me that the good opinion of society—children included—was not worth having because society places too much emphasis on appearances and not enough on head colds.

Armed with that knowledge, I face the new year.

The Misery of Chickenpox

A GREAT MANY things are funny: life, Jack Benny, a fat man doing the twist, the collected works of Mark Twain, the Congressional Record, the Polk County Jail.

And there are several things that are not funny. High on this list is chickenpox.

While this would seem self-evident, there are a number of persons on whom this fact seems to be lost, all of them persons who don't have chickenpox and are in no danger of getting them.

These people, most of whom would not think of laughing at a man in traction or in an oxygen tent, grow giddy at the sight of an adult friend stricken with a childhood disease.

"Ho, ho," they wittily exclaim in the presence of their sick friend, "So you've got chickenpox, eh?"

The only adequate response to this is a silver bullet through the heart, a tactic too seldom used.

An adult suffering from a child's disease is a helpless individual. The considerable misery of being very ill is deepened by the awareness of the ridiculousness of his situation.

He is like a man being attacked by a savage toy poodle; his danger lacks dignity.

HIS FEVER might be as high as that of a veteran who

contracted malaria in the war; the pain he suffers might be equal to that of a hero who received minor burns while rescuing a child from a flaming building, but his predicament is totally lacking in glamour.

Chickenpox does not capture the popular imagination.

The lonely misery of the chickenpox sufferer is further intensified by the knowledge that he looks like a beekeeper at a leper colony.

Each day he looks into the mirror and says, "Well, I think I've hit bottom. I certainly can't look any worse than this." And the next day he looks worse.

He sits at home, looking awful, feeling awful, sinking deeper and deeper into self-pity.

His friends visit him freely— they've all had the disease years ago—and not all of them are laughers. Many attempt to cheer him up with stories of their own recent illnesses.

He hears detailed accounts of cases of viral pneumonia, mononucleosis, c h r o n i c asthma, arthritis, neuritis, n e u r a l g i a and dandruff. He is forced to examine hideous scars, the mementos of major surgery.

All of which would be enough to make him ill if he were well, which he isn't.

The friends are well enough intentioned. They're operating on the theory that if they explain to the patient just how sick he could be, he will feel fortunate that he's no sicker than he is.

A ND IT MIGHT work, except that the sufferer of chickenpox is itching—all over.

A man who itches in several hundred different places and is unable to scratch even one cannot be persuaded that he is more fortunate than anyone, excluding not even the starving children of India.

Finally the peak of the disease passes and he ventures out into the world, his unshaven, wounded face a source of terror to small children and pregnant women.

Acquaintances see him and say, "Say, I heard you were sick. I'm glad to see you looking . . . er . . . better." Presumably they mean looking better than an exhumed body or a victim of a Mau Mau uprising.

But he feels better. He notices how fresh the wind smells and that his backyard lawn is coming alive and that pleasant-sounding birds are back after a winter's absence.

And he takes heart in the fact that he is now immune to chickenpox.

Keats, Kaline, And Kaul

A WOMAN walked into her living room to find her husband staring into infinity.

"What's wrong, Dear?" she asked.

"Do you realize," he said, that at my age Keats already had been dead for three years?"

"Don't tell me you're still worried about your pen gleaning your teeming brain?"

"No, it's just that I happened to run across a roster of the Detroit Tigers the other day and do you know that only three or four players on the whole team are older than I am?"

"What's that got to do with John Keats?"

"Nothing, I suppose. It's just that everyone seems so young these days. One of the Tigers, Al Kaline, has been a major league star for 12 years and he's only six days older than I am."

I WISH YOU wouldn't let things like that get you down, Dear. It's not your fault that you're astigmatic in your left eye and could never hit a curve."

"I could never hit a fast ball either, if you want to know the truth, but that's not the point. It's sobering to realize that you're as old as those aging veterans you read about on the sports pages."

"**All right. For a baseball player you're an old man; but for a writer, you're a kid.**"

"Well, maybe; but just to be on the safe side I'm going to renew my membership in the Y.M.C.A. Too many men get old before their time because they let their bodies go to pot."

"That's what you said last year when you renewed your membership. And how many times did you work out at the 'Y'?"

"*I was pretty busy last year.*"

"**Not once, that's how many. It was $40 out of the window.**"

"I know, but this time it's going to be different. As a matter of fact, I think I'll go downtown tomorrow and play a little handball."

AND SO HE did. When he came home that evening his wife said, "Well, how did the handball go, Dear?"

"Not bad, not bad. I'm a little stiff but that's only natural. Give me six months of this and my muscles will be like spring steel."

"**I hope you didn't overdo it the first time out. You know you haven't done anything more strenuous than crack ice in a year and a half.**"

"No, I took it easy. Just an hour or so of handball, then 10 laps around the gym."

"Well, I suppose you know what you're doing."

THE NEXT morning the woman was preparing breakfast when she heard a long moan coming from the direction of the bedroom. She hurried upstairs and found her husband lying on the bed.

"What's wrong?" she asked.

"**Me,**" he said. "**I can't move my arms or my legs or my back or my neck.**"

"Where does it hurt?"

"Put your hand on my forearm . . . now move it a little to the left . . . a little more, there. That's where it doesn't hurt. Everyplace else hurts."

"**Even right here in the middle of your back.**"

"*EEARGHOWOO!*"

"I guess you overdid yesterday after all."

"Brilliant deduction."

"**The only thing for it is to go back and play more handball. You know what pilots say, if you have a crash you should go right up in a plane.**"

"Right. As soon as I can walk again I'll go up in a plane. In the meantime get me some liniment."

'Ha,' Rang The Battle Cry, And the Marital Bit Began

A DES MOINES MAN'S contemplation of the advisability of admitting Red China to the United Nations was shattered recently by an explosive "Ha" coming from the direction of his wife.

He knew the sound well; one part discovery, one part indignation and one part battle cry. He let the challenge hang in the silence that followed for a few moments, then said:

133

"What do you mean, 'Ha?' "

"This article," she said, jabbing her forefinger at the newspaper she'd been reading, "is very revealing," She pronounced "very" as if it had three Rs.

"What does it reveal?" he asked mildly.

"It says that studies show that money is at the root of most marital strife."

He shrugged. "If you needed a newspaper article to find that out you haven't been paying much attention to most of the marital strife around here."

"But," she continued, *"it also says that this is misleading. The arguments about money have hidden roots. People use them to disguise more serious inherent differences."*

She stopped and looked at him coolly. He fancied he could hear his watch ticking.

"Well?" she said, finally.

"I think I'll take out the garbage," he said, rising.

N EVER MIND the garbage for now," she said. "What I want to know is what is the real reason you're always nagging me about the way I spend money?"

"It's not the way you spend money but the amount you spend that I find objectionable," he answered.

"What serious inherent differences are you attempting to disguise?" she demanded.

"Oh come off of it. You don't really. . ."

"Is it another woman?" she asked, her face like stone.

"Another woman?" he cried.

"Ignoring the fact that I love you more than life itself and ignoring the fact that I am an essentially moral person, I couldn't possibly afford another woman. Sin does not come cheap and you manage to take care of my bankroll quite nicely."

"You see?" she said pointing her finger at him. "You can't even say something nice without doing it."

"Doing what?"

"Nagging me about money. I don't really spend money foolishly and yet you insist on nagging me about it. Why?"

He lengthened his face. "I'm not sure you really want to know."

"What do you mean?"

"I mean that if I tell you you'll be sorry you asked. You're happier not knowing."

"I think I'm the best judge of that."

He smiled a sad, enigmatic smile. "Well, if you insist, I suppose there's nothing to do but tell you."

"Be absolutely frank," she said. "I can take it."

"It is true that I've been making a special effort to hold our expenses down recently. I hadn't realized I'd been so hard on you. Remember that dining room set that we saw a few months ago, the one you liked so much? Well, I've been trying to save enough money to buy that for you for our wedding anniversary next month."

S HE NARROWED her eyes. "I don't believe you," she said without conviction.

"It was to have been a surprise," he answered, allowing a slight huskiness to enter his voice.

"But we talked it over and decided that we couldn't afford that dining room set," she said.

"I know and we were probably right, too. At the same time, half the fun of buying something is not being able to afford it. Besides, anything we can afford isn't good enough for you. You deserve only the best."

He turned and walked into the kitchen and momentarily considered taking out the garbage as a grand gesture. But he decided against it.

A Perilous Ad Campaign

A MAJOR AIRLINE has embarked on one of the most perilous advertising campaigns of modern times.

The theme of the campaign—the phrase that jingles in your mind—is "Take Me Along."

The idea is that men are supposed to take their wives along on business trips, paying a reduced rate for the extra ticket.

Now this presupposes that men WANT to take their wives along on business trips, an analysis that, for accuracy, could rank with Neville Chamberlain's assessment of Adolf Hitler's trustworthiness.

Surely there must be many men who, for reasons of their own, would prefer not to take their wives along on business trips. How will these men react when their wives, inspired by the ads, demand to accompany them?

FOR EXAMPLE, a man is on his way out the door, headed for Chicago.

"Goodbye, dear, I'm off for Chicago," he says. "Wish me luck. . . . Say, how come you're all dressed up? And why do you have your bag packed?"

"Take me along," she says.

"Quit kidding around, honey. I'm going to miss my plane. Say goodbye to the kids for me. Tell them I'll bring them back something from the big city."

"Take me along, Charlie."

"Why do you keep saying that?"

"Because I want to go along."

"WITH ME? Now? To Chicago? Baby, I thought you knew. This is a business trip. It wouldn't be any fun for you, sitting around a hotel, wandering aimlessly around a strange city."

"It beats trying to carry on an intelligent conversation with a 2-year-old all day. Take me along."

"Look I know what you're thinking. You're thinking that I have a good time when I go out of town on these trips. You're thinking that I enjoy myself."

"That's what I'm thinking."

"You couldn't be more wrong. These trips are a chore; they're the part of my job I like least. Take tomorrow, for example. Tomorrow I'm booked solid all day. I won't even be able to enjoy dinner; I'm entertaining some clients. It's just going to be work, work, work for three days."

"Where are you having dinner?"

"Uh . . . as a matter of fact, I don't remember, offhand. It doesn't make much difference, really. One place is like another when you're having a business dinner."

"Where are you having dinner, Charlie?"

"The name's right on the tip of my tongue. It's called the Playroom, something like that."

"The Playboy Club?"

"Yes, I think that is what they call it, now that you mention it. It's funny how a name like that will slip your mind."

"You're taking me along."

"LOOK, ETHEL. I understand how you feel, I really do. The grass always looks greener on the other side of the fence. But you have to remember that a marriage is like a partnership, a team. And members of a team have different jobs to perform, each as important as the others in relation to the overall success of the team. Take the Indians, for example. The men went out to hunt and fish. . . ."

"While the women stayed in the tepee chewing blubber."

"You're getting the Indians confused with the Eskimos."

"No. You're getting me confused with a squaw. You're taking me along, Charlie, and that's all there is to it."

"Okay, Ethel, if that's the way you feel, I'll take you along."

"I knew you'd see it my way, dear. And just think, the airline will give us a discount on my ticket. Isn't that nice of them?"

"Ethel. Nice isn't the word for it."

The Great Outdoor Eating Hustle

SOCIETY, BY ITS very nature, relies heavily on its myths for support. People generally are uncomfortable in the face of the unknown or when confronted by an unpleasant truth, so they make up stories that explain away their discomfiture.

These stories make up the mythology of the society.

One of the great myths that now bolsters the American civilization is the fiction that food tastes better when eaten outdoors. **This is a relatively recent invention. The caveman didn't think much of eating outdoors; that's why he searched out caves to live in.**

The charm of open air dining escaped our pioneer forefathers almost entirely. After enduring months of fresh air fun while camping out on the trail, the first thing they did on reaching their destinations was build homes to protect themselves from the elements while they ate.

A contemporary man, otherwise sane, will build himself a $35,000 shack with central air *conditioning, then rush out onto his hot, humid patio to give the old rotisserie a whirl.*

The myth of the attractiveness of outdoor eating is largely the invention of women. It serves to disguise an unpleasant but unassailable truth—women don't like to cook indoors during the summer.

INDOOR COOKING is hot, they claim. And it is, but so is the food, which is more than you can say for outdoor meals. It is an unexplained but verifiable fact that outdoor meals, no matter how hot the weather, are cold when served.

Women have achieved this monstrous fraud by playing upon the vanity of their husbands.

First of all they remind men that the great chefs are all men; meaning, of course, that men have a natural talent for cooking. This puts the would-be cook in the proper frame of mind.

Before he knows what's happening he's in the backyard,

wearing a silly cap and slaving over a hot charcoal burner while his wife sips a refreshing drink.

He can incinerate a batch of hamburgers badly enough to make a vegetarian cringe and all his wife will say is: "These burgers are simply marvelous dear. I don't know how you do it. That charcoal flavor is just out of this world and so good for the teeth too."

She's probably on a diet anyway and doesn't care whether she eats or not. It's the children who suffer.

If they refuse to eat the mess that dad cooked up, mother is quick to say:

"I swear I don't know how those children survive, they haven't eaten anything in a week. The hot weather has just taken away their appetites." So the kids go hungry.

Even with a cook who has mastered the techniques of culinary primitivism, eating outdoors leaves something to be desired.

The bugs, of course, consider each cookout as an ideal opportunity to hold a convention. It remains a mystery why so many people who would never think of ordering mosquitoes with their meal at a restaurant so amiably accept mosquitoes in their back yards.

YET, no matter how densely the insects swarm or irritations mount, a wife will smile through it all, tranquil in the knowledge that she doesn't have to lift a finger.

At the end of the meal she may consent to scooping up the paperware and dumping it into a sack.

"You know, it's true," she says. "Food really does taste better outdoors."

As an eminent Lover of the Great Indoors, informed of this, once said: "Better than what?"

How to Save
Some Money

A MAN recently was torn away from the work he loves so well by a phone call from his wife.

"Honey," she said, with the rising inflection he had long since learned to be wary of. "I've done something that will make you proud of me."

CAREFULLY CHOOSING his words, he answered: "Hmmm?"

"I've saved some money."

"Well, that is a surprise. Unprecedented, as a matter of fact. And it does make me proud of you. How much have you saved?"

"Seventy dollars."

"Wonderful," he shouted. "Why you little devil, you've been holding out on me. I didn't think you could be spending all of that grocery money on the food we've been having. You were saving a little of it, week by week, weren't you? It's a lucky man who has a frugal wife."

WAIT a minute, dear. I don't think you're grasping what I'm trying to say."

"What are you trying to say?"

"I bought a piece of furniture for $65."

"And that's what you call saving $70?"

"Certainly, it's worth $135."

"I should have known. If all savers were like you, banks wouldn't need vaults. What was it you bought?"

"A dry sink."

He took the receiver from his ear and shook it. "Excuse me, honey, we've got a bad connection here. It sounded like you said—this will break you up—a dry sink. Ha, ha, ha." He noticed she wasn't joining him in laughter.

"That's what I did say," she stated.

"What in heaven's name is a dry sink?"

"It's what pioneer families used for a sink. It's a cabinet with a basin in it and the water was hand poured into the basin."

OF COURSE, and I suppose no modern American home should be without one. No matter, I've got work to do. You let me hang up now and I'll take a look at your buy when I get home."

It was after 6 p.m. when he walked into his kitchen and was confronted by a rather large, wooden, box-like structure.

"Say," he called out. "You didn't do so badly after all. This crate that it came in must be worth five or ten dollars all by itself."

His wife walked slowly into the kitchen, her face stony. "That is not the crate," she said. "That is it."

"All of it?" he asked. She nodded.

He cleared his throat. "Did you get the license number of the guy who sold it to you?"

"It happens to be a rather good example of a primitive American antique."

"Rather good? It's darn near perfect. It looks as if a nearsighted cave man built it with a stone ax. It's got more gouges in it than a three-hour wrestling match."

"Those aren't gouges, they're distress marks."

"That thing isn't in distress, it's in a state of total collapse."

"You don't like it," she said.

"I didn't say that," he answered, squinting at the sink. "Admittedly, it has a certain offbeat, beat-up charm to it. Isn't it going to be rather difficult to wash dishes in it after being used to a double sink with running water?"

"Don't be ridiculous," she said. *"You don't wash dishes in a dry sink any more. I'm going to move it into the dining room and put a plant in it."*

"You mean you laid out sixty-five bucks on something that you're going to use as a planter?"

"Yes, and before I forget it, there's something else I want to talk to you about."

"What?"

"You're going to have to increase my food allowance. I simply can't make ends meet on what you're giving me."

• • •

A WEEK ago, with the flood season hard upon us, it occurred to me that Over the Coffee had been negligent in failing to supply tips on What to Do When the Water Reaches the Upstairs Bedroom.

So I looked up an article on floods and it said one good way to protect your house from flood water is to wrap it in plastic sheeting.

The house will stay nice and dry, the article said. There's just this one catch. A house wrapped in plastic sheeting becomes buoyant and tends to float away.

• • •

Ain't Love . . . ?
Yeah, Ain't It?

A VETERAN HUSBAND was slumped in his easy chair, practicing his shallow breathing exercises, when his wife put down the paper with a rattle and said: "Do you think we're happily married?"

"Is this a true or false quiz or an essay exam?"

"Twenty-five words or less."

"It's a hard question to answer. After all, what is happiness? And whatever it is, what has it got to do with marriage?"

"**What do you mean by that?**"

"Happy is a pretty pallid term to describe the years we've had together. They've been more than happy, they've been memorable. And I want you to know I'll cherish them always; or at the very least for the foreseeable future. We've had nearly 10 years and that, as they say, is a lot. I'll just get a few of my things and go over to my club. Don't move, I want to remember you just as you are."

"You don't have a club."

"You moved."

"Will you explain what you're talking about?"

"You're asking me for a divorce, aren't you?"

"No."

"THEN what's all this about being happily married? Of course we're happily married. There hasn't been a more ideal couple since Debbie Reynolds and Eddie Fisher."

"And we're compatible?"

"Certainly."

"*That's what I thought. I want a divorce.*'

"Because we're compatible?"

"Yes. It says right here in the newspaper that a lot of so-called happy marriages are merely dull; that instead of being compatible these couples are merely unexciting."

"Who says that?"

"**A psychologist at the National Institute of Mental Health. He warns against the 'unexamined idea that compatibility is a good thing.'**"

"We're in a war in Viet Nam, the world is being threatened by over-population, our water and air are being destroyed by pollution and some clown for the National Institute of Mental Health is warning against compatibility."

"Scoff if you will. That doesn't change the fact that our marriage is dull."

"DULL? Don't be ridiculous. Our marriage is about as dull as a sword swallower with the hiccups."

"What's so exciting about us?"

"I'll tell you what. The other day I took out the garbage and when I came back I was going to put out a fresh bag, but there wasn't any."

"That's exciting?"

"**It is if you consider the significance of it. Where do we get our garbage bags?**"

"We use the bags we bring the groceries home in, of course."

"Now, do we throw any of those bags away?"

"No. We save them all for garbage."

"Do we use them for anything but garbage?"

"No."

"THERE you have it. Then running out of garbage bags means that we throw away more garbage than we bring in food."

"But that's impossible."

"*I know; and that's the kind of thing that makes living with you so exciting.*"

139

"God must have loved th[e

He made s[o

common people;

many of them rich"

Make Mine Cash

IF YOU TAKE the trouble to seek out a rich man—particularly a very rich man—and ask him, "Can money buy happiness?", you are very apt to get a response that goes something like this:

He will place one hand on your shoulder and the other on his wallet, look you in the eye and say, "I swear, I don't know where you young people pick up such foolish ideas. Of course money can't buy happiness. Money and its attendant responsibilities are merely the price a man pays for possessing ability and foolish ambition. It is more of a curse than a blessing. What with taxes the way they are and all, your average welfare recipient is better off than your average millionaire. Here's a bright shiny quarter for you, boy. Run on home and show it to your wife and kiddies."

Now, if you consider yourself a particularly cunning individual, you might very well refuse the quarter, saying "I'd rather have your advice, sir. I'm sure it will prove more valuable to me in the long run."

And the rich man will take back the money and, smiling, reply with: "You want some sound advice, sonny? Okay, here it is. When someone offers you a quarter; take it." Then he will walk away.

That is the way of the world.

THE RICH MAN'S contempt for money is well-known, and unsurprising. He's got a pretty good thing going for him; why should he let the rest of us in on it?

The poor man's contempt for money is less publicized and entirely inexplicable.

This was brought home to me the other day when The Register's "What Do You Think?" reporter asked four persons, none of whom looked to be a millionaire, whether money could buy happiness.

Although they exhibited varying enthusiasms for doing without money, they were in general agreement that it couldn't buy happiness.

Which is, of course, nonsense.

Money can buy time, space, respect, power and freedom, why can't it buy happiness? A guy who can have all of those things and remain unhappy, deserves what he gets.

YOU ALWAYS HEAR the stories about the poor little rich boys and girls who can't seem to have a good time on 350 thou a year.

Look at it this way—could they have a better time on $5,000?

One well-known New York millionaire who became famous a few years back for his habit of marrying random showgirls was considered by most of his associates to be a raving lunatic, harmless but nutty.

Had he been the member of a poor but honest family, chances are he would have lived his life in an upstairs room, hidden away from public view.

But because he inherited an enormous fortune he spent his life bopping around the great cities of the world, having a grand time.

OF COURSE there are certain things that money can't buy; poverty, for example. Also:

Health. It can only buy the finest medical attention.

A happy home. Unless your wife can be bribed.

Wonderful children. It can

143

merely keep bad children away at boarding school.

The thinking classes vastly underrate materialism. They forget that the Bible condemns not money itself but LOVE of money as the root of evil. And surely poor men covet money more than rich. You always want most what you don't have.

There are some very rich persons, however, who retain the poor man's view of things.

H. L. Hunt, the oil billionaire, says that he gave up chain-smoking cigars because he considered it too expensive a luxury.

"I figured out that it was costing $300,000 of my time per year just to unwrap them," he says.

But he sounds happy when he says it.

Can We Trust You, Baby?

THE YOUNG have always been an unwieldly lot but they seem to be carrying their rebellions to extremes these days. As one veteran observer put it:

"Kids today are a different breed. There was nothing incomprehensible about me when I was a kid. I understood myself. All my friends understood me.

"But these kids today; I can't understand them and neither can my friends."

It is reactions like this that have prompted the philosophy now current in younger circles: "Don't trust anyone over 30."

WHILE THIS is a valuable rule of thumb for youngsters, it is hardly accurate in its implications. The flush of youth does not leave a man—WHOOSH —on his thirtieth birthday.

No, it happens gradually. Some persons are middle-aged at age 20, while others remain hip as senior citizens.

What's needed is a test that will help identify those of us who are spiritually over thirty. As it happens, I have such a test right here.

You are not where it's happening, baby, if you:

Identify LSD as a World War II landing craft.

Think Simon and Garfunkel is a law firm.

Consider yourself pretty hep to the jive.

Used to wonder whether girls thought about the same things that boys think about.

Think of aspirin when someone mentions "The Pill."

Wonder what ever happened to Butch Jenkins.

Are still learning the Twist.

Remember Frank Sinatra's comeback.

Think of Walt Disney primarily as the man who filmed "Snow White."

Fell in love with the horse at your first Elizabeth Taylor movie.

Said that Hubert Humphrey was too honest to get anyplace in national politics.

Believe that the knee is one of the ugliest parts of the body.

Root for the good guys at the movies.

Want your son to grow up to be like J. Edgar Hoover.

Get winded watching the Pepsi-Cola ads on television.

Somerset Maugham was never considered a profound thinker, not even by himself. Yet he would, at times, get off a sharp observation on the human condition. For example, in his Ashenden stories, from which all modern spy stories spring, he says of his secret agent-hero: "Though he had both esteem and admiration for the sensibility of the human race he had little respect for their intelligence; man has always found it easier to sacrifice his life than to learn the multiplication table."

144

T. J.'s Long, Hard Road To Oblivion

CALL HIM T. J., he's been called worse. He is what is commonly known as a drifter or, more properly, a vagrant.

He arrived in town like something out of a hobo cartoon, carrying his belongings wrapped in a bundle on a stick.

He was cold, broke and friendless, but it was not a new experience and he understood the solution to his problems.

He took a can of beans from his bundle and threw it through a $75 store window. Then he went to a nearby drugstore and told people what he'd done.

They called the police and T. J. got a free ride downtown and a nice, warm jail cell to sleep in.

His ingenuity in this exploit gave promise of a colorful character with perhaps an amusing story to tell. I went down to the County Jail where he was serving a three-day jail sentence to talk with him and write an amusing Knight-of-the-Open-Road story.

It didn't turn out.

He shuffled into the basement of the jail; a small, dry, brittle man with uncut black hair and a ragged white beard.

He said he was 58 years old but he could have said 78 and no one would have given him an argument.

He spoke softly, in a cracked voice.

"I broke that window to get medical attention," he said. "I got a rupture so bad I can hardly stand and I need an operation. When it gets cold it just knocks me down and rolls me over.

"When I was young I could take the cold but I can't do it anymore."

Did he get the medical attention?

"They took me down to that hospital, Broadlawns, and a doctor gave me a diagnosis. He said something about an operation but he didn't make any promises."

Did he want anyone to call Broadlawns and find out what the deal was?

"Do me a favor. Don't call Broadlawns. I've got enough problems already."

T. J. is a frightened, beaten man. He's weary in a way that can't be helped by sleep and rest. He moves around from town to town looking for a place to die, afraid he'll find it.

He's been on the road 38 years. He was a porter in a Massachusetts shoe factory in 1926 when he decided to see what the West looked like.

He's been at it ever since, endlessly criss-crossing the country in search of a full stomach and a warm place to sleep.

"I've been arrested all over the country," he said. "Vagrancy mostly. Traveled on about every railroad line, too. I pick up a job picking cotton here, doing something else there. Sometimes people give me money.

"It seems that everytime I try and get help, though, people mock me. I guess I make an amusing story.

"I only went to grammar school. When I first went west I was just going to travel around for a couple of years. I guess I sort of broke down and started drifting. A fellow gets in the habit and it's hard to break.

"I've got no plans. Everytime I plan something, something else happens. I'll probably go south when I get out of here, or maybe Omaha. I don't know how I'll get there; walk, I guess.

"Can't work no more, not with this rupture. I guess I'm just a victim of society."

And while one can rebel at accepting this self-pitying assessment, it is difficult to do so when a c t u a l l y confronted by the wretched old man.

For the Big Rock Candy Mountain, the hobo heaven where the bulldogs all have rubber teeth, exists only in song. A drifter has to settle for oblivion.

Puts
A Price
On Sight

SIGHT IS priceless; you know it, I know it, and Kenneth Jernigan, who has been blind since birth, knows it.

Yet, on occasion, Jernigan, director of the Iowa Commission for the Blind, asks his students to set a cash value on their lost sight. He does it as a demonstration, framing the question this way:

Suppose a genie or wizard appeared and offered to restore your sight with a wave of a wand if you, in exchange, would mortgage your future to him.

Once sighted you would be assured of the bare essentials of existence but you would have to pay off the mortgage out of your excess income. Under those conditions what would you be willing to pay to gain sight?

"The persons who have been at our training center the shortest time usually bid the highest, up to about $100,000," says Jernigan.

Ask Jernigan, whose salary is $8,500 a year, what dollar figure would he pay to be able to see?

"I'd give about $4,500. I could come by that amount conveniently and it would be convenient to have sight."

$4,500? Convenient? Jernigan is not unaware of the shock value of his casual statement.

"It's a difficult concept for sighted persons to accept emotionally. I would have the same problem if we were talking about the loss of an arm.

"I'm not trying to play down the importance of sight. It's an important sensory perception. If you have sight you wouldn't take $1 million for it, not unless you're an idiot.

"But blindness is not an absolute tragedy. Once you do not have sight you develop new patterns of living. To gain sight I certainly wouldn't be willing to give up all of the modest pleasures I now have; the owning of books, boating, having my choice of foods and wearing good clothes."

Blindness is not an absolute tragedy. This is the point of the demonstration and the point Jernigan has been striving to make throughout his life.

JERNIGAN, who is 38, does not attempt to deny his blindness, rather he accepts it as a limiting characteristic; more limiting perhaps than a missing finger, but less than a low I.Q.

"Even when I was a boy growing up on a Tennessee farm I felt that blindness wasn't what people thought it to be. I wanted to know why, for example, I couldn't play checkers. My mother told me I'd have to learn to accept my limitations.

"So I made my own checkerboard, outlining the squares with string. I also had rock fights with the other kids. I was at something of a disadvantage there but you'd be

amazed at the accuracy you can develop by sound."

The rock-throwing aspect of his personal history serves to illustrate one of Jernigan's chief characteristics. He's a fighter.

He was the only blind child of a Tennessee farmer and his wife. The doctors still aren't sure what caused the blindness.

H E ATTENDED the Tennessee School for the Blind, then made and sold furniture of his own design to earn his way through college. The first blind person ever to attend Tennessee Polytechnic Institute, he missed being an all-"A" student by the margin of three "Bs."

After serving on the staff of the California Orientation Center for the Blind in Oakland, Calif., he came to Iowa to take over direction of the poorly supported Commission for the Blind in 1958.

With the help of a sympathetic Legislature and various civic groups, he has built a training center here that is internationally recognized as one of the best in existence.

"We're just beginning to get a payoff on our capital investment now," he says. "The tax savings that come from the rehabilitation of the blind are important; that's what we very often use to sell our program.

B UT WHAT'S really important is the new hope, the new sense of purpose that is coming to the blind persons of Iowa. This state has the best climate of public opinion toward the blind, of any state in the nation.

"We believe that the blind are not helpless but are simply normal people who cannot see. Remember, in this world you do not compete with an image of yourself as you might have been, sighted, smarter, whatever; you compete with other people—as they are."

You're In The Leisure Generation

A N IMPRESSIVE body of thought has been built around the theory that machines are not evil.

Proponents of this theory, many of them people, contend that machines, far from being the oppressors of the human race, are its liberators.

This, the zealots say, is because machines can free man from many routine tasks, thereby giving him leisure time in which he may search for his true destiny.

However, even the most ardent supporter of the machine age will admit that the increase in leisure time recently experienced by persons—Americans in particular—presents certain problems; largely the one called "What To Do With It."

In an effort to illuminate this beclouded issue, a Des Moines man, himself a narrowly-quoted authority on leisure, sought the guidance of Dr. Otto von Helper, noted scholar of the Isle of Corfu.

Dr. von Helper is exceptionally qualified to speak on the subject of leisure. It has been said, with justice, that the doctor, pound for pound, has known more leisure than a 2,000-year-old, 12-ton statue of Buddha.

He recently authored a book, "Bear Down and Relax," notable for his coining of the truism, "All jack and no dull work makes a playboy."

What follows is a partial transcript of a conversation with the master.

Q. What is leisure?

147

A. Leisure is a concept that differs with each individual. For a bus driver, paying for a bus ride might constitute leisure; for a fisherman, working in a factory might fill the bill.

Q. What is your personal idea of leisure?

A. Not answering stupid questions.

Q. Does the entire spectrum of leisure activity lend itself to any sort of logical grouping or categorization?

A. Yes. There are four very definite and distinct classes of leisure activity.

First, there is the leisure of concentration, for persons who aren't happy unless they're straining their heads on a bridge or chess problem.

Second, there is constructive or do-it-yourself leisure, for persons whose idea of fun is to lose two fingers in a power saw.

Third, there is running-jump-ing-throwing leisure, favored by persons who are trying to prove something.

Last, there is standing-sitting-lying down leisure, favored by those who know what they're doing.

Q. You, then, believe that the best possible way to spend leisure time is by standing, sitting or lying down.

A. Yes, preferably lying down with eyes closed. Remember that the Lord, on the seventh day, after creating the heavens and the Earth, rested; he did not play handball.

Q. You obviously do not subscribe to the commonly held theory that idle hands are the Devil's workshop.

A. No. The Devil is too busy running four-fifths of the civilized world to play hand games with idlers.

Q. What about the proposal, offered by a number of leisure experts, to create a federal Department of Leisure?

A. We already have one. It's called Congress.

Q. There are those who claim that leisure activities, both mental and physical, should be a compulsory part of school training along with reading, writing and arithmetic. What are your thoughts on this?

A. I think it would meet with the same success that the teaching of reading, writing and arithmetic has. You could make playing hookey unpopular by requiring kids to do it.

Q. What role do spectator sports play in your philosophy of leisure?

A. A major role. As a matter of fact I would say that spectator sports are one of the two pillars on which my philosophy of leisure is built. The other is shallow breathing exercises.

Q. Shallow breathing exercises?

A. Yes. Shallow breathing exercises, if practiced according to the principles laid down by me in my forthcoming book, "The Fruitful Uses of Fruit," insure that even when you get the urge to go out and play a sport instead of watching it, you can't.

Q. In your vast experience, is there one man, through the ages, who stands out as the ideal man of leisure?

A. Certainly. Rip Van Winkle.

● ● ●

THE MOST AMUSING news story of last week was the one about the New York state cop who spent nine months among the hippies, gathering evidence which led to the arrest of 70 of them.

The amusing part was his description of the youths as "paranoiac" because they were constantly concerned about the police.

That's not paranoia; that's knowing where it's at.

● ● ●

Dick Gregory

Words That Cut Deep

DICK GREGORY is an angry man.

And when you listen to him, you understand why.

He begins his talks slowly, with a few light jabs at the establishment, at himself.

"I knew the money was no good as soon as L.B.J. said it *was*. I didn't need any more proof than that."

"With my political views, if I tried to volunteer for the draft, the *government* would burn my draft card."

THEN HE TALKS about rats and begins to cut a little deeper:

"This country says it can't get rid of its rats, but they wiped out that big buffalo."

And deeper still:

"The only thing wrong with Rap Brown and Stokely Carmichael is that they dared to become as bitter as Patrick Henry.

"Remember when he said, 'Give me liberty or give me death'? He wasn't talking about singing no freedom songs to the British, Baby."

He hits his stride about an hour into the speech. That's when he gets to the real nitty-gritty. He talks about the white racist attitude that most Negroes are "dirty and greasy and will depreciate property."

149

"Sure we are, Baby," he says in fury and anguish. "But old mad Hitler, as crazy as he was, when he went down to look at the concentration camps and saw 50,000 Jews living in a place built for 500 people and smelled the stench, he wasn't insane enough to believe he was smelling Judaism.

"That was pure Naziism he was smelling, Baby, and he knew it.

"And when you go down to the ghetto to see all them stinking Niggers, that's not those colored folks you're smelling. That's Democracy."

HE SLASHES at what he calls the insanity of our society.

"L.B.J. goes before Congress and talks about crime in the streets and they applaud for five minutes. Are you out of your minds? L.B.J. talking about crime in the streets.

"L.B.J. went to Congress when he was 26 years old, a poor, humble Baptist schoolteacher—and now he's a multimillionaire. And you don't want to know where he got that money?

"If Bobby Baker worked for Adam Clayton Powell, both of them would be in jail by now."

While Gregory professes nonviolence as a personal code of conduct, he does not urge it on others.

"Two young men—Rap Brown and Stokely Carmichael—say 'Black Power' and the whole country gets scared.

"When Khrushchev said he was going to bury us, we didn't get scared and he had the missiles to do it. We said, 'Come on, Baby.'

"Stokely Carmichael doesn't have no missiles. Rap Brown hasn't even got a canoe.

"White folks think Negroes are going to be violent because deep down inside they know they should be."

BUT FOR ALL his rage, he never forgets to be funny. He expresses some regret at the success of the heart transplant operation in South Africa, in which the heart of a mulatto donor was given to a white man.

"The last thing in the world we want you white folks assuming," he says, "is that us black folks are going to supply you with spare parts."

The Beatle Beat

JOHN LENNON, the egghead Beatle, nearly created a world crisis with his recent suggestion that, in this lunatic world, the Beatles might be more popular than Jesus Christ.

The already shaky English pound threatened to disappear, the Vatican issued a position paper, several Southern radio stations considered seceding from rock 'n' roll and the group's manager came to the United States to explain things away.

It was said that Lennon offered his analysis as a deplorable fact, not as a cause for rejoicing—which seems reasonable.

The interesting thing is that there was a need to explain the statement. This is a phenomenon of modern mass communications.

In this day of instantaneous relay of information, let a Leo Durocher say "Nice guys finish last," or a Charles Wilson say "What's good for General Motors is good for the United States," and they are forced to spend the rest of their lives explaining what they REALLY meant.

150

IT WAS NOT always so. In previous centuries an important person could stick his foot in his mouth and by the time everyone heard about it and got mad, the guy had died of old age. No apologies.

It made for neater history.

What, however, would have been the result if famous people had been called to task immediately for their offhand remarks? They undoubtedly would have hired press agents who would have called press conferences soon after their clients had made immortal bloopers. And the press agents would have rendered them innocuous. Like this:

MARIE ANTOINETTE, on hearing that the people of France have no bread to eat, says "Let them eat cake." And her press agent says:

"First let me say that the queen had no idea the microphone was turned on when she made that remark the other day. More importantly, she had no intention of giving the impression that she lacked sympathy for the poor. Taken in context, her statement was merely a plea for a rise in the standard of living for her beloved countrymen. She further expressed confidence that, given continued prosperity under King Louis' ever-normal granary policy, it will come to pass."

ADOLF HITLER says, "Today, E u r o p e . Tomorrow, the world." And:

"The remark made by the Fuehrer yesterday in his press conference should not be interpreted as a desire for world conquest. The reference was to publication of his book, 'Mein Kampf,' which has been published throughout Europe. He is now negotiating with the Book-of-the-Month Club for worldwide distribution. In addition, there is a strong possibility that it will be condensed by the Reader's Digest and then be serialized as a comic strip for American and South American newspapers."

JOHN PAUL JONES says "We have not yet begun to fight," and the Defense Department says:

"Admiral Jones, in his recent statement, was not commenting on the defense posture of our nation nor was he attempting to cast doubt on our military preparedness. Lieutenant Commander Jones was speaking of a very specific and relatively unimportant engagement during which a retaliatory gap developed. This was closed almost immediately. Lieutenant (j.g.) Jones regrets having misled you."

P T. BARNUM says "There's a sucker born every minute." His press agent responds with:

"Mr. Barnum is understandably concerned over the interpretation placed on his remark the other day. He was not using 'sucker' in the idiomatic sense of simpleton or boob. Mr. Barnum never uses slang. He instead was referring to the ever-expanding lollipop market in this country, symbolic of an upturn in the economy."

KARL MARX says, "The ends justify the means." But:

"He was misquoted, gentlemen. It was a direct misquote. Mr. and Mrs. Marx were getting ready to go out to dinner and Mrs. Marx was having trouble getting her stockings straight. She tried and she tried to straighten them but without success. Finally, she asked her husband for help and he said, 'Wear a longer skirt and let the hem justify the seams.'"

Little-known facts—Pound for pound the most vicious animal on earth is the amoeba.

A Detroit
Liberal

IF PRESSED for my political orientation, I suppose I should have to admit to being a so-called liberal.

That is to say, when Barry Goldwater or Ronald Reagan says "the so-called liberals who . . .," the words that follow generally describe my heartfelt political convictions.

And when the Newark riot broke out a couple of weeks ago, I reacted as a so-called liberal should. I deplored the violence, at the same time recognizing that its seeds had been sown by racial injustice.

It was a comfortable position, allowing me to express concern over a regrettable situation without having to pay the price of personal involvement.

Then the Detroit riot broke out.

I WAS BORN and reared on the near west side of Detroit, on the fringes of the riot area, and my family lives there still. I called my parents as soon as I heard of the rioting Sunday and my mother informed me that THEY were at Weatherby and Warren avenue.

Weatherby and Warren! I crossed that intersection every Saturday of my boyhood on the way to the movies. The neighborhood five-and-ten was at Weatherby and Warren.

What right did THEY have there?

Technically, I suppose, THEY meant the rioters, but emotionally, I must confess, it meant Negroes. To hear the word "riot" these days is to summon the image of a Negro throwing a rock.

I felt resentment rising within me. What did THEY want anyway? How could THEY hope to profit by terrorizing my old neighborhood? I hoped that the governor would be able to do something about THEM before it was too late.

AND THEN it occurred to me that I was thinking like a a white racist, that I was being sucked up into the whirlwind of racial hatred that seems to be sweeping across the country.

I had, for a moment, allowed myself to begin thinking of Negroes as people all pretty much alike and as people quite different from me and mine. That's not the kind of thing a so-called liberal likes to find himself thinking. So I reconsidered the problem—dispassionately this time.

The fact is that there are more than 500,000 Negroes in Detroit. I haven't seen estimates on the numbers involved in the disorder but one would think that 10,000 persons could stage a hell of a riot. Ten thousand would be less than 2 per cent of the Negro population.

Moreover, a fact that is often lost sight of is that the chief victims of the Detroit riot and of all similar riots of recent years have been Negroes.

There has been a certain amount of "Kill Whitey" sentiment expressed, but it is the Negro who has suffered the heaviest casualties, who has had his home destroyed.

IF I FEAR for the safety of my parents on the fringe of the area, how much more would I fear were I a Negro whose parents lived in the heart of the ghetto, surrounded by random shooting and looting?

To say, as many have recently, that Negro rioters are hurting the cause of the Negro is as irrelevant as saying that the criminal activities of the Mafia are hurting the public image of Italian-Americans.

The point is that neither the Mafia nor the Negro rioter cares about causes or Negroes or Italian-Americans. They're out to get as much as they can from whomever they can.

Rioters, white or black, are largely hoodlums and punks. They riot not in protest but for the thrill of rioting, for the profit in it, because it makes them feel powerful.

No race or ethnic group is without its share of hoodlums and punks. It might be well for my fellow so-called liberals to remember that in the difficult and dangerous months ahead.

Two-Prices Crisis

THERE ARE certain aspects of the current world monetary crisis that I don't understand; I admit that.

The gold standard—that's one of the aspects I don't understand. Balance of payments—that's another. Also imports, exports, excise taxes, tariffs and free trade.

But when you get to the two-price system, that's another story. I am an expert in the two-price system.

The two-price system, you'll remember, is the gimmick the un-French free world used to head off an international gold rush several weeks ago.

It involved shutting off the open sale of the gold stores of cooperating nations, reserving them for intramural trading at $35 an ounce, while allowing the rest of the world's gold supply to be bought and sold at whatever price

the market set. Or maybe it was the other way around.

In any case, it was a two-price system and that's what I know about.

Every major purchase I have ever made involved two prices; the price I paid and the price some friend of mine would have paid for the same item.

I RECALL buying a television set, for example, one of those little Japanese-made portables. A friend came over to admire it and said: "That's a nice little set. How much did you pay for it?"

"A hundred and twenty dollars," I told him.

"Sure, that's the list price, but how much did you actually *pay?*

"A hundred and twenty dollars."

"You're joking! You paid list price for that television set? Hey, Mabel, guess who paid list for his television set?"

"Fan-TAS-tic," his wife shrieked from across the room.

"I happen to think it's worth $120," I said, as coldly as possible.

"That's not the point. The point is they put those list prices on merchandise as a come-on to suckers—so that they'll think they're getting a good deal when the price comes down a few bucks. They don't even expect the suckers to pay list."

I accepted the man at his word, and from that day onward I attempted to make the two-price system work for me, rather than against me.

I SHOPPED at discount houses, I stalked sales, I haggled. It was no use. No matter how little I paid for something, the first person I met after the purchase would inform me he could have got it for less.

I bought a $22.37 radio for $18.33, only to learn that the man across the street had a cousin who could have bought it for me for $12.44.

I waited until the last day of a closing out sale at a bankrupt appliance store to buy a refrigerator at what was described to me as "absolute cost." The very next day I saw an ad for the same model, being sold by another store at 10% less than I paid.

The crowning insult took place when I went to an after-Christmas sale at a men's clothing store and bought what was advertised as an $80 overcoat for $50. I liked the coat and none of my friends told me they could have gotten it for me cheaper. I was pleased.

Until the following year at the same store, during the after-Christmas sale, I saw the same coat on sale for $30.

Yes, I know about the two-price system.

The only thing I can't figure out is how the United States hopes to stop the outflow of gold with it.

Inevitable Tragedy

THEY SAY THAT a lone assassin pulled the trigger on Martin Luther King, jr.; a single white man, demented, sick. They say that every society has its demented individuals and that a society cannot be held responsible for their acts.

They said the same thing when John F. Kennedy was shot . . . and Medgar Evers . . . and James Meredith.

It would be comforting to believe that were so—but it is not.

Given the nature of our society, Martin Luther King's death—and its manner—can be viewed only as an inevitable tragedy, an event woven into the fabric of our national life.

ONE WONDERS only how he survived so long. The youngest man to win a Nobel Peace Prize is dead at 39.

That's our society.

A few hours after Dr. King's death Thursday, I received a call at my home. It was from two young men, high school students. They were obviously shaken by an incident they had just witnessed.

They had been in a bowling alley earlier that evening. It was ladies' night or something of the sort and the alley was crowded with about 75 women.

News that Dr. King had been shot in Memphis was general knowledge and some of the women sat talking of the event as they waited their turns.

Then the word came that Dr. King was dead. The proprietor announced the fact over the public address system—and 10 or 15 of the women burst into applause.

There they were, these women — housewives, m o t h e r s , members of clubs — and their immediate reaction to the death of a great man was one of glee.

That's our society.

Reports of similar occurrences filtered in throughout the evening, as they had five years before after the assassination of President Kennedy.

Technically, I suppose, one man (or two or three, the exact number is irrelevant) did kill Martin Luther King, jr.

154

But, in a larger sense, the killer was the agent of the forces of hatred that are set loose within our society. He was the elected representative of those 10 or 15 bowlers and of all persons who felt no pain or shame at the news of Dr. King's death.

HE WAS ELECTED by people who felt no loss at President Kennedy's assassination and, yes, by those who felt a lift in spirit at the news of George Lincoln Rockwell's murder and those who are gladdened by Lurleen Wallace's terrible illness.

And he shares his constituency with others, men like H. Rap Brown and Stokely Carmichael. For they, too, are elected representatives of our society, as surely as if we had ever pulled the lever opposite their names in a voting booth.

If the killer is a sick man, it is because we are a sick society; sick with hatred, sick with racism, black and white.

As long as a man can use the word "nigger" in public without fear of social ostracization, as long as businessmen can practice racism without feeling the lash of economic reprisal—not merely from blacks but from whites as well—as long as we allow politicians to play word games while our cities burn, we will remain a sick society.

And we cannot escape responsibility for our acts.

● ● ●

The Chicago Art Institute is presenting a photographic exhibit depicting the boot camp training of a U.S. Marine.

Only in Chicago would boot camp be considered art.

● ● ●

Faint
Praise

THE COMPLAINING cries coming from the Iowa National Guardsmen at Fort Carson, Colo., last week produced recollections of my own military career.

Oh yes, I did my little bit. I served in the U.S. Naval Reserve during the Korean War and after.

I'll never forget my first year in the service. The war wasn't going well in Korea; the winter was harsh, casualties high.

The hardships were made bearable only by the fact that I was attending a school for communications technicians in Chicago at the time.

That was the closest I ever got to Korea, but I'd rather not talk about it. I lost some good friends in the service. Three of them through court martial, one by lending him money.

Another time I lived through two hurricanes while aboard an attack transport off the coast of Virginia. I slept through them, as a matter of fact. Everybody did. In the Naval Reserve you did what was asked of you.

ADMITTEDLY, I did complain some, but I differed from Iowa's National Guardsmen in that I was never foolish enough to commit my complaints to writing.

I suppose you might call my military career an average one. It was not so glorious as that of Lyndon Johnson who, according to the World Almanac, was a lieutenant commander in the Naval Reserve in 1941-42, "winning the Silver Star for a flight over Japanese positions at New Guinea." (I've always wondered what they gave the pilot.)

But I was a bigger hero than Hubert Humphrey who, I am told, was deferred from service during World War II for physical defects that included a hernia and color blindness.

The most memorable portion of my naval service came, interestingly enough, when I was a student at the University of Michigan attending reserve meetings once a week.

Talk about hardships! They were two-and-a-half-hour meetings with only one coffee break.

Most of the members were graduate students and instructors in the math department, and they spent most of the training time trying to work out solutions to a game of three-dimensional tic-tac-toe they had invented.

It was a loose ship, but a happy ship.

THE ONLY TIME I can remember a n y o n e getting chewed out in public was once when the commander noticed that one of his enlisted men was wearing blue suede shoes with his dark winter uniform.

The seaman argued—persuasively, I thought—that he always wore blue suede shoes to reserve meetings and no one had objected to them before. He didn't own a pair of regulation black shoes, he said.

The "old man" was a real stickler for detail, however, and he made the sailor buy a pair.

It was that same sailor who gave our reserve unit its finest hour.

A ritual of our reserve meetings was "muster." That was when we'd all line up in rows in the hallway (Passageway, we called it) and wait for the executive officer to call out our names, at which time we'd yell

"yo" or "here, sir," depending on what they were yelling in John Wayne cavalry movies at the time.

One evening we were all standing there at attention, answering the roll call when we heard this crash, as though someone had fallen heavily to the floor.

As it turned out, someone had fallen heavily to the floor. The kid with the blue suede shoes had fainted—CRASH.

NOW ONE'S natural inclination in a situation like that is to go to the aid of the fainted party. You can never tell, it might be a heart attack.

But that's not the Navy way. We were at attention and we weren't supposed to move, no matter what.

The commander who, I suppose, had seen his share of John Wayne movies, too, went right on with the roll call just as though that sailor wasn't lying there in ranks.

After the inspection we carried the fallen sailor to the commander's office and revived him. He was all right.

But for weeks afterward we all carried our heads a little higher in the knowledge that we'd reacted in a military way to the only emergency that reserve unit would ever know.

• • •

SOME SAY it's part of the "See America First" movement. Others claim it owes more to the "See America Last" campaign.

But I say a driving vacation is something masochists take when they don't have enough money to hire someone to beat them up.

• • •

The Perils of Cape Horn

Sir Francis Chichester

AT A TIME when most of our national heroes are young men who earn enormous sums playing boys' games, England—*England* of all places—has given the world a hero worthy of the name: Sir Francis Chichester.

Chichester's feat of single-handedly sailing a 53-foot ketch around the world is truly an incredible one. It perhaps cannot be fully appreciated without some knowledge of the sea.

Certainly the dangers of sailing around Cape Horn at the tip of South America cannot be overestimated.

NO WRITER who has lived to tell of the experience has spoken of storms in those waters with anything but awe.

Charles Darwin, he of the theory of evolution, said, upon seeing the breakers beat against the shore near the cape in 1833:

"The sight . . . is enough to make a landsman dream for a week about death, peril and shipwreck."

Captain Felix Reisenberg was a Nineteenth Century mariner who wrote extensively about the sea. He said that he first rounded the cape in a sailing vessel as a seaman and his captain pointed it out to him and said:

"That's Cape Horn, Felix. Take a look at it. You may never see it again—if you were born lucky."

Here is how Reisenberg describes riding out a Cape Horn storm a few days later:

"The noise was so great that it numbed the ears. No one could shout and be heard; we were alone, wondering what might happen if a plank started or a hatch failed, for many tons of thundering water pounded the deck."

And he adds:

"Small wonder the surviving sailor holds a private measure of disdain for the landsman, the lubber, the fellow who never gets beyond call of Mother's dinner gong."

AND SMALL WONDER that Sir Francis said of the experience, "You'll only survive down there in a small boat by luck—just luck."

But perhaps Herman Melville—Melville the metaphysician—who first sailed around the Horn in 1843 as a seaman, has the final word on the matter. He writes:

"Sailor or landsman, there is some sort of a Cape Horn for all. Boys! Beware of it; prepare for it in time.

"Graybeards! Thank God it has passed. And ye lucky livers to whom, by some rare fatality, your Cape Horns are as placid as Lake Lemans, flatter not yourselves that good luck is judgment and discretion; for all the yolk in your eggs, you might have foundered and gone down had the Spirit of the Cape said the word."

It's Segregation
To the CORE

WORD CAME through the other day that the new constitution adopted by the Congress of Racial Equality (CORE) limits membership in the organization to Negroes; that is to say, it excludes whites.

Naturally, I was outraged. I quickly called a friend of mine—a Negro—who happens to be a member of CORE.

"I've just been banned from CORE and I want to know what you're going to do about it," I told him.

"I didn't know you were a member of CORE."

"I'm not, but I was thinking of joining. Until I was discriminated against. It's segregation, that's what it is."

"It looks like it."

"How would you blacks like it if we whites started excluding you from our civil rights organizations?"

"You mean like the Ku Klux Klan?"

"No, I mean like the N.A.A.C.P. Can I help it if my skin is white? How do I explain to my children that they can't join CORE because they're the wrong color?"

"I don't envy you that task."

WELL, WHAT are you going to do about it?"

"What do you expect me to do about it?"

"You could resign in protest."

"I don't see that that would serve any useful purpose. I think I'll keep my membership, and work from within to change policy."

"Ha! Just what I expected. All of you bleeding-heart moderates are alike, afraid to put your convictions where your mouth is."

"Now just a minute. What you seem to forget is that it takes time to change the hearts and minds of people. It doesn't happen overnight. It wasn't so long ago that your ancestors were painting themselves blue, you know."

"Racist!"

"That's going too far. Why I was practically raised by a white woman—our maid—and we thought of her as one of the family."

"Yeah, sure; I know. Some of your best friends are white folk. But you continue to live in the black ghetto and send your kid to a racially segregated school, don't you?"

"I bought that house because it overlooks the urban renewal area and my kids go to their school because it's the only one within walking distance."

YOU COULD bus them into a white district, couldn't you?"

"I don't believe in busing, on philosophical grounds."

"You're a hypocrite. I'd rather deal with a Black Nationalist any time. At least with those guys you know where you stand."

"Is this what it's come to, then? A lifetime of being called raghead and Uncle Tom by black militants, and now this?"

"I'm sorry, I lost my head."

"That's all right. We all say things we don't mean occasionally. Look, why don't you come over for dinner Friday and we'll let bygones be bygones."

"Great. What's on the menu, fried chicken with gravy and greens?"

"Let's keep politics out of it shall we? We'll have lobster Newburg."

Pipe Dream

KANSAS CITY pipefitters got a raise the other day; a raise that, in three years, will bring their pay rate to $9.18 an hour in wages and fringe benefits.

Let's hear it for the Kansas City pipefitters. Too long have they been ill-clothed, ill-housed and ill-fed. It's about time they were paid a living wage.

It would be fascinating to go back 35 years into the young manhood of one of those pipefitters, to the time when he chose his career.

A young man carrying a suitcase walks down a Midwestern street, past a man selling apples. He climbs the stairs to a weather-beaten frame house and enters without knocking.

"Hi, Mom, I'm home," he says. His mother comes out of the kitchen, wiping her hands on her apron. "Georgie," she says, "what are you doing home so early? I thought Harvard didn't let out for two weeks yet."

"It doesn't. I've quit school, Mom."

"Quit school! Two weeks from graduation and you quit school? Georgie, you're not in any kind of trouble are you?"

"No, it's just that I've found something I'd rather be than a Harvard man."

"What?"

"A pipefitter."

"A pipefitter?"

"YES. I began to get interested in it last fall. We had a crew of plumbers working in the dorm, fixing a water basin, and they had a piece of pipe that was too long. One of them let me use his cutter and I cut three-quarters of an inch off one end. When I saw that pipe fit right in where it was supposed to go, I knew right then what I wanted to do with the rest of my life."

"This will kill your father; you know that."

"Mom, be reasonable."

"Be reasonable, he says. Your father and I scrimp and save to get enough money to send you to Harvard, and you quit two weeks before graduation and tell us to be reasonable."

"You don't understand the thrill of taking a length of pipe that won't fit anything and making something useful out of it."

"Thrills! That's all you young people think about is thrills. Can you feed a family on thrills? How much can a pipefitter make?"

"Gee, you mean they actually pay you for fitting pipe? I thought I'd have to do it for nothing."

"GEORGIE, WE had hopes for you—dreams. Your father wanted you to grow up to be a professional man; a social worker maybe, or a high school teacher. Something that pays."

"Money isn't everything, Mom. Look at Dad. He went into fruit peddling for the money and he hates it."

"But you never lacked for Vitamin C."

"A man has to do what he has to do, Mom. My mind is made up."

"But what about your wonderful education? Four years at Harvard. Are you going to throw that down the drain?"

"It's not down the drain, exactly. A lot of it will come in handy when I'm a pipefitter."

"How?"

"Well, I took a course in labor economics last semester. That shouldn't do me any harm."

Being enchanted with the idea of "Gentle Thursday," which was conducted at Iowa State University Friday, I decided to try it myself. The idea of Gentle Thursday was to "engage in much handholding and smiling to break down barriers between people."

So I went out on the streets of Des Moines and beamed at people and held girls' hands and was beaten to a pulp three times. Next time they should hold it on a Wednesday.

Americans Not Gentle

AND YET AGAIN we have lived through a weekend of national mourning; endured the sight of a widow at the grave of her slain husband, of fatherless children dazed by an event they cannot fully comprehend. And yet again we ask, what does it mean? What is happening to us, as a nation?

Those seeking to find meaning in the death of Senator Robert Kennedy have tended to find what they chose to look for.

Proponents of stricter gun laws have seen in the killing a need for stricter gun laws. For opponents of the war in Vietnam, it was a demonstration of that war's corrosive influence; to believers in the sanctity of law and order, a need for more punitive law enforcement.

One Iowa Republican leader even saw in it a need to elect more Republicans, although it must be said that such political opportunism, at such a time, beggars the imagination.

It is difficult to come to terms with Senator Kennedy's death, particularly for one who was most critical of him in life. Previous criticisms of the man, however honest, now seem mean-spirited —certainly unworthy of repetition.

IN THE SHADOW of so cruel and unjust a fate, it is the positive qualities of the man—his compassion for the underdog, his intelligence, his vitality — that stand out most clearly.

One's first inclination in trying to make sense of the tragedy is to find parallels between the senator's death and that of Martin Luther King, jr., and draw similar conclusions from them.

But while there are striking similarities in the deaths, there are also differences—crucial differences.

Dr. King, as nearly as we know, was killed by a racist, the product of a racist society. To the degree that we shape that society, we are involved in his death.

Senator Kennedy, on the other hand, appears to have been the victim of a product of an alien society, motivated by reasons that have little to do with the forces that are tearing our nation apart.

And so one is tempted to agree with President Johnson's statement that 200 million Americans did not strike down Senator Kennedy. One is tempted, but not persuaded.

If the assassination of Senator Kennedy was the work of a single man, if it was an isolated incident of madness, unrelated to our society, then why form a presidential commission to study our violence?

Why not just pay due respect to the memory of a brilliant man —for Kennedy was that—and go on about our business?

ERIC HOFFER, the longshore-man-philosopher and a member of the president's commission, made an impassioned statement in the wake of the assassination, protesting against the idea that we are a violent people. We Americans are a gentle people, he said.

Why then, the commission?

The answer, of course, is that Hoffer's contention is absurd. It is made grimly ludicrous by the scene at the airport when the senator's body was brought back to New York.

Disembarking from the plane were the widow of the murdered Senator Kennedy, the widow of the murdered President Kennedy, the widow of the murdered Martin Luther King, jr., and the brother of the murdered civil rights leader, Medgar Evers.

A gentle people?

Does a gentle people buy out its gun shops, arming for interracial war?

Does a gentle people indulge in an orgy of vicariously experienced violence in its books, its films, its television shows?

Does a gentle people burn down areas of its cities?

Can a people, any people, fight three nightmarish wars in 25 years and expect to remain untouched by their unspeakable brutality?

Apparently so, but only at the cost of appalling self-deception.

Senator Kennedy's assassin may or may not have been formed by our society, but most assuredly he committed his crime in its atmosphere, an atmosphere characterized by a rising level of anarchy and violence.

I do not know the meaning of Senator Kennedy's death, or even if it has a meaning, but this I know:

We Americans are not a gentle people.

The Firing of
A Saint

THE ROMAN Catholic Church dumped 30 saints from its calendar of Official Feast Days a couple of weeks ago, which couldn't have been the easiest thing in the world to do.

I mean, how do you fire a saint?

The most notable of the deletions was Saint Christopher, patron of travelers. Vatican officials questioned whether he had ever actually existed.

Which must have caused a good deal of consternation in the Upper Reaches of the heavens. One can imagine the Relevant Authority calling Saint Christopher into His office and saying:

"Come in, Christopher. Sit down, I'll be with you in a minute."

HE WORKS at his desk for a few moments, then continues:

"Sorry to keep you waiting. Had to fill out these requisition forms for some electrically amplified harps. It sounds like a lot of noise to me but the young people seem to like them. Christopher, how long have you been with us?"

"It'll be 16 centuries next April, sir."

"And you've been patron saint of travelers all that time."

"Pretty much, yes, sir."

"And you've done a good job for us, too. . . ."

"Thank you, sir."

". . . until recently."

"Sir?"

"There's no sense kidding

ourselves, Christopher. Your work has not been up to par lately."

"I've been doing my best."

"I know that, but times change. We have to change with them. Your performance record has been going down ever since the invention of the automobile; not to mention the flying machine."

"I DON'T WANT to seem to be making excuses, sir, but the competition is getting a lot more help than it used to. Look what I've got to contend with — jet planes with inadequate airport facilities, 350-horsepower family cars, double-bottomed trucks, trains carrying mustard gas and now they're even talking about a supersonic transport."

"That's just the point. You can't be an effective patron saint of jet-age travelers when you have an ox cart philosophy of travel safety."

"I'm only a saint, sir, and my division is badly understaffed."

"You said that the last time I spoke to you. That's why I gave you Ralph Nader as a helper."

"Yes, but the other side turned right around and gave me John Volpe as secretary of transportation of the United States, don't forget that."

"I KNOW, I know. It hasn't been easy. Still, I have to judge performance on results, and accident rates of travelers have been skyrocketing over the past few centuries. They don't know you down there anymore. Christopher, I'm afraid we're going to have to let you go."

"What! After all these years you're going to turn me out? Sir, you can't eat the orange and throw away the peel. A saint is not a piece of fruit."

"I think you need a good long rest. Perhaps when you're feeling better we can find a place for you here in the Home Office; a desk job."

"But I've always been a field man."

"I know. This isn't an easy thing for me to do. The thing most people don't understand is that there's no rock bottom to being a patron saint.

"He's the saint way out there in the blue, riding on a prayer. When he gets a couple of spots on his halo, that's a catastrophe. And when they stop believing in his existence—he's through."

"That's your final word, then."

"I'm afraid it is."

"All right. But I don't know how I'm going to break this to Gina Lollobrigida."

A Shortage Of Slums

THEY SAY that necessity is the mother of invention and inspiration its father.

Nowhere is this more forcefully demonstrated than in the recent case of Charles Blitzer, director of education and training at the Smithsonian Institution in Washington, D.C.

Blitzer was sitting around, trying to think up ways of improving the program of the museum, sometimes called "the nation's attic," when it occurred to him that middle-class America is losing touch with an important aspect of its cultural heritage — slums.

What with the War on Poverty and urban renewal, he reasoned, young people today don't have the opportunity to experience the slum conditions that were common to preceding generations.

Then it hit Blitzer. Why not set up a slum as a Smithsonian exhibit? Go out and buy a slum building, dismantle it and install it in the museum, complete with smells, sounds, filth and rats. Why not indeed?

Blitzer admits that the idea is still in the talking stage but he expects to go out shopping for a potential exhibit soon.

CAN YOU imagine how things will go at the realtor's office?

"Good afternoon, sir, what can I do for you?"

"I'd like to see what you've got in slums."

"Ha, ha. I like you Old Left people; always joking. You're a fun group. I have a 17-room cottage in Chevy Chase that you might be interested in."

"You don't understand. I really want a slum."

"I see; the old redecorating bug bit you, eh? Well, here's something in Georgetown that's quite run down. A real challenge for . . ."

"Not run down. A slum. I want a slum."

"Oh. How big a slum did you have in mind?"

"Fourteen stories."

"You have a large family?"

"I'm not going to live in it."

"YOU'RE BUYING it for a friend then; I should have known. Let me take another look in our files. Uh huh, here's a lovely tenement that might interest you. Until recently it was owned by a religious organization whose communication with its tenants was almost exclusively through legal documents."

"It doesn't look too bad."

"That black-and-white photo doesn't do it justice. In color it's really ghastly."

"The elevator doesn't work, I suppose."

"Not since 1932."

"And the stairs are in bad repair."

"After dark, not even Batman and Robin would use them."

"Heating bad?"

"Only during the winter."

"And the plumbing?"

"I'm sorry about that."

"Oh?"

"ABOUT THREE years ago the health department cracked down and made the owner install all new plumbing."

"That's too bad."

"You can't expect to find your dream slum at the price you're willing to pay, you know. You're going to have to compromise and take a little good with the bad."

"I know, but plumbing's such an important item."

"We could take hammers and bang it a little before you took possession."

"I wouldn't feel right about it. I would be cheating, don't you see?"

"Right. Well, that about exhausts our slum supply. With the stock market as uncertain as it is these days good slums aren't easy to find."

"I appreciate that, but I wish you'd keep me in mind if you run across an exceptional piece of condemned property."

"Don't worry, sir. You'll be the first to know."

• • •

THE SECOND most amusing story of the week dealt with the results of the recent sex survey entitled "On Sexual Life in Sweden."

The survey discovered that nearly half of Sweden's brides are pregnant at the time of their marriage, and the report went on to call Sweden "the contraceptive society."

I mean, with statistics like that the most you could call them would be "the semi-contraceptive society."

• • •

163

Biggest Drag:
Unhip Adults

A THIRTYISH Des Moines man awoke in the middle of the night last week with a question exploding in his brain:

What is young America thinking?

He decided to find out. The next day he went out and bought a pair of checked Carnaby street slacks, a wide leather belt, a flowered shirt with French cuffs, a Ringo Starr cap and a pair of flamenco dancer boots.

He put them on, smiled at himself in the mirror and went straight to Teen Town at the Iowa State Fair. A dance was in progress when he got there.

He walked up to a neatly dressed young man and said:

"Where is it happening at, baby?"

"Pardon me?" the young man answered.

"Would you believe, at where is it happening?"

"Are you sure you're not looking for the Lawrence Welk show, sir?"

"Welk? That square? I came to make the scene, man. The Beatles. Bobby Dylan. Kicks. That's my bag. You know; fab, gear, that sort of thing."

"WE DON'T HAVE any detergents here, but we do have a car with gears. Over there."

The man winked broadly. "I get it. You're putting me on. Cool it, I'm hip. I'm on your side; dig?"

"I'm afraid not, sir. What exactly is it that you want?"

"I want to find out about your hangups."

"Hangups?"

"Yeah. You know, what's bugging kids these days? Are you still worried over the mess the older generation has put the world in? Has the H-bomb got you all shook up? Does the draft turn you off?" He threw a quick look over his shoulder and lowered his voice. *"What about LSD?"*

"Isn't that some sort of federal agency?"

The man decided that he'd fallen in with the wrong sort of teen-ager so he said, "Later, man," and went in search of a more typical youth.

HE MOVED OVER to a group of young men dressed like foppish London dock hands. "How you hitting 'em, baby?" he drawled.

One of the boys looked up and said, "Another one."

"Huh?"

"You want to know what the younger generation is thinking, right?"

"Why yes, but how did you know?"

"You're the third Senior Citizen this week who's come around wanting to know the same thing. There must be a sociologists' convention in town or something."

"Well, what about it?"

"Sit down and I'll tell it to you the way it is. The biggest drag kids face today is adults who want to be kids."

"What do you mean?"

"I understand that way back in the 1950s adults had their gigs, the kids had theirs and never the twain met. I mean,

old people dressed old and they had their own music and dances and pretty much left the kids alone."

"That's more or less true."

IT'S NOT THAT way anymore. As soon as kids today think up a new dance or find a new sound or something, the adults jump in and take over. For example, the other day I went over to my girl's house and her mother was wearing a mini-skirt. Her mother, for crying out loud. The dame must be 37 or 38 at least."

"That's too old, huh?"

"It's embarrassing. A middle-aged woman shouldn't be doing the Monkey and Watusi, it doesn't look right. It's like me copying my 8-year-old brother. It used to be that when a kid got older and got tired of teen dances and clothes styles and music, he could step up into the adult world. It sort of gave him something to look forward to. That's all gone now."

"Don't you feel, though, that this sort of thing helps your parents understand you better?"

"Naw. If they understood us, they'd leave us alone. A kid doesn't want his parents to be pals. He's got plenty of pals. He wants them to be parents."

The Phrases of Mize

PARKER MIZE retired last week. He was the "assistant managing editor of The Des Moines Tribune"; he ran the paper.

I worked for him for a couple years when I first came to Des Moines and, although my spelling kept us from becoming close, I shall never forget him.

Bud Mize is the most brilliant phrase-maker I have ever met or ever hope to meet. He has what amounts to a genius for vivid expression.

He'd preface a tentative thought by saying:

"I'm not binding this idea to my breast with hoops of steel."

And when someone came to him with a go or no-go problem, he'd be apt to say:

"Well, why don't you just wade out into the cold water belly-deep and see how it feels?"

HE WOULD disapprove of a column like this, because he felt that the people who put out a paper should not appear in the paper, except as births, deaths and OMVIs. The Tribune was his obsession and when he came to work each morning, he would roll his sleeves high on his arms, as if preparing to engage in physical combat with the day's news.

And most days he just about had to. He'd look at a 60-page Thanksgiving paper that had to be filled by the next day and say:

"It's like feeding a 12-year-old boy on a hunting trip."

Or, looking at page one after a particularly hectic day:

"That's put together like a backward boy's tree house."

HE WAS a newspaperman of the old school and had most definite ideas of what should and should not be done to readers.

Once, reading a rival publication, he was forced to turn to page 48 to continue a story that had begun back on page 64.

"It's like making a seven with two threes and a one," he said, with righteous crapshooter's indignation.

Sloppy headline writing was particularly offensive to him. On seeing the word "DynaSoar" in a headline, he said:

"You can't tell whether it's a space capsule, an animal or a nightclub at Carter Lake."

This was his philosophy on headline writing:

"We want to leave some veils on Salome, but not so many that they can't be seen through."

On being handed a story that you had to read and read before discovering its theme, he would say, accusingly:

"You don't have to go to the back of the cave to feel the dragon's hot breath."

THE REMARKABLE thing about these phrases is that they never gave any suggestion of having been shaped by their author. They sprang from his lips almost as though they had a life of their own.

One time he spotted a colleague across the newsroom with a telephone at each ear. "Looks like a bigamist calling home for the weekend," he said.

Bud dabbled in the stock market and he expressed a preference for stocks that paid dividends.

"I don't like these cows that never get into the milking stanchion," was the way he put it.

As an editor, he was a man of almost puritanical sensibilities. He never embraced the idea that four-letter words had any place in public print, and a film like "Midnight Cowboy" could truly shock him. But he was no prude. One of his timeless quotes was uttered upon hearing of a new scheme to automate bartending.

"I hope that I shall never see a martini made by machinery," he said.

He was a hell of a newspaperman. There! That probably will ruin his whole day.

Famished Is Fashionable

THE BIGGEST news in women's fashions these days is something called "Twiggy." Usually reliable sources say it is a girl, a 17-year-old girl.

With Twiggy it's a little hard to be sure, because she is somewhat on the slim side. She looks like Anita Ekberg after a famine. Make that two famines.

She is so skinny that, next to her, Audrey Hepburn looks like a Las Vegas chorine. As a matter of fact, next to Twiggy, Bob Hope looks like a Las Vegas chorine.

IN A WELL-ordered society, a girl like Twiggy, who seems like a nice sort, would be sent to a hospital to be fattened up.

In our society she has become the top fashion model of the western world. This means that fashion designers are designing clothes that look good on figures like Twiggy's.

Unfortunately (or fortunately, depending on your outlook), most figures like Twiggy's belong to 12-year-old boys, who have an understandable antipathy toward high fashion.

The woman who is cursed with all of the standard womanly equipment—hips, bosom, shapely legs, etc.—has to try to transform herself into a reasonable facsimile of Twiggy if she wants to be in style this season.

HERE IS HOW she might go about it. Naturally, she consults her physician.

"Doctor," she says, "I'd like you to help me with my weight problem."

"You mean you're having trouble lifting things? When did you first notice the onset of symptoms?"

"No, you don't understand. I want to lose weight."

"How much?"

"Sixty pounds."

"Oh. Which leg would you like me to cut off first?"

"Is that necessary?"

"How else do you expect to lose 60 pounds: you only weigh 120 now. Why do you want to lose that much weight anyway? Does your husband have a broom fetish?"

"No. It's my dressmaker. He says that unless I lose 60 pounds I won't be able to wear any of his new clothes."

"Who's your dressmaker — Adolf Hitler?"

"No. He owns the local Twiggy dress franchise."

"He sounds more as though he's the local franchise holder of Malnutrition Institute of America. What are your measurements, anyway?"

"38–22–36"

"And that's bad, huh?"

"Disastrous."

"What should measurements be to look good in a Twiggy dress?"

"24–24–24."

"Those aren't measurements,

Twiggy
24-24-24

they're a bad stutter. Look, I'll put you on a diet if that's what you want, but short of getting a terminal case of tapeworm, you're not going to lose 60 pounds."

"WELL, DO the best you can, doctor. And if you could give me something to help my 12-year-old daughter's appetite, I'd appreciate it."

"Why, what's wrong with her appetite?"

"For breakfast she has a half a slice of dry toast and a cup of coffee. For lunch a whole slice of dry toast, some cottage cheese and a bottle of soft drink. For dinner she has a slice of dry toast, one stewed prune and a glass of water."

"I can see why you're concerned."

"Certainly. Is it normal for a girl her age to stuff herself with dry toast all day?"

Motherhood Is Dead

AMERICAN motherhood, as we once knew it, is dead. No longer is the American woman content to limit her horizons to the nursery and kitchen stove. The modern woman is a vital, vibrant creature who has achieved social equality and, in many cases, professional equality with her husband.

Yet there are those who question whether she has found real happiness in her emancipation. These critics suggest that she suffered less anxiety and led a truly richer life when her role was limited to that of housekeeper, cook and governess.

To help shed light on this complex and controversial matter, Over the Coffee called on Professor Otto von Helper, famed scholar of the Isle of Corfu. Dr. von Helper is the author of the classic study on women, "I Wonder What She Meant by That," and is internationally recognized as an expert womanizer.

Following is a partial transcript of an interview with the great man:

Q. How long have you been a student of women, doctor?

A. Ever since I found out they weren't just soft boys.

Q. Would you say that, in recent years, women have achieved relative equality with men?

A. Very definitely.

Q. And how has this equality manifested itself?

A. In the increasingly important role women have carved out for themselves in society. When I was a boy a woman was a wife and mother, little else. Today a typical woman will be a wage earner, an active participant in community affairs and the financial manager of the household, as well as filling her traditional roles of wife and mother.

Q. Do you feel that this increased responsibility has been a liberating factor?

A. Certainly. It has liberated the American man to play golf.

Q. How does the modern woman differ from her Victorian predecessor in terms of sexual behavior and attitudes?

A. *The Victorian woman was much better at keeping a secret.*

Q. What is your opinion of the latest women's fashions; the mini-skirt, for example?

A. There is nothing wrong with it but it should not be worn by women past a certain age.

Q. What age is that?

A. Six and a half.

Q. Do you find any social significance in the popularity of the mini-skirt?

A. Yes. I find it a very strong indication that boys like girls.

Q. Many have called the girls portrayed in the center foldout of Playboy magazine the living symbols of modern American womanhood, serving much the same function as the Gibson girls of another era. Would you agree?

A. I really couldn't say. I get Playboy magazine but I never look at the pictures. I just read the articles and stories and throw the issue away.

168

Q. Oh. Who's your favorite author?

A. Miss November.

Q. Do you find merit in the argument that the modern woman is unhappy in her freedom, that she would be better off back up on her pedestal?

A. To a degree, yes. I think it is unrealistic to expect a woman to play a full masculine and a full feminine role in our society. I think she would be happier and society would function more efficiently if we could lighten her load of responsibility.

Q. If you had just one responsibility to rid her of, which one would it be?

A. Voting.

On Holding
The Bag

I WAS SITTING at my desk the other day, wondering what ever became of Butch Jenkins, when a friend came up and said: "Hey, have you heard about the new manbags?"

"You mean the purses for men?" I replied. "Yeah I've heard of them. Pretty funny."

"What do you mean, funny?"

"Well, the idea that men would carry around hand and shoulder bags, like women, is fairly ridiculous, isn't it? I mean, what do those designers think we are, a bunch of sissies?"

"I had expected a more enlightened view from you."

"Are you trying to tell me that you're *in favor* of men carrying purses?"

"Of course I am. It's a great idea; it's got all kinds of advantages."

"Like what?"

"Did you ever try to fend off an assailant with a wallet?"

"Okay, but if men started carrying purses, your assailant would probably have one, too."

A ND THEN there's the problem of finding things. Whenever a man is trying to find a nickel, for example, he digs around in all of his pockets until he finally jabs the point of a pencil under his fingernail. Manbags would do away with infected fingers."

"I'm a fast healer and I say they're for sissies."

"Nonsense. Why, in the Eighteenth Century, gentlemen wore powdered wigs and no one thought of them as effeminate."

"Then how come Errol Flynn always beat the wigged guys in sword-fighting?"

"I see I am casting my pearls of wisdom before a swinish sensibility," said my friend, flouncing off.

I GOT TO thinking about it, though; if this manbag thing catches on, it's going to make for some pretty weird situations. Take, for example, a wife getting ready to go to the store.

"Dear," she yells at her husband from the back door, "where are the keys to the car?"

"In my purse," he yells back.

"The brown one?"

"No, the electric blue one. I wore my linen suit yesterday . . . Find it?"

"I've got the purse but no keys. Look at this mess you've got here

169

—so far I've found a credit card, three cigars, a packet of golf tees, a deck of playing cards, last Wednesday's paper, a ham and cheese on rye, a compass, a Win With Stassen button, a feather with a fish hook on it and three gum drops with lint sticking to them—I don't understand why you men can't keep your purses neat."

"Hey, bring me the feather with the fish hook. I've been looking for that."

"But where are the keys?"

"I don't know; look in my fishing creel, why don't you?"

OR, FOR another example, a boy talking to his father: "Hey, Dad, Billy stole my purse."

"Did you do anything about it?"

"Sure, I cried a lot."

"That's all? A kid steals your purse and all you do is cry? When I was your age if someone stole my purse, I'd have belted the kid."

"Yeah, but you went to an all-girl school. Besides, it wasn't my fault."

"What do you mean?"

"I started to hit him but he broke my necklace and while I was picking up the beads, he ran away."

The future looks gloomier every minute.

• • •

HOLLYWOOD FACTS: Ross Hunter is perhaps best known as the movie producer who made Doris Day a virgin.

• • •

Paper Husband

THE FREE spirit of American manhood lost its most glittering symbol last week. George Plimpton got married.

Plimpton has made a career of acting out the fantasy life of the American male.

A man of no particular athletic ability, he has tried out for quarterback with the Detroit L i o n s, an experience which produced the best-selling book, "Paper Lion."

He has pitched an inning of baseball against a team of major league all-stars and played in a big-time golf tournament, writing of both experiences amusingly.

He has performed as a percussionist—amateur, of course—with the New York Philharmonic. They made a television show out of that.

He has done, in short, just about everything a red-blooded American man watches professionals do on weekends, and dreams of doing himself.

Plimpton has been miserably inept at all of his adventures which, of course, is the whole point. It is doubtful whether we armchair amateurs could have forgiven him had he been able to succeed in fields where excellence is reserved to dedicated professionals, but we were glad to have him out there representing us.

THAT PHASE of his life is now over. He probably doesn't know it yet, but it is. Acting out masculine fantasies and being married are not compatible activities.

The first thing that will happen is that his wife will suggest that they move out of his

swank Manhattan apartment to a house in the suburbs, 40 minutes from Broadway—by plane.

Then, one day soon, he'll get up on a Sunday morning and say:

"I think I'll go into the city today, Honey."

And his wife will reply: "Why?"

"Oh, Alex Karras and a few of the guys are in town and I thought we might go over to Central Park and play a little touch football."

"George, when are you going to grow up? Touch football, honestly."

"What's wrong with touch football?"

"All of this time you spend playing boys' games, pretending you're an athlete. Don't you think you're getting a little old for that sort of thing?"

"I'm only 40. Besides, I never felt better in my life."

"But it's so embarrassing, seeing you making a fool of yourself."

"I'm not making a fool out of myself; I'm having fun. You knew I was like this when you married me, you said it gave me a kind of boyish charm."

"And it does, dear. It's just that I can't stand to see you humiliated."

"I'M NOT humiliated."

"Then why do all of your friends laugh at you behind your back?"

"My friends laugh at me behind my back?"

"I'm afraid so. Just the other night I overheard Art Buchwald telling Truman Capote you can't go to your left the way you used to."

"Art Buchwald said that?"

"Yes, and Capote said that you never could."

"If Truman Capote ever lost his caterer he'd be a nothing."

"Perhaps, dear, but all the same I wish you'd give up these silly games. Why give them the satisfaction of making you the butt of their cruel jokes?"

"But I'm committed to running in the Olympic marathon for the United States at Mexico City."

"Hasn't President Johnson got enough troubles?"

"I never thought of it that way. Maybe you're right. Gee, somehow I don't feel like playing touch football today. I'll call up Alex and tell him to count me out."

"I think that's wise, love. And, as long as you're up, why don't you take out the garbage?"

The Barbs of Saul Alinsky

SAUL ALINSKY is a troublemaker.

He has made a career of washing dirty linen in public, discussing politics and religion at the dinner table and turning away soft words with wrath.

His idea of togetherness is an economic boycott.

For more than 20 years, Alinsky worked primarily in the Chicago area, organizing the poor into politically effective groups. Recently he has branched out into other areas of the country.

Like Cedar Rapids.

He recently gave a lecture at Coe College in Cedar Rapids in which he called the community "smug and segregated," among other things.

He spoke and answered questions for a couple of hours, giving everyone in sight a pretty good working over. Then, at 9:30 p.m., just in case there was someone present whom he had not yet offended, he looked at his watch and said:

"I've done many things in my life for which I deserve to be punished. But I've never done anything that would cause me to deserve spending a whole night in Cedar Rapids. I'm leaving so I can catch that damn plane."

ALINSKY is an expert at leaving towns unfriendly to him. He told this story in private conversation:

He found himself in a small Texas town, confronted by a gang of Ku Klux Klansmen. They did not seem to want his autograph.

They were closing in on him, meaning no good, when Alinsky pointed to the leader (who was wearing a sheet but no mask) and said:

"I studied anthropology in college and have become an expert on the races of man. And I tell you this man is a Negro!"

While the Klansmen were clustering around their leader, studying his features, Alinsky made his escape.

That's Alinsky's story, anyway.

Remember the story about Dean Martin paying his lady love emeritus $500,000 to go fly a kite? How will he treat that expenditure on his income tax return?

In any case, to quote an ancient Japanese proverb: "Desire exacts its cost, but $500,000 is a lot of yen."

Stop me before I kill.

More Men's Toiletries

LIPSTICK for men is just around the corner. A leading manufacturer of men's toiletries announced that it will go on the market in May.

It will be called a "lip conditioner stick." The firm, Zizanie de Fragonard, says that it's part of a trend that has seen men begin to use cologne and hair spray and lay out $25 for a haircut.

Well . . . maybe. In any case, the most interesting aspect of the phenomenon is sure to be the television commercials they devise to peddle the stuff. Here's a preview of what they'll probably be like:

AN ENORMOUS semi-trailer truck is seen rolling into a truck stop. The driver, a beefy, rough-looking man with an unshaven appearance, addresses the camera with, "Hey you! You want a real he-man lipstick? Try 'Autowreck' by Virile Brothers; it's da brand used by tree out of four over-da-road truckers. We meet a lot of pretty waitresses in our job and, believe you me, we have to look our best at all times. Take my advice. Try 'Autowreck.' You won't regret it."

WE SEE an undernourished young man playing catch with several beautiful girls at a beach. One of the girls throws the ball past him and he runs toward the camera to retrieve it. He picks up the ball, looks at the camera and says, "Would you believe that I was once a 98-pound weakling and that bullies used to kick sand in my face and girls laughed at me? Then I started using 'Bullfight,' the man's lipstick made by Phermia, Inc. Suddenly girls began to flock to me. I became the most popular fellow on the beach. I'm still a 98-pound weakling but now when bullies kick sand in my face I hit them with my purse."

A SINCERE-LOOKING young man stands in the foreground. Behind him are two men, identical twins, and a pretty girl. The sincere one says, "Here is scientific proof that 'Pheasant Hunt,' by Jodphur, is the most effective men's lipstick on the market today. Watch as our model kisses Burt who is wearing Brand X. See there . . . she is staggering away and going 'Ptuie' on the sidewalk. Look now as she kisses Burt's twin brother Bart, who is wearing new, improved 'Pheasant Hunt.' Notice how much longer a 'Pheasant Hunt' kiss lasts. AND there are no unpleasant afterthoughts."

A FAMOUS football star is shown playing catch with a boy of about high school age. He gives the lad a few pointers and we switch to the locker room. They have showered and combed their hair and are now putting on their makeup. The athlete looks at the boy applying his lipstick and says, "Say! Are you still using that greasy kid stuff? Let me show you something. Kiss that mirror." The boy does so, leaving a big smear. "Now watch this," the athlete says. He kisses the mirror and leaves no mark. "See? Here, start using my brand, 'Red Dog,' by Super-Colossal, Ltd."

W E SEE a weather-beaten old farmer standing in front of his barn. He says, "I got to admit that I was a little leery about trying out the lipstick when I first heard about it. I was afraid the chickens would laugh me out of the hen house, not to mention what the fellows at the feed store would do. Well sir, my wife kept after me about it so until I tried it and now, let me tell you, I wouldn't be without it. My cows have been giving 25 per cent more milk ever since I started wearing 'Sheep Dip' by Barnyard."

A ND FINALLY, a man with the look of a tired basset comes on the screen and says, "Fellow Americans. Less than a year ago I looked at a picture of myself and said, 'That's the ugliest thing I ever saw.' Then friends and neighbors persuaded me to try a man's lipstick, 'Patriotism' by Jingo Cosmetics. I did and the next time I looked at a picture of myself I said, 'It's beautiful.' "

Workings of An Idle Mind

T HIS IS A true story; it really happened and I can prove it.

Three gentlemen were about to take their daily coffee-break at a diner in downtown Des Moines.

As they reached the door an elderly woman—a little old lady, as a matter of fact—came into view. She dragged behind her a heavily laden shopping cart and she obviously was headed for the diner.

The first man said, "Here let me help you with that," and he opened the diner door and helped guide the cart.

The second man said, "I'll get the other door for you," and he ushered her into the place.

The third man said, "Let me get that out of the way for you," and he parked the shopping cart for her.

They all sat down at the counter and the waitress came up and said, "What'll it be this morning, fellows?"

And the little old lady said:

"I was here first, Miss."

I can prove it.

Beauty Only
Year Deep

YOU CAN imagine my surprise when I turned to the women's page of the newspaper the other day and found out that many, if not most, women are walking around with last year's face.

I had noticed that a good many of them looked familiar to me but I hadn't been able to analyze it until I ran across that article about Estee Lauder.

Mrs. Lauder is a cosmetics manufacturer in New York and she has the real lowdown on this year's face versus last year's face and vice versa.

Of the current style in faces, she said:

"This year a lady's eyes do not precede her into a room."

I WAS standing on the Locust Street bridge, mulling that over, when a young lady near me climbed up on the railing and made as if she were going to jump into the churning water of the Des Moines River below.

"Here," I shouted. "You can't do that." And I pulled her back to the relative safety of the sidewalk. She was sobbing uncontrollably and it was some time before I could get her quieted.

"There, there," I said. "Now, what is all this? Why should a pretty girl like you want to pass herself away?"

"I have last year's face."

"What?"

"It's true. I found out last night when I went to a party."

"Somebody told you?"

"Worse than that. My eyes preceded me into the room."

"I'll bet you're imagining things. I'll bet that everyone at the party thought you'd left your eyes out in the car."

"You're just saying that to be nice."

"No, I'm not. What does last year's face look like anyway?"

"GAUDY. HEAVY white lines or colored shadow above the eyes; that sort of thing."

"Doesn't sound so bad. And this year's?"

"Once over lightly. Everything fresh, delicate and moist, moist, moist."

"Well, you've got one of the moistest faces I've ever seen."

"That's just because I've been crying for the past hour. When I'm happy my face is dry, dry, dry."

"It still doesn't seem like enough to kill yourself over."

"It's not just that. I don't even have this year's legs."

"They look all right to me," I said, understating the case.

"How can you say that? Look at them; shapely and muscular."

"That's bad, huh?"

"Last year they were okay, good even. But this year you've got to have straight and skinny legs, like a 12-year-old girl."

"That makes it pretty nice for 12-year-old boys, I guess."

"JUST LOOK at the rest of me, 38–22–36. I look ridiculous in a mod jumper. And look at my hair."

"Wait a minute, I'm still looking at the rest of you."

"Naturally curly. I've tried to have it straightened. Lord knows I've tried, but it keeps its wave. I don't know what to do."

"Yeah, you're a mess all right."

"And the worst thing of all is that people keep telling me I look like Sophia Loren."

AS A MATTER of fact, she did look like Sophia Loren; a lot

like her, but I decided to sacrifice my integrity for her emotional well-being.

"You don't look a bit like Sophia Loren," I told her. "Do you want to know who you really look like?"

"Who?"

"Bobby Dylan."

She threw her arms around my neck and kissed me. "Oh, thank you. I know you don't mean it, but I love you for saying it anyway." And she skipped off down the street.

Last year was a very good year for faces.

The Incredible Awards

IOWANS HAVE chosen Gen. Charles de Gaulle as 1965's Incredible Man of the Year in the second annual survey conducted by the Incredible Poll.

De Gaulle won the honor for waiting until he was 75 years old before making his first political speech.

"Any politician who can keep his mouth shut that long deserves everything we can give him," a silo manufacturer from Cylinder said.

The absolutely unreliable polling agency also found a great deal of support for the general because of his recent election victory over a Communist opponent.

"De Gaulle is the only man who can get 55 per cent of the vote and still suffer a moral defeat," one woman said.

The general won out over stiff competition. Other Incredible Awards:

WAR ON Poverty Award — For efforts above and beyond the call of duty in eliminating poverty: To the mayor of Selma, Ala., who donated $107 to a Negro flimflam artist while visiting Washington, D.C.

Socrates Award — For self-knowledge: To Brigitte Bardot for her statement, "There's nothing wrong with being a sex symbol if you have a good figure."

Old Testament Award — To Sandy Koufax who, by sitting out the first game of the World Series because of Yom Kippur, did more to promote Judaism among the young than anyone since Moses.

Roman Empire Award—For decline and fall: To Des Moines' bridges.

Courage in Government Award —To the Des Moines City Council for coming out strongly against liquor billboards near churches, thereby alienating all clergy who enjoy drinking.

• • •

LAST WEDNESDAY, Apr. 1, marked the sixth year this column has been operating under new management. Yes, it was a balmy April Fool's Day in 1965 that Son of Over the Coffee first surfaced. That's roughly 1,615 columns ago.

The amazing part is, if you took all the columns I've written in the past six years and laid them end to end, they wouldn't reach a conclusion.

• • •

175

Title Index

177